John Bancks

A Short Critical Review of the Political Life of Oliver Cromwell

Lord protector of the commonwealth of England, Scotland, and Ireland. His descent, alliances, and first advances to popularity, his military exploits and his civil government.

John Bancks

A Short Critical Review of the Political Life of Oliver Cromwell
Lord protector of the commonwealth of England, Scotland, and Ireland. His descent, alliances, and first advances to popularity, his military exploits and his civil government.

ISBN/EAN: 9783337328672

Printed in Europe, USA, Canada, Australia, Japan

Cover: Foto ©ninafisch / pixelio.de

More available books at **www.hansebooks.com**

A SHORT CRITICAL
REVIEW
Of the POLITICAL LIFE of
OLIVER CROMWELL,
LORD PROTECTOR of the Commonwealth of England, Scotland, and Ireland.

Comprised under the following Heads:

His descent, alliances, and first advances to popularity; with a view of the motives to the civil war, and the sentiments of Mr. Locke and a British parliament concerning resistance.

His military exploits, and wonderful success in the civil wars, during the life of king Charles I.

His military actions after that king's death, during his government in Ireland.

His war against the Scots under king Charles II. till he totally routed them at Worcester.

A view of his conduct towards king Charles I. with a vindication of him in many particulars.

His management towards the parliament, the army, and the parties he had to deal with, till he assumed the sovereignty.

A view of his civil government, from his dissolving the long parliament to his death.

His behaviour towards foreign princes and states; his zeal for the honour of England, the protestant religion, and the liberties of mankind.

A summary of his character, and of that of king Charles I. with a parallel between them in such points as will admit of it.

By the late JOHN BANKS, Esq;

With an APPENDIX, containing many curious Pieces relating to the History and Character of the LORD PROTECTOR.

The FIFTH EDITION.

LONDON:
Printed for J. BUCKLAND, J. and F. RIVINGTON, L. DAVIS and C. REYMERS, S. CROWDER, and T. LONGMAN.

PREFACE.

THE *Author of the following Sheets, who professes no attachment to any party, had often heard Oliver Cromwell applauded and condemned by the same gentlemen, almost in the same breath; or spoken of in the words of the noble historian, as a great wicked man. This made him inquisitive into the life of so extraordinary a person; that he might know what was that series of conduct which could make him deserve so singular a character.*

As this inquiry demanded some application, he began to think it might be made more generally useful than just to satisfy himself, and a few private friends, to whom he might communicate the result of it. This determined him to try the judgment of the public, in order to know how far what he should think truth would take place; and whether a character so much declaimed against, might, at the distance of almost an hundred years, be suffered to stand the test of a fair examination.

To accomplish this, he found it requisite to give the matter a new form, very different from any it had hitherto appeared in: that by throwing together facts of a similar nature, the picture might be view'd in all possible lights, with the greatest advantage.

The first chapter discovers the origin of the civil war, which gave those great talents an opportunity to exert themselves. We were then to consider Cromwell in his rise to authority, and his exercise of it when in full possession. In his rise he appears under two different characters, as a soldier, and a politician. His actions under the first fill up

A 2   three

PREFACE.

three remarkable periods, each of them terminated by a triumphant return to his seat in parliament; which we have therefore divided into so many chapters. As a politician he had to deal with the king, the parliament, the army, and the predominant parties: his behaviour to all these is examined in two chapters, which make the fifth and the sixth.

The administration at home, and influence abroad, are the two grand criteria of any government. We have survey'd Cromwell's under both titles, and given a distinct chapter to each. The ninth and last contains some reflections on his character, with a parallel, which, however ungrateful it may sound to some, can be supported from history. Other remarks will be found in the body of the work, all written with an honest freedom, and not intended to give offence.

It seems manifest from the whole, that Cromwell's character, however it has been misrepresented, is more capable of a vindication, than that of most other invaders of royalty, who are now ranked among the heroes of ancient and modern story. Such a chain of events contributed to his advancement, that with such great abilities, and so much ambition, it was hardly possible for him to be less than he was. Even Cæsar, whom he the most nearly represented, had not so fair a way open to the supreme power, as Cromwell had when he assumed it. But those very causes which give him some right to a vindication, remove him intirely out of the reach of imitation. Nothing but such a crisis as that wherein he did it (which has never yet had a parallel in history) could either support or justify such an attempt in any other.

As the success of the first impression of this work was much greater than the author expected, he thought it his duty to give the second, which he is told has been long wanted, some considerable additions, and other necessary improvements, especially in the article of authorities for what he had advanced. This he has done through the whole, sometimes in the body of the work, and at other times in notes; but chiefly in the appendix now intirely added. Notwithstanding that the book, by these means,

became

PREFACE.

became more than twice as large as before, he thought it best to keep the old title of "Short Critical Review", that it might not seem to be a new work; and because a much larger volume might have been writ upon a subject that affords such an abundance of matter. All he has farther to say, is, that the prose panegyric at the end of the whole contains only part of that printed in Latin; and in some places, where the spirit of the original appears, is very little altered from the translation already published.

CONTENTS.

CHAP. I. Reflections on party prejudices. Effects of them with regard to the parties concerned in the troubles of king Charles I. Cromwell's descent, alliances, and first advances to popularity; with a view of the motives to the civil war, and the sentiments of Mr. Locke and a British parliament concerning resistance, Page 1.

CHAP. II. Cromwell's military exploits, and wonderful success in the civil wars, during the life of king Charles the First, 18

CHAP. III. The military actions of general Cromwell after the king's death, during his government of Ireland, 35

CHAP. IV. Cromwell's war against the Scots under king Charles the Second, till he totally routs them at the battle of Worcester, 47

CHAP. V. A view of Cromwell's conduct towards king Charles I. with a vindication of him in many particulars, 78

CHAP. VI. Cromwell's management towards the parliament, the army, and the parties he had to deal with, till he assumed the sovereignty, 112

CONTENTS.

CHAP. VII. *A view of Cromwell's civil government, from his dissolving the long parliament till his death,* Page 139

CHAP. VIII. *Protector Cromwell's behaviour towards foreign princes and states, his zeal for the honour of England, the protestant religion, and the liberties of mankind,* 177

CHAP. IX. *The characters of Cromwell and king Charles I. with a parallel between them in such points as will admit of it,* 213

APPENDIX.

N° I. *A letter of the marquis of Montrose to king Charles I. delivered during the treaty of Uxbridge, and which was the occasion of breaking off the conferences,* 241

N° II. *The substance of Cromwell's first conference with the members and officers concerning settling the nation,* 245

N° III. *A remarkable conference between general Cromwell and Whitelock on the same subject,* 247

N° IV. *List of the number of representatives chosen in Cromwell's last parliament for the counties, cities and boroughs,* 253

N° V. *A debate between the committee of the house of commons in 1657, and O. Cromwell, upon the humble petition and advice of parliament, by which he was desired to assume the title of king,* 255

N° VI. *Poems on Oliver Cromwell, by Mr. Waller, Mr. Dryden, Mr. Sprat, Mr. Locke, &c.*
 1. *A panegyric on O. Cromwell, by Edw. Waller, Esq;* 287
 2. *A war with Spain, and fight at sea, by Mr. Waller,* 292
 3. *To*

CONTENTS.

3. *To Oliver Cromwell, by Mr. John Locke*, Page 295
4. *Heroic stanzas on Oliver Cromwell, written after his death by Mr. Dryden*, ibid.
5. *To the memory of the protector Oliver Cromwell, by Mr. Sprat*, 299
6. *Upon the late storm, and the protector's death, by Mr. Waller,*. 309
7. *In obitum serenissimi domini, Olivarii Cromwelli, hujus, reipublicæ protectoris,* 310

N° VII. *Substance of a panegyric of the lord-general Oliver Cromwell, as presented to him by the Portuguese ambassador Don John Roderiguez de Saa Meneses, Conde de Penaguaia. Written in Latin, as pretended, by a learned Jesuit, his excellency's chaplain; but, as more probably supposed, by the celebrated Mr. John Milton, Latin secretary to Cromwell,* 311

A

A Short Critical

REVIEW

OF THE

POLITICAL LIFE

OF

OLIVER CROMWELL.

CHAP. I.

Reflections on party prejudices. Effects of them with regard to the parties concerned in the troubles of king Charles. CROMWELL's *descent, alliances, and first advances to popularity; with a view of the motives to the civil war, and the sentiments of Mr. Locke and a British parliament concerning resistance.*

PUBLICK heats and animosities are very aptly compared by an * author of the first reputation, to the heat contracted by a comet, in its approach to the sun. When a people have been so unhappy as to fall into them, it is long before they recover their natural temper. We cannot judge

* Mr. Addison, in the Spectator.

judge, with any certainty, either of the merits of a cause, or of the persons engaged in it, from the representations of authors, who write while that fervour continues, by which themselves have been generally affected. Hence it is, that the characters of men who act in a high capacity, are seldom impartially drawn till a long time after their sphere of action is over, especially by writers of their own country. Former concurrence and present approbation on the one hand; contracted prejudice and inveterate enmity on the other; opinion, interest, and the remains of passion on both, make it a task impossible, at least too difficult for human nature in general, to enter sincerely on the matter in question. Affection rises into reverence, resentment dwindles into contempt, and histories of the times immediately past are usually either panegyrick or satire. The common people receive the impressions, made by the party which succeeds in power; and even reason and experience are found too weak, till after many years, to make things appear in their genuine light.

From these considerations, which have the experience of all ages to support them, we may account for the different Pictures that are left us, of men who acted on the same principles, and with the same views; nay more, we may learn, why the villain in design, who has prospered, has been called the father of his country, and the unprosperous hero and patriot neglected or martyr'd. How many brave and virtuous persons, who boldly contended for the liberties of their fellow-citizens, have been branded with publick infamy, and suffered as rebels and traitors, only because they have not succeeded in attempts, which would otherwise have crowned them with immortal honour? How many enemies of publick liberty, who had nothing in view but the gratification of their own ambition, and no pretence to superiority but from their wealth and influence, have been complimented by those very people, whose rights they had invaded and subverted, with pompous titles and extravagant concessions;

conceffions; which have afterwards, by their defcendants, been made the foundation of another fort of claim; that of divine appointment, and hereditary, indefeafible right? It is true, future ages generally do juftice to particular merit, where the traces of it are by any means preferved. But when it has been fafhionable, for whole centuries together, to infult the memory of any great perfon, it will not be eafy for the moft impartial writer, who can have only fuch partial materials, to draw a picture worthy the original. It is therefore neceffary, that we fhould be as careful as poffible in preferving fuch lineaments of public characters, while they can be known, as may enable pofterity to imitate the whole features, when truth fhall venture to appear, and party and prejudice are no more.

§. 2. The revolutions in England, between the years 1640 and 1660, which, indeed, can hardly be paralleled in hiftory, have been the fource of more virulent parties than any other circumftance in our chronicle. We need not wonder, if we are fenfible of thefe divifions, even at the diftance of fourfcore years. We need not wonder, if the leading men on the country fide, though in reality perfons of great abilities and virtue, were reprefented as a fet of hypocritical fcoundrels and blind enthufiafts, by the partizans of king Charles II. after that prince was reftored to the dignity which he thought his natural inheritance, but which he had long been deprived of by the prevailing party. And, as the notions of divine right, and abfolute unlimited power, were afterwards carried to a great height during his and his brother's reign, by the court and the corrupt part of the clergy, it is not ftrange, that the friends of liberty fhould fall into contempt, and be ftigmatized as fo many enemies to government; that all the mifchiefs of a civil war, which a weak and mifguided king had been led into by his ambitious minifters, fhould be charged on thofe principles which alone could preferve a harmony between the fovereign and his people. And while the accusation ran thus high in general, it was not likely that particular characters should escape. Those, especially, who had been any way concerned in the administration of affairs during the king's exile, were to be stript of every humane virtue, and made to appear worse than cannibals. Their sobriety, temperance, justice, moderation, piety, were to be represented only as hypocrisy and affectation. OLIVER CROMWELL, to be sure, must stand foremost in the black list. It was not enough to call him usurper, tyrant, traitor; but even those very personal qualities, which enabled him to assume and support the first character in the age, were to be rendered ridiculous and contemptible, as well as odious. A very odd method of procedure this! to persuade us that a man, without the capacity requisite in a common justice of peace, should be not only too hard for the whole royal family, but even for his own masters, and all the ministers and crowned heads with whom he had any thing to do: that a man without principle, or whose standing principle was no better than this, * " that moral laws are binding only on ordinary occa-" sions," should be more exact and circumspect in the administration of justice than any sovereign who had gone before him; should seek out capable and worthy men for all employments, more especially for those of the law, so as to give a general satisfaction. Yet all this, however, we have been taught to believe. Cromwell, it seems, was possessed of no real virtues, either civil or military; yet acted more like a person possessed of them all, than almost any other we can meet with in our ancient chronicles.

But facts are very stubborn things, and it is in vain to resist their evidence. The most prejudiced historians on the other side, have related such actions of our British hero, as shew their characters of him to be partially drawn; nay, even in the pictures of their own invention, they have not been able to avoid some
lineaments

* Burnet's history.

lineaments that contradict the general idea they give of him, and shew him to be another sort of a man than they are willing we should believe. The present age begins to see through all this, and the name of Cromwell is now thought no dishonour to the English nation. At this favourable conjuncture, therefore, when there are not wanting those who wish our publick conduct, in particular with regard to a certain haughty, though contemptible people, were copied from that of this great man, I shall venture to draw together such passages of his life, and range them under proper heads, as may shew what he really was, and remove, upon the principles of our best writers on the part of liberty, much of that load of calumny which he has hitherto borne. The task, I apprehend, will not be difficult.

§. 3. His assuming the regal power at a time when he did, will be considered in a chapter by itself. But it is necessary here to obviate one common objection; " That being born a private man, he could not, by any means, have a legal right to the sovereignty over others at all." This maxim has been much contended for under established hereditary monarchies, and might have been universally received, if reason and history did not prove it to be without foundation. But the most impartial disquisitions of the matter, founded on the common sense and practice of mankind, have long ago convinced the wise and unprejudiced, that no individual, however nobly born, has a right over the person or property of another, except only from mutual compact, entered into for general benefit, the conditions of which are as obligatory on the governing, as on the governed parties. No man, therefore, in the nature of things, is any way superior, or inferior to his fellow-citizens, but on such conditions as they are supposed to have reciprocally consented to. It is only to prevent the confusion that riches, interest, or ambition might create, among persons equally qualified, that the sovereignty has been settled in particular

lar families. It is in regard only to conveniency, that the succeffion fhould remain uninterrupted, as long as it can be confiftent with the good of the whole. But where this is infringed, difpenfed with, fuperfeded, the obligation is cancelled, the people are free, and may either chufe a new form of government, or put their old into other hands. Where this has happened indeed, the choice, for very manifeft reafons, has ufually fallen on fome one of the greateft fortune and figure. But this cannot be attributed to any natural right in the perfon, unlefs we fuppofe authority to be the neceffary confequence of riches and intereft; which would produce more confufion than any other fyftem that has yet been advanced. In a word, the natural and moral qualifications of the perfon, where the election is entirely free, are the moft probable recommendations to the community, whofe confent alone can conftitute a lawful authority. If I can prove therefore, that Cromwell had more of thefe qualifications than any other man of his age, and as much of this confent as was confiftent with the temper of the times, I fhall do an act of juftice to his memory, which feems to be hitherto wanting.

§. 4. This great man, notwithftanding what fome have ignorantly afferted, was very well defcended *. The original name of his family was not Cromwell, but Williams. Morgan Williams, fon and heir of Williams, married the fifter of the famous Lord Cromwell,

---

* He fays thus of himfelf, in a fpeech to the parliament, Sept. 12, 1654. " I was by birth a gentle-
" man, living neither in any confiderable height,
" nor yet in obfcurity. I have been called to feveral
" employments in the nation, and to ferve in parlia-
" ments: and I did endeavour to difcharge the du-
" ties of an honeft man in thofe fervices." Mr. Milton calls his houfe " noble and illuftrious;" and fays,
" the name was formerly famous in the nation, when
" well

well, who was made Earl of Effex by king Henry VIII. By her he had a fon named Richard, who was knighted by king Henry, and took the name of his uncle Cromwell, though he kept the arms of Williams. He married Frances, daughter and coheir of Sir Thomas Murfyn; and upon the diffolution of the monafteries, obtained all the lands that belonged to them in Huntingdonfhire, which amounted to a prodigious value. This Sir Richard Cromwell, at a folemn triumph held at Weftminfter, anno 1540, before king Henry VIII. and which was proclaimed in France, Spain, Scotland, and Flanders, overthrew two of the combatants, Mr. Palmer and Mr. Cufpey. He had a fon, Henry, who was knighted by queen Elizabeth in the fixth year of her reign. This Sir Henry married Joan, daughter and heir of Sir Ralph Warren, and refided chiefly at Hinchingbrook, where had been a houfe of nuns. He is faid to have been a/ worthy gentleman, that lived in high efteem both at court and in his country. The father of our protector, Robert Cromwell, Efq; was fecond fon of Sir Henry. There were five more: Sir Oliver was the eldeft, who had a vaft eftate, and after whom his nephew Oliver feems to be named: the others were Henry, Richard, Philip, and Ralph. We read of Sir Oliver, that at his houfe at Hinchingbrook, on the acceffion of king James I. he made the moft noble entertainment that ever had been made by a private fubject in honour of his fovereign.

" well governed by kings; but more famous for or-
" thodox religion, then either firft reftored or efta-
" blifhed among us." " He is well born, fays an-
" other author, and of a noble and ancient extract."
Unparalleled Monarch, page 69. Father Orleans, in his hiftory of the revolutions of England, expreffes himfelf thus, " Cromwell was well enough born, not
" to be contemptible; and yet not fo well as to be
" fufpected of afpiring to fovereignty."

But Mr. Robert Cromwell's estate was much inferior to his brother's. He had not above three hundred pounds a year, when his wife, daughter of Sir Richard Steward, brought him a son that was to have at his command the persons and fortunes of three wealthy nations. It was on the 25th of April, 1599, that this prodigy was given to the world, at the town of Huntingdon, where his father then inhabited. The accounts we have of his youth are imperfect and unsatisfactory; for he never distinguished himself till he was called upon to do it in a public capacity. We only learn, that his father took care of his education, sending him when grown up, to Sidney-college in Cambridge, where he discovered more inclination to an active than a speculative life: though there are proofs sufficient that his advances in learning were not despicable, since they made him master of a genteel stile. It was owing, perhaps, to his turn for action, that we read of his running into some excesses, when he retired from Cambridge after his father's death; which occasioned his mother to enter him at Lincoln's-Inn. The study of the law, however, did not long agree with him; and having five hundred pounds a year left him by his maternal uncle, Sir Richard Steward, over and above what he inherited from his father, he fixed entirely in the country, growing as remarkably sober and religious, as he had been before vicious and extravagant. For some time after his reformation he adhered to the church of England, but at last fell in with the puritans.

§. 5. The grievances of the people were at this time many and great, occasioned by the encroachments of the court and clergy, on almost every branch of civil and religious liberty. Cromwell's engagement on the puritan side, at his first coming into the house of commons, made him a warm stickler for the country interest. He was one of the committee of religion in king Charles's third parliament; and made himself taken

notice

Life of OLIVER CROMWELL.

notice of on this occasion by the people, as a person well affected to the legal constitution of his country. But what made him the most popular, was his opposition to an undertaking in which the king himself was concerned, for draining the fens in Lincolnshire and the Isle of Ely. At this time, by heading the town's people of Cambridge, he got to be elected one of their burgesses, to serve in the parliament of 1640, afterwards called the long parliament.

In this parliament he shewed himself a zealous and forward opposer of the publick grievances. The whole senate, indeed, were earnestly bent on prosecuting the affair; and work enough they had on their hands. And as Cromwell's conduct herein was no ways different from that of the representatives in general, I shall here, in order to his justification, give a character of that assembly, as drawn by an author who wrote at the request of one of the royal family. I shall also, chiefly from the same writer, insert a general view of the state of the nation at that time, and of the causes of the unhappy breach that followed.

§. 6. * No age ever produced greater men than those who sat in that parliament: they had sufficient abilities and inclinations to render the king and their country happy, if England had not been, thro' a chain of concurring accidents, ripened for destruction. At their sitting down, a scene of grievances, under which we had long groaned, was laid open, and all topicks made use of to paint them out in the liveliest colours. The many cruelties and illegal practices of the star-chamber and high commission courts, that had alienated peoples minds from the hierarchy, were now insisted on, to throw down those two arbitrary tribunals; and with them, some time after, the bishops out of the house of peers, and at length episcopacy itself out of the church. It was not a few of either house, but indeed all the great patriots, that concurred at first to make an enquiry

* Wellwood's Memoirs.

quiry into the grievances of this reign. Sir Edward Hide, afterwards earl of Clarendon, and lord chancellor of England; the lord Digby; the lord Falkland; the lord Capel; Mr. Grimstone, who was chosen afterwards speaker of the house of commons that brought in king Charles the second, and was master of the rolls; Mr. Hollis, afterwards lord Hollis; and in general, most of those who took the king's part in the succeeding war, were the men that appeared with the greatest zeal for the redress of grievances, and made the sharpest speeches upon those subjects. The intentions of those gentlemen were certainly noble and just, and tended to the equal advantage of king and people: but the fate of England urged on its ruin step by step, till an open rupture between the king and parliament made the gap too wide ever to be made up again.

Sir Thomas Wentworth, earl of Strafford, and Dr. Laud, archbishop of Canterbury, had too great a share in the ministry, to escape being censured; and they were the first that felt the effects of a popular hatred. These two gentlemen, and James duke of Hamilton, first advised king Charles to call this parliament; and all three fell by it, tho' not at the same time. King Charles now, from the necessity of the times, did every thing to satisfy the parliament: he passed the bill for attainting the earl of Strafford, tho' with reluctancy, as believing he deserved not such hard measure: he took away monopolies, that had been a discouragement to trade: he expressed himself to their contentment in the matters of loan, ship-money, tonage and poundage, and other unwarrantable methods that had been used in raising money; and shewed a settled resolution to comply with them, in every thing that might tend to the ease and security of the subject. As in the preceding parliament he had passed the petition of right, so in the beginning of this, he had agreed to the acts for triennial parliaments, and for abolishing the starchamber and high-commission courts, which had been great grievances; and with chearfulness passed that act which seem'd inconsistent with his own just prerogative,

tive, "That that parliament should not be dissolved but by act of parliament; nor prorogued or adjourned but by their own consent."

The king having, upon these concessions, received the thanks of both houses, and the loud applauses of his people, took a journey to Scotland in August, 1641, to settle matters there, that required his presence; that kingdom having just before been at war with England, on account of the grievances there introduced. He left the parliament sitting, which they continued to do for some time, and then adjourned themselves to October following. At the king's going away, affairs had been already settled betwixt the two kingdoms by an act of pacification, and both armies ordered to be disbanded, the Scots returning home for that purpose.

§. 7. But while the king was in Scotland, the Irish rebellion broke out, which became a new bone of contention between him and the parliaments of both nations. He seemingly took measures in Scotland about suppressing that rebellion, and is said to have made haste back to England to concert with the parliament concerning it. He did not act, however, with so much vigour, as to convince every one of his sincerity in the affair: and it appeared that the queen, who very much governed his majesty, kept up a correspondence with lord Antrim, one of the chief agents in that bloodshed. Nevertheless the king was received in London, at his return, with all demonstrations of affection. The lord mayor and aldermen, the nobility, gentry, and train'd-bands, met him without the city, and conducted him in great state, amid the acclamations of the people, the city companies lining the streets on each side, to Guildhall, where he was royally feasted, and after dinner conducted with the same pomp to Whitehall. "What man, says Dr. Wellwood, that had seen a
" prince thus received into his capital city, could have
" imagined that within less than seven weeks he should
" be obliged to leave it upon the account of tumults,
" never to see it again, but as a prisoner brought thi-

"ther to die upon a scaffold? yet this was king
"Charles's hard fortune."

The house of commons had begun, some few days before his return, to fall into heats about innovations in religion; the rebellion in Ireland; plots said to be laid in Scotland; the disabling of the clergy to exercise temporal jurisdiction; and excluding the bishops from votes in parliament: all which matters, together with some reports that were spread about of some designs against the parliament, led the house into that remarkable petition and remonstrance of the state of the nation, in which they repeated all the mismanagements in the government since the king's coming to the throne, and attributed all to evil counsels and counsellors, and a malignant party about the king. The billeting of soldiers contrary to law, the dissolution and suspension of parliaments, the severe imprisonment of several members, the raising of money by unparliamentary ways, violent prosecutions for non-payment, arbitrary proceedings in the courts of law, the late behaviour and doctrines of the high-flown clergy, continuance of those abuses since the late concessions, were some of the topicks insisted on. This remonstrance met with great opposition in the house, the debate lasting from * three o'clock in the afternoon till ten o'clock the next morning, when it passed by a small majority. It was presented to his majesty the eighth day after his return from Scotland. This petition and remonstrance, together with the king's answer to them at their delivery, and the declaration which he published at large afterwards to the same purpose, contain the matters of almost all those fatal differences, that came, within a very short time after they were drawn up, to be decided by the sword. But they being very long, and to be met with in most histories of that time, I shall not swell this volume with them.

§. 8. Crom-

---

*. This is Wellwood's account: others say, from nine one morning till three the next, which seems most probable by what follows.

§. 8. Cromwell was a great promoter of this remonstrance; and we have this remarkable passage concerning him, while it was in agitation. A day having been appointed for retaking it into consideration, upon its not being called for till late, the matter was put off till next morning. Cromwell, hereupon, asked the lord Falkland, why he was for deferring it, since that day would have put an end to the business. His lordship answered, " There will not be time enough; for sure it will take up some debate." To which the other replied, " A very sorry one;" concluding it would be opposed by very few. But the day after it was over, when upon so hard a struggle it passed only by a majority of nine, lord Falkland asked Mr. Cromwell if there had been a debate. " Yes, said he, and I will take your word another time." Then whispering in the lord Falkland's ear, he added, " If the remonstrance had not passed, I would have sold all I had the next morning, and have never seen England more; and I know many other honest men that were of the same resolution."

Some years before this, indeed, on account of the severe proceedings of archbishop Laud against the puritans, Cromwell had formed a design, together with several other gentlemen of fortune and worth, to go to the American plantations; which design they were very near putting in execution, being only prevented by a proclamation and order of council, when they were actually embarked, in order to transport themselves. This shews, that Cromwell, at that time, as well as the other * excellent persons before-mentioned, acted entirely from a principle of conscience in his opposition against the court, which, without dispute, had been guilty of numberless oppressions: and by these means his reputation increased, both in the house and without, as a steady and zealous patriot.

§. 9.

* The famous Mr. John Hampden was one of that number.

§. 9. † Things were now going fast on towards lessening the confidence betwixt the king and parliament: and yet there were not wanting endeavours, on both sides, to accommodate matters by soft and healing methods, when the king's coming to the house of commons in person, to demand ‡ five of their members, whom he had ordered the day before to be impeached of high treason, put all into a combustion, and gave occasion to the house to assert their privileges with a greater warmth than ever. This was the most unlucky step king Charles could have made at this juncture: and the indiscretion of some that attended the king to the lobby of the house, was insisted upon as an argument that the king was resolved to use violence upon the parliament. These five members had hardly time to make their escape, just when the king was entering; and upon his going away, the house adjourn'd in a flame for some days, ordering a committee to sit at Guildhall in the mean time, as if they were not safe at Westminster.

Whoever they were that advised the king to this rash attempt, are justly chargeable with all the blood that was afterwards spilt; for this sudden action was the first and visible ground of all our following miseries. It was beleived, that if the king had found the five members in the house, and had called in his guards to seize them, the house would have endeavoured their defence, and opposed force to force; which might have endangered the king's person. But the consequences were bad enough without this; for immediately upon it there was nothing but confusion and tumults, fears and jealousies every where, which spread themselves to Whitehall in the rudest manner: so that his majesty not thinking himself safe there, retired with his family to Hampton-court.

The

† Wellwood.

‡ These five members were, Mr. Pym, Mr. Hampden, Mr. Hollis, afterwards lord Hollis, Sir Arthur Hallerig, and Mr. Strode: lord Kimbolton was also accused by his majesty of the same crimes.

Life of OLIVER CROMWELL.

The king leaving his parliament in this manner, there were scarce any hopes of a thorough reconciliation. But when, after a great many removes from place to place, his majesty came to set up his standard at Nottingham, there ensued a fatal and bloody war, which, it is reasonable to believe, was never designed at first by either side.

§. 10. I shall not give a particular account of this war, but take notice only of such facts in which Cromwell was personally concerned, as help to set his character in a clear light. But having said thus much concerning the motives and beginning of it, I shall add a few reflections of the great * Mr. Locke, in defence of subjects taking arms against their prince; and leave it to the reader's determination, how far they regard the present case, and may be urged in vindication of Cromwell, and the other members of this famous parliament.

" Wheresoever law ends, says this excellent reasoner, tyranny begins, if the law be transgressed to another's harm. And whoever in authority exceeds the power given him by law, and makes use of the force he has under his command, to compass that upon the subject which the law allows not, ceases in that to be a magistrate; and acting without authority, may be opposed, as any other man, who invades the right of another. This is acknowledged in subordinate magistrates. He that hath authority to seize my person in the street, may be opposed as a thief or a robber, if he endeavours to break into my house to execute a writ, notwithstanding that I know he has such a warrant, and such a legal authority, as will impower him to arrest me abroad. And why this should not hold in the highest, as well as in the most inferior magistrate, I would gladly be informed. Is it reasonable that the elder brother, because he has the greatest part of his father's estate, should thereby have a right to

---

* In his second essay on government, ch. xviii.

to take away any of his younger brother's portions? or, that a rich man, who poſſeſſed a whole country, ſhould from thence have a right to ſeize, when he pleaſed, the garden and cottage of his poor neighbour? The being rightfully poſſeſſed of great power and riches, exceedingly beyond the greateſt part of the ſons of Adam, is ſo far from being an excuſe, much leſs a reaſon for rapine and oppreſſion, which the endamaging another without authority, is, that it is a great aggravation of it: for the exceeding the bounds of authority is no more a right in a great, than in a petty officer, no more juſtifiable in a king than a conſtable; but is ſo much the worſe in him, in that he has more truſt put in him, has already a much greater ſhare than the reſt of his brethren, and is ſuppoſed, from the advantage of his education, employment, and counſellors, to be more knowing in the meaſure of right or wrong."

And in another * place, ſpeaking of the chimerical notion of reſiſtance with reverence, and without retribution or puniſhment, he ſays, " How to reſiſt force without ſtriking again, or how to ſtrike with reverence, will need ſome ſkill to make intelligible. He that ſhall oppoſe an aſſault only with a ſtick to receive the blows, or in any more reſpectful poſture, without a ſword in his hand, to abate the confidence and force of the aſſailant, will quickly be at an end of his reſiſtance, and will find ſuch a defence only to draw on himſelf the worſe uſage.—He therefore who may reſiſt, muſt be allowed to ſtrike, and then let any one join a knock on the head, or a cut on the face, with as much reverence and reſpect as he thinks fit. He that can reconcile blows and reverence, may, for aught I know, deſerve for his pains a civil reſpectful cudgelling, where-ever he can meet with it.—It is true an inferior, generally ſpeaking, cannot reſiſt a ſuperior. But to reſiſt force with force being the ſtate of war, that levels the parties, cancels all former relations of reverence, reſpect, and ſuperiority: and then the odds that remains

---

* Chap. xix.

mains is, that he who oppofes the unjuft aggreffor, has this fureriority over him, and he has a right, when he prevails, to punifh the offender, both for the breach of peace, and all the events that followed upon it."

A little farther he proceeds thus: " Here, 'tis like, the common queftion will be made, Who fhall be judge, whether the prince or legiflature act contrary to their truft? This, perhaps, ill-affected and factious men may fpread among the people, when the prince only makes ufe of his juft prerogative. To this I reply, The people fhall be judge; for who fhall be judge whether his truftee or deputy acts well, and according to the truft repofed in him, but he who deputes him, and muft, by having deputed him, have ftill a power to difcard him, when he fails in his truft? If this be reafonable in particular cafes of private men, why fhould it be otherwife in that of the greateft moment, where the welfare of millions is concerned; and alfo, where the evil, if not prevented, is greater, and the redrefs very difficult, dear, and dangerous?"

§. 11. But we have a ftill greater authority than that of any private man, to vindicate the proceedings of the long parliament. That very convention which brought in king Charles II. tho' ready to run mad with loyalty, would not fuffer any reflection on the conduct of their brethren, except only in the article of deftroying the king.

* Mr. William Lenthal, who had been fpeaker of the long parliament, and was a member of the reftoring one, happened to drop this expreffion, in the debate about the general pardon: "He who firft drew his fword againft the late king, committed as great an offence, as he who cut off his head." Upon which he was feized by the ferjeant, and Sir Harbottle Grimftone, by order of the houfe of commons, reprimanded him in the following words. " Sir, the houfe hath taken great offence at fome words you have let fall in this

---

* Critical hiftory of England, Vol. II.

this debate; which in their judgments, contain as high a reflection on the justice and proceedings of the lords and commons of the last parliament in their actings, before 1648, as could be expressed. They apprehend there is much poison in the said words, and that they were spoken out of a design to inflame, and to render them who drew the sword, to bring delinquents to punishment, and to assert their just liberties, into a balance with them who cut off the king's head."

Thus, says the author who gives us this passage, are all the lord Clarendon's and Mr. Echard's reflections on those actings declared to be highly injurious; and the history of England, and that of the grand rebellion, which treat that glorious parliament as rebels, are condemned in the most solemn manner, by the declaration of the house of commons, pronounced by their speaker. After which, I think all future critics upon them would be superfluous and needless.

CHAP. II.

CROMWELL's military exploits, and wonderful success, in the civil wars, during the life of king Charles the first.

§. 1. WHEN the differences between the king and parliament were come to an open rupture, the active genius of Cromwell would not suffer him to be an idle spectator. He got a captain's commission from the commons, and immediately raised a troop of horse in his own country. They consisted of select men, whose bravery he proved by the following stratagem. He placed about twelve of them in an ambuscade, near one of the king's garrisons, who advancing furiously towards the body, as if they had been of the enemy's party, put some of their raw companions to the flight. These he immediately cashiered, and filled their places with others of more courage.

Other men, in what profession soever, have generally advanced very slowly, or by some other means than pure merit, to the highest dignities. But this was not Cromwell's case: his advances from a captain to a lieutenant-general were so sudden, that they could not but surprise all that were witnesses to them. His securing the town of Cambridge, when the college-plate was upon the point of being sent to the king at Oxford, and his taking Sir Thomas Connesby, high-sheriff of Hertfordshire, just as he was going to St. Alban's, to proclaim the parliament-commanders all traitors, were such actions as procured him the thanks of the house, and soon after recommended him to the dignity of a colonel. In this post, having raised a thousand horse by his own interest, he obstructed the levies for the king in Cambridgeshire, Essex, Suffolk, and Norfolk, with incredible diligence: he also defeated the project of a counter-association on the king's side, contrived by Sir John Pettus and others, by surprising the parties in the town of Leftoff, and seizing all their provisions and stores: then, going to convoy some ammunition from Warwick to Gloucester, he by the way took Hifden-house, made Sir Alexander Denton, the owner, and many others, prisoners, obtained a large booty, and gave an alarm to Oxford itself.

§. 2. Being now made lieutenant-general to the earl of Manchester, he levy'd more forces. With these marching towards Lincolnshire, he disarmed the parliament's enemies by the way, relieved captain Wray, who was distressed by the Newarkers, made a great slaughter, and took three troops. Afterwards meeting with twenty-four of the king's troops near Grantham, he with seven troops only entirely routed them.

Lord Willoughby of Parham having got possession of Gainsborough for the parliament, colonel Cavendish was sent by his brother, the earl of Newcastle, with a great party of horse, to summon it. Cromwell attacked him with only twelve troops, near the town; and

and though Cavendish had three times the number of men, and prodigious advantage of situation, his party was entirely routed, and himself killed, among a great number of other officers. " This, says Whitlock, was the beginning of Cromwell's great fortunes; and now he began to appear in the world. He had a * brave regiment of horse of his countrymen, most of them freeholders, and freeholders sons, who upon matter of conscience engaged in the quarrel under Cromwell. And thus being well armed within, by the satisfaction of their own consciences, and without

by

* At a general muster in 1644, no men appeared so full, and well armed, and civil, as Colonel Cromwell's horse did.

Bate says, that " Cromwell used them daily to look after, feed, and dress their horses, and, when it was necessary, to lie together on the ground; and besides taught them to clean and keep their arms bright, and have them ready for service; to chuse the best armour, and to arm themselves to the best advantage. Trained up in this kind of military exercise, they excelled all their fellow-soldiers in feats of war, and obtained more victories over the enemy. These were afterwards preferred to be commanders and officers in the army, and their places filled up with lusty strong fellows, whom he brought up in the same strictness of discipline."

But the fullest and best authority for what is here advanced, may be found in Cromwell's own words, as quoted by the Reverend Mr. Peck from his conference on the parliament's desiring him to take on him the title of king. " I was a person that from my first employment was suddenly preferred and lifted up from lesser trusts to greater. From my first being captain of a troop of horse, I did labour, as well as I could, to discharge my trust; and God blessed me, as it pleased him.. I had a very worthy friend then, Mr. John Hampden, and he was a very noble person, and

I know

by good iron arms, they would as one man stand firmly, and charge desperately." He was obliged, however, after this victory, to retreat the same night to Lincoln; which he did in good order, and marched the next day to the earl of Manchester at Boston. Colonel Cavendish's troops rallying, after the death of their leader, and joining the earl of Newcastle, Cromwell thought it not prudent to engage against such prodigious odds; so drew off with all the conduct of an experienced general.

His next action was against Sir John Henderson, an old commander, at the head of eighty-seven troops. They

I know his memory is very grateful to all. At my first going out into this engagement, I saw our men were beaten on every hand: I did indeed; and desired him that he would make some additions to my lord Essex's army of some new regiments; and I told him it would be serviceable to him in bringing such men in, as I thought had a spirit that would do something in the work. Your troops, said I, are most of them old decayed serving-men and tapsters, and such kind of fellows; and their troops are gentlemens sons, younger sons, and persons of quality: and do you think that the spirit of such base and mean fellows will ever be able to encounter gentlemen, that have honour, and courage, and resolution in them? You must get men of a spirit, and (take it not ill what I say) of a spirit that is likely to go on as far as gentlemen will go; or else I am sure you will be beaten, still. I told him so. He was a wise and worthy person, and he did think that I talked a good notion, but an impracticable one. I told him, I could do somewhat in it. And I raised such men as had the fear of God before them, and made some conscience of what they did. And from that day forwards they were never beaten, but whenever they engaged against the enemy, they beat continually." Peck's memoirs of the life and actions of Oliver Cromwell, p. 52. in the notes.

They met near Horn-caftle, at a place called Windſby-field. Here Cromwell was in great danger, having his horſe killed in the firſt ſhock, and being ſtruck down again as he attempted to riſe. But his good fortune ſtill protected him; in about an hour the royaliſts were routed, the lord Widdrington, Sir Ingram Hopton, and other perſons of quality, with about fifteen hundred ſoldiers and inferior officers, were left dead on the field, very few being loſt on the parliament ſide. Many priſoners, arms, and horſes, were taken; and it was in conſequence of this victory, that the earl of Mancheſter made himſelf maſter of Lincoln.

§. 3. Soon after this followed the battle of Marſtonmoor. The parliament army, under the earl of Mancheſter, lord Fairfax, and general Leven, had been obliged by prince Rupert to raiſe the ſiege of York. His highneſs, not contented with this advantage, reſolved to give them battle, and accordingly came up with them at the above-mentioned place. In the engagement, the left wing of the royal army, commanded by the prince in perſon, put to flight the parliament's right wing, and in it the ſaid three generals. But the prince purſuing them too far, Cromwell, who commanded the left wing, found means to draw over the victory to his ſide, and get the whole honour of it to himſelf. He engaged cloſely the earl of Newcaſtle, who had before only cannonaded at a diſtance, and the action on both ſides was warm and deſperate. The horſe having diſcharged their piſtols, flung them at each other's heads, and then fell to it with their ſwords. But after a very obſtinate diſpute, Cromwell's ſuperior genius prevailed, and the king's right wing was totally routed. And now the prince returning with his victorious party, was alſo charged at unawares, and entirely defeated, by the reſerve of Cromwell's brigade.

In this action, above four thouſand of the king's forces were ſlain, and fifteen hundred taken priſoners, among whom were above a hundred perſons of diſtintion, and confiderable officers. All their artillery, great number of fmall arms, and much ammunition, together with the prince's own ftandard, were alfo taken: the parliamentarians lofing not above three hundred men. The whole glory of it is univerfally afcribed to Cromwell, who, according to fome, was abfent when Manchefter, Fairfax, and Leven, were put in confufion, being gone off to have a wound dreffed, which he received at the firft charge: but returning to his poft, he fhewed what good fenfe united with valour could do; for by his own prowefs he infpired the troops with frefh courage, and immediately gave a new turn to the fortune of the day. For his behaviour in this memorable battle, which was fought on the fecond of July 1644, Cromwell gained the name of Ironfides, alluding to his invincible bravery, and the impenetrable ftrength of his troops. The confequences on the king's fide were, diffenfion and feparation between the prince and his confederates, and foon after the furrender of the city of York, by Sir Thomas Glenham.

I am very fenfible that Sir William Dugdale, in his fhort view of the late troubles, and lord Hollis, in his memoirs, have accufed Cromwell of egregious cowardice, the former in the battle of Edge-hill, and the latter in this battle of Marfton-moor: but as they both do it only on hearfay, and were befides profeffed enemies of our commander, and as all the concurrent and fubfequent facts and circumftances, in particular his great reputation from this time, entirely contradict and overthrow every calumny of that nature, it is certainly needlefs to ufe any other means to wipe off their afperfions.

§. 4. In fact Cromwell began now to be fo very much taken notice of, that fome dreaded, others envy'd, and all admir'd him. It is reported, that the character given of him to the king by archbifhop Williams, made fuch an impreffion on his majefty, that he was heard to fay, " I would fome one would

do

do me the good service to bring Cromwell to me, alive or dead." The earl of Essex grew jealous of him: the Scotch commissioners, * at his instigation, held a conference with some of the parliament's members, how to get rid of him, in which he was vehemently accused by the chancellor of Scotland. He had also a difference with the earl of Manchester, whom he accused of cowardice at the second battle of Newbury, which ended in an irreconcileable breach between them. Yet, amidst all his enemies and rivals, Cromwell still carry'd his point, so far, that when the army was new modelled, by what was called the self-denying ordinance, which excluded all members of parliament from military posts, he continued a single exception to this general law, and kept his command, when the earls of Essex, Manchester, Denbigh, and Warwick, the lord Grey of Groby, Sir William Waller, major-general Massey, and many others, were removed from theirs. Of such importance did his services now appear, that envy and opposition could have no effect against him, though promoted by persons in the highest stations.

I do not pretend to give a regular narrative of all the actions of this great man, and therefore shall hasten over those of less moment; such as his defeat of the earl of Northampton and lord Goring at Islipbridge; his taking Bletchington-house, for the surrender of which colonel Windebank was shot to death at Oxford; his taking Sir William Vaughan, and lieutenant-colonel Littleton, with most of their men, prisoners; his storming of Faringdon-house, where he was repulsed by Sir George Lisle: it is sufficient to take notice, that a little before the battle of Naseby he was appointed † lieutenant-general of the horse,

notwith-

---

* Vide Chap. VI.

† This was in consequence of some letters from the chief officers of horse to the parliament, desiring that colonel Cromwell might be lieutenant-general of the

horse

notwithstanding the self-denying ordinance, and the complaints of those gentlemen upon whose ruins he was now visibly raising. Whitelock informs us, that he now began to increase in the favour of the people, and of the army, and to grow great to the envy of many.

There is a passage in the Portuguese embassador's panegyrick to the protector, which I cannot help inserting here. " A way being made, says the author, thro' the inferior posts, he rose to be lieutenant-general of the army; where, with a singular prerogative of experience, acquired through all the military offices, he so suited himself to all persons, that he seemed to be born only to that trust which he then exercised. He commanded both the horse and foot forces with the same ease, though in their use and ordering so different from each other; and performed such great and wonderful things with the help of each, that he made it a doubt, which of them may be of the most service in an engagement, since it was evident that both stood in need of so great a captain for the gaining of those happy successes which he won in battle.*"

§. 5. Fairfax was the parliament's chief general, in the room of the earl of Essex. Cromwell joined him and the main army at Gilsborough, bringing with him six hundred horse and dragoons. The king, having been some time at Borough-hill, drew off from thence towards Harborough, and designed to march to Pomfret; thinking, if he were followed by the parliament's forces, he should fight with greater

horse under Sir Thomas Fairfax. After some debate, says Whitelock, the house ordered, " That Sir Thomas Fairfax should appoint Cromwell to command the horse under him as lieutenant-general, if he thought fit."

† Memoirs, &c. p. 52. This piece is supposed to have been written by Milton.

advantage northward. But Ireton, by Cromwell's advice, being sent out with a flying party of horse, fell upon a party of the king's rear, quartered in Naseby town, and took many prisoners, being some of prince Rupert's life-guard, and Langdale's brigade. This gave such an alarm to the whole royal army, that the king at midnight left his own quarters, and for security hastened to Harborough, where the van of his army lay. Here calling up prince Rupert, he summoned a council of war, in which it was resolved (chiefly through the prince's eagerness, the old commanders being much against it) to give the enemy battle; and since Fairfax had been so forward, they would no longer stay for him, but seek him out. Accordingly, being come near Naseby, there they found him; and both armies being drawn up in battalia, faced each other. The princes Rupert and Maurice commanded the right wing of the royal army, Sir Marmaduke Langdale the left, and the king himself the main body; the earl of Lindsay and Jacob lord Astley, the right-hand reserve; and the lord Bard and Sir George Lisle, the left reserve. The right wing of the parliament's army was held by lieutenant-general Cromwell, the left by colonel Ireton, the main body by general Fairfax and major-general Skippon, who fought stoutly, though severely wounded in the beginning of the fight; and the reserves were brought up by Rainsborough, Hammond, and Pride. The place of action was a large fallow field, on the north-west side of Naseby, above a mile broad; which space of ground was wholly taken up by the two armies.

All things being disposed, on the 14th of June, at ten in the morning, the battle began with more than civil rage; the royal word being, " God and queen Mary," and the others, " God with us." Prince Rupert gave the first charge, and engaged the parliament's left wing with great resolution. Ireton made gallant resistance, but was forced at last to give ground, the horse being shot under him, and himself

run

run through the thigh with a pike, and into the face with a halbert, and taken prisoner, till upon the turn of the battle he regained his liberty. The prince chased the enemy to Naseby town, and in his return summoned the train, and visited his carriages, where was good plunder. But here, as in the battle of Marston-moor, his long stay so far from the main body, was no small prejudice to the king's army.

For Cromwell, in the mean time, charged furiously on the king's left wing, and that with good success, forcing them from the body; and prosecuting the advantage, quite broke them, and their reserve. After which, joining with Fairfax, he charged the king's foot, who had beaten the parliament's, and got possession of their ordnance, and thought themselves sure of victory; but being now in confusion, and having no horse to support them, they were easily over-borne by Fairfax, and Cromwell. By this time the king was joined by prince Rupert, returned from his fatal success; but the horse could never be brought to rally themselves again in order, or to charge the enemy.

Upon this, lord Clarendon says, "that this difference was observed all along in the discipline of the king's troops, and those commanded by Fairfax and Cromwell (it having never been remarkable under Essex and Waller, but only under them) though the king's troops prevailed in the charge, and routed those they charged, they seldom rally'd themselves again in order, nor could be brought to make a second charge the same day; which was the reason they had not an entire victory at Edge-hill: whereas the troops under Fairfax and Cromwell, if they prevailed, or though they were beaten and routed, presently rally'd again, and stood in good order, till they received farther directions.

And the glory of all that happened under Fairfax, ought, according to most writers, to be ascribed solely to Cromwell. Father Orleans says, "Fairfax his birth, service, courage, and warlike temper, sufficiently qualified him to represent a prime actor: his mean capacity and want of forefight (which made him active without thought, though heavy and hypochondriac) made him fit to receive the impreffions given him by another, and be guided by Cromwell. Thus Fairfax made the fhow, and Cromwell managed all. The former being as pliable as he was ambitious, the latter ruled by appearing fubmiffive." Agreeably to which we find the panegyrift before quoted expreffing himfelf thus of Cromwell; "Whatever military honours he bore, he moft religioufly obeyed his fuperiors in them all; in atchieving the moft gallant acts, he gave the glory of all the conduct to the chief generals, and that with fuch a modefty, that he bound them moft ftrongly to himfelf, and obtain'd the admiration of all. Becaufe a conqueft of himfelf, is ever reckon'd more honourable in a foldier, than to triumph over the enemy. For this and his other virtues Fairfax valued him at fo high a rate, that he would take no cognizance of the greateft affairs, becaufe he would leave them intirely to Cromwell: and Cromwell, in thofe things which he himfelf only performed, and gave an account of to the parliament, ftill made Fairfax the author."

In fine, with all that the king and the prince could do, they could not rally their broken troops, which ftood in fufficient numbers upon the place: fo that they were forced at laft to quit the field, leaving a compleat victory to the parliament's party, who purfued them within two miles of Leicefter; and the king finding the purfuit fo hot, fled from thence to Afhby-de-la-Zouch, and then to Litchfield, and for a fafer retreat into Wales.

Thus ended the famous battle of Nafeby, in which the wonderful fuccefs of the parliament's party was chiefly owing to Cromwell's valour and good conduct, who flew like lightening from one part of the army to the other, and broke through the enemy's fquadrons with fuch rapidity, that nothing either could or durft ftop him. 'Tis faid, that in this action a commander of the king's knowing Cromwell, advanced

brifkly

briskly from the head of his troops, to exchange a single bullet with him, and was with equal bravery encountered by him, both sides forbearing to come in; till their pistols being discharged, the cavalier, with a slanting back blow of a broad sword, chanced to cut the ribbon that held Cromwell's murrion, and with a draw threw it off his head; and now, just as he was going to repeat his stroke, Cromwell's party came in and rescued him; and one of them alighting, threw up his head-piece into his saddle, which he hastily catching, clapped it on the wrong way, and so bravely fought with it the rest of the day, which proved so very fortunate on his side.

The king's loss in this battle was irreparable; for besides that there were slain above a hundred and fifty officers, and gentlemen of quality, most of his foot were taken prisoners, with all his cannon and baggage, eight thousand arms, and other rich booty; among which was also his majesty's own cabinet, where were reposited his most secret papers, and letters between him and his queen, which shewed how contrary his counsels with her were to those he declared to the kingdom. Many of these, relating to the publick, were printed with observations, and kept upon record, by order of the two houses; who also made a publick declaration of them, shewing what the nobility and gentry, who followed the king, were to expect; but of these letters, and his majesty's insincerity in other particulars, we shall have occasion to take notice in a following chapter.

§. 6. I have inserted a particular description of this battle, as I find it in the histories of those times, because it was in effect the decisive action between the two parties. It is observed, that from this grand period, the king's affairs became desperate, and his whole party began to moulder away, and most sensibly to decline every where. The parliament's army had no sooner gained this wonderful advantage, but like a torrent they soon overflowed the whole kingdom,

dom, bearing down all before them. Leicester, which the king had lately taken from them, was immediately regained. Taunton, which had been closely besieged by lord Goring, and defended by the valiant Blake, was relieved: lord Goring was beaten, and pursued almost to Bridgewater. In this latter action the prudence of Cromwell was very conspicuous: he would not suffer part of the horse to pursue the enemy, till they were all come up together; then putting himself at their head, he performed the work with such success, that he took almost all the enemy's foot, and their ordnance.

After this victory, the strong garrison of Bridgewater was taken by storm. This was of great advantage to the parliament; for thereby a line of garrisons was drawn over the country, from the Severn to the south coasts; whereby Devonshire and Cornwall, still chiefly at the king's devotion, were cut off from any communication with the eastern parts.

§. 7. Cromwell's next expedition was against the club-men, a kind of third army, which started up suddenly in several counties, on occasion of the rapines and violences practised by the royalists in the west. Both parties endeavoured to gain them over, and they were formidable to both; till Cromwell's presence, and excellent conduct, put an end to the insurrection.

Immediately after we find him before Bristol, in company with Fairfax, whom he advised to storm that important city. Prince Rupert held it, with about 5000 horse and foot, for the king, and had declared he would never surrender it, unless a mutiny happened. But Cromwell's counsel prevailing, an attack was made with so much fury, that the prince thought not fit to run the hazard of a second assault, but delivered up the place, and with it most of the king's magazines and warlike provisions. His majesty hereupon discharged the prince, and wrote him a letter to retire out of the kingdom.

From Briſtol, with a brigade of four regiments, Cromwell flew to the Devizes, and ſummoned the caſtle. The place was ſo ſtrong, that Sir Charles Lloyd, the governor, returned no other anſwer but "Win it and wear it. Yet, as if nothing was defenſible againſt our victorious commander, he was ſoon maſter of this fortreſs. Thence haſtening to Wincheſter, he by the way diſarmed and diſperſed the Hampſhire rioters: and being come before the city, he fired the gate, and entered; made a breach in the caſtle, which held out, and reduced it to the parliament's obedience. He did the ſame by Baſing-houſe, which was held by the marquis of Wincheſter, its owner, and thought almoſt impregnable; the colonels Norton and Harvey, and Sir William Waller, having aſſaulted it in vain. Seventy-two men were here loſt on the king's ſide, and about 200 taken, among which were the marquis himſelf, and ſeveral other perſons of diſtinction, whom Cromwell ſent up to the parliament, and received the thanks of the houſe for theſe important ſervices.

Langford-houſe, near Saliſbury, upon his coming before it, was ſurrendered at the firſt ſummons. Then marching beyond Exeter, at Bovy-Tracy he fought the lord Wentworth, taking 400 horſe, and about 100 foot, priſoners, with ſix ſtandards, one of which was the king's. Then joining with Fairfax, they in conjunction took Dartmouth by ſtorm, defeated the lord Hopton at Torrington, and purſued the only remains of a royal army into Cornwall, where prince Charles had a body of about 5000 horſe, and a 1000 foot: but unable to make head againſt the victors, he embarked with ſeveral noble perſons, and fled to the iſles of Scilly. Lord Hopton, who was left to command the forces, was obliged to diſband them: ſoon after which Exeter ſurrendered, and Cromwell came up to London, where he took his place in parliament, and received the hearty thanks of the houſe, for his great and many ſervices.

§. 8.

§. 8. The king's affairs were now entirely ruined, and an end was put to the firſt and longeſt civil war. The few places that held out for him were ſurrendered, and his majeſty threw himſelf into the hands of the Scots, then lying before Newark. The Scots ſoon after delivered him to the Engliſh parliament, who ſecured him in Holmby-houſe, where he was ſeized the next year by the army, and after ſome ineffectual treating, which we ſhall take notice of elſewhere, made his eſcape from Hampton-court to the iſle of Wight, remaining there till he was brought up to London in order to his trial. During all this time Cromwell was managing the parliament and the army, who were both jealous of him in their turns, and both of them, in their turns, outwitted by him. It was now perceived, that though Fairfax was general in name, Cromwell commanded in fact, the other doing nothing without his concurrence.

But the whole time between the end of the firſt war and the death of the king, was not ſpent in intriguing, and circumventing of parties. In the year 1648 the diſcontented part of the nation had again recourſe to arms. The firſt that appeared in a hoſtile manner were the Welſh, under major-general Langhorn, colonel Poyer, and colonel Powell. Theſe men, though formerly active parliamentarians, being to be diſbanded by order of the council of war, refuſed to ſubmit; and the better to ſecure themſelves, declared for the king, acting by commiſſion under the prince of Wales. Others joining them, they ſoon had a formidable body, and got poſſeſſion of ſeveral caſtles. There was alſo a conſiderable riſing in Kent, under the earl of Norwich; and another in the north, under Sir Marmaduke Langdale. The duke of Buckingham and his brother, the earl of Holland, and the earl of Peterborough, appeared in arms ſo near as Kingſton; and part of the fleet, under captain Batten, revolted to the prince. In a word, there was ſcarce a county in England, where there was not ſome aſſociation forming, in favour of the king. This put the parliament

ment upon vigorous measures; which proving successful, several of the insurrections were immediately quelled, and a powerful body of the royalists were shut up in the town of Colchester; where being obliged, after a long siege to surrender, Sir George Lisle, and Sir Charles Lucas, two of their heads, were shot to death by order of a council of war.

§ 9. Cromwell's part in this second war was very considerable. Being sent into Wales, colonel Horton, whom he dispatched before him, defeated Langhorn's army, slew 1500, and took 3000 prisoners. Cromwell himself besieged Chepstow, which was taken by colonel Ewer, whom he left behind him for that purpose. Proceeding in the mean time into Pembrokeshire, he took Tenby by storm. Then advancing to Pembroke, where Langhorn, Poyer, and Powell had strongly fortified themselves, he reduced both the town and castle by famine. The three chiefs surrendered at mercy, and being condemned by a court-martial, were ordered to be shot to death; but having the favour given them of casting lots, Poyer was the only one who suffered. The other prisoners were used with more lenity, and none of the town's people plundered.

The Scots, about this time, invaded England under duke Hamilton, who had carried the command from the marquis of Argyle, and was for restoring the king without conditions. Cromwell was ordered to advance against these, and fight them. Accordingly, having compleated the reduction of Wales, he marched towards the north with all his forces; sending to major-general Lambert, who was already in those parts, to avoid engaging 'till the whole army came together. While Cromwell was on this march, a charge of high-treason was drawn up against him by major Huntingdon, which proved ineffectual in the house of commons. At last, having joined Lambert, he met the Scots on the 17th of August, near Preston in Lancashire. The English under Langdale,

dale, who had joined the Scots, behaved resolutely, but were so pressed upon by Cromwell's men, that they were obliged to retreat: which the Scots perceiving, they soon followed their example, and left Cromwell master of the field; who pursuing them closely, slew many, and took abundance of prisoners, with all their baggage, artillery, and ammunition. The next morning marching towards Warrington, he made a stand at a pass, which for many hours was resolutely disputed with him: but at last he drove on the enemy, slew 1000 of them, and took 2000 prisoners. He was again opposed at Warrington-bridge by lieutenant-general Bayley, who was obliged to surrender himself prisoner of war, and all his men, to the number of 4000, with arms and ammunition. As for duke Hamilton, he fled from place to place with about 3000 horse, 'till he was taken at Uttoxeter in Staffordshire, with all his men, and sent prisoner to Windsor-castle. Thus the whole Scotch army, which had occasioned so much terror, was totally routed and defeated by Cromwell, with scarce a third part of the same number of forces, very few of which were lost in this important expedition. General Monroe, who was come into England as a reserve to the duke, hearing of what had happened, and that Cromwell was advancing towards him in order to prosecute the advantage, thought it his best way to march back again with all expedition.

Having rid the nation of this great fear, and the north in particular of the burthen it groaned under through the oppression of the Scots, Cromwell resolved to enter Scotland itself, that he might effectually root out whatever threatned any farther disturbance. In his way he reduced Berwick and Carlisle, both which had revolted from their former obedience. And just upon entering the kingdom, he ordered proclamation to be made at the head of every regiment, that no one, upon pain of death, should force from the Scots any of their cattle or goods. He also declared to the Scots themselves, " That he came with an army to
free

free their kingdom from the Hamiltonian party, who endeavoured to involve both the nations in blood; without any intention to invade their liberties, or infringe their privileges." His proceedings were agreeable to this declaration; for marching to Edinburgh, he was received with great solemnity by the marquis of Argyle, and others; and having difpoffefs'd the Hamilton party of all public trufts, he returned to England loaded with marks of honour, leaving behind him, at the requeft of the Argyle party, three regiments of horfe under major-general Lambert. Upon his arrival at London, he took his place in parliament, and was prefented with the thanks of the houfe; which he received, according to cuftom, with great appearance of humility. This was his laft military expedition before the death of the king, which happened foon after, but which we fhall leave to be fpoken of in another place, and purfue our hero into Ireland.

CHAP. III.

The military actions of general CROMWELL *after the king's death, during his government of Ireland.*

§. 1. THE Irifh rebellion, which broke out in 1641, had, thro' the neceffity of the times, been much neglected till 1649. The parliament, indeed, had long before got poffeffion of Dublin, which was delivered up to them by the marquis of Ormond, who was then obliged to come over to England. But being recalled by the Irifh, Ormond made a league with them in favour of the king, and brought over moft of the kingdom into a union with the royalifts. Londonderry and Dublin were the only places that held out for the parliament, and the latter was in great danger of being loft. This made colonel Jones, the governor, fend over to England for fuccour; and a confiderable

fiderable body of forces were thereupon ordered for Ireland. The command of thefe was offered to Cromwell, who accepted it with feeming reluctance; profeffing, " that the difficulty which appeared in the expedition, was his chief motive for engaging in it; and that he hardly expected to prevail over the rebels, but only to preferve to the commonwealth fome footing in that kingdom.*"

The parliament was fo pleafed with his anfwer, that on the † 22d of June, 1649, they gave him a commiffion to command all the forces that fhould be fent into Ireland, and to be lord-governor of that kingdom for three years, in all affairs both civil and military. From the very minute of his receiving this charge, Cromwell ufed an incredible expedition in the raifing of money, providing of fhipping, and drawing the forces together for their intended enterprize. The foldiery marched with great fpeed to the rendezvous at Milford-Haven, there to expect the new lord-deputy, who followed them from London on the 10th of July. His
setting

* The parliament, fays his panegyrift, offers the Irifh expedition, with the lieutenancy of that kingdom, to Cromwell; but that command appears inglorious to him, as it leffens the authority of his general. He acquaints him with it, and affures him, that he will never accept of it, tho' threatened with the greateft punifhment if he do not comply, or tendered the higheft reward if he do.—By this title and inftance Fairfax perceived how much more deferving Cromwell was than himfelf, whom he before knew to be no way his inferior: and at the fame time, he vied in kindnefs, and fhewed that he deferved well of his country, by refufing the charge, and affigned it wholly to Cromwell. Peck's memoirs, &c. p. 54.

† The council of ftate had nominated him as long before as the 15th of January 1648, and the parliament voted their approbation of him March the 31ft; fo that he deliberated a long while about the accepting of this commiffion.

setting out was very pompous, being drawn in a coach with six horses, and attended by many members of the parliament and council of state, with the chief of the army; his life-guard consisting of eighty men, who had formerly been commanders, all bravely mounted and accoutered, both them and their servants.

§. 2. Never did general more distinguish himself, either for valour and conduct, than Cromwell in this Irish expedition. Having called at Bristol, where he was received with great honour, and given orders for the train of artillery, he went over to Wales, dispatching three regiments before him for Dublin, to strengthen the brave colonel Jones, who was appointed lieutenant-general of horse by the parliament. With the assistance of these, that gallant commander raised the siege of Dublin, and entirely routed the marquis of Ormond, who had treated him with contempt. About four thousand were killed in this action, and 2500o taken prisoners, with the loss of only twenty on the parliament side. All the great guns, ammunition, provisions, and about 4000 l. in money, belonging to the royalists, were obtained in this battle; the great success of which was unexpected on both sides: Jones having at first only attacked a party, by whose defeat he was led on to a complete victory. The marquis, upon this misfortune, fled to Kilkenny, and from thence to Drogheda, whither many of his scattered forces had betook themselves before.

There was work enough, however, left for Cromwell, notwithstanding this advantage before his arrival. The beating an army in the field was not the greatest part of the business; while most of the fortified places, which were numerous, were in the hands of the enemy: yet a victory so complete, when he expected rather to hear of the loss of Dublin, was matter of great encouragement to his excellency. He embarked at Milford-haven full of the good news, and arrived at Dublin in a short time, where he was received with all possible demonstrations of joy. As he passed

passed thro' the city, at a convenient place he made a stand, and in a speech to the people, "declared the cause of his coming, promising not only favour and affection, but rewards and gratuities, to all that should assist him in the reduction of their enemies." He was answered with loud applauses, the people crying out that they would live and die with him.

§. 3. After the soldiers had refreshed themselves, Cromwell drew them out of the city to a general muster, where there appeared a complete body of 15,000 horse and foot, out of which 10,000 were drawn for present service. With this army he advanced towards Drogheda, or Tredagh, a strong place, garrisoned by 2,500 foot and 300 horse, the flower of the royal army, under the command of Sir Arthur Aston, an experienced old soldier. The marquis of Ormond foresaw that this place, by reason of its situation, would be first attempted; and he was in hopes he should have time to recruit his army, while Cromwell was waiting his forces against the town. But no sooner was the general come before Tredagh, than he summoned the governor to surrender; which not being regarded, he immediately hung out the red ensign, blocked up the town by land, and ordered Ayscough with his fleet to do the same by sea; and being sensible of the mischiefs of a long siege, he would not submit to the common forms of approaches, but prepared directly for an assault.

Having planted a battery on the south-side of the town, which continued firing for two days, two breaches were made in the walls, by which some regiments of foot immediately entered. But these being repulsed by the defendants, Cromwell drew out a fresh reserve of foot, and in person bravely entered at their head. This example inspired the soldiers with such courage, that none were able to stand before them; and having now gained the town, they made a terrible slaughter, putting all they met with, that were in arms, to the sword. Cromwell had given such orders, to discourage

rage other places from making opposition, to which purpose he wrote to the parliament, " that he believed this severity would save much effusion of blood." Afton's men, however, did not fall unrevenged; for they desperately disputed every corner of the streets, and finding these too hot, they retired to the churches and steeples. About an hundred of them were blown up together in St. Peter's church; only one man escaping, who leaped from the tower, and had quarter given him. Those who would not surrender upon summons, were closely shut up and guarded, in order to starve them out; and of those who did surrender, all the officers and every tenth private man were killed, and the rest thrust on shipboard for Barbadoes. The winning of this town was so surprising, that O-Neal, at the hearing of it, swore a great oath, " that if Cromwell had taken Tredagh by storm, if he should storm hell he would take it."

§. 4. The slaughter at Tredagh, though cruel in itself, had the good effect that the general desired. All the other places round about surrendered, few of them waiting so much as for a summons. Dundalk was abandoned so precipitately, that the garrison left their cannon behind them on the platforms. Cromwell therefore, finding his name sufficient at this time in the north, did not march any farther that way, but returned to besiege Wexford, taking in Killingkerick and Arkloe-castle by the way.

Having summoned Wexford, and received a dubious answer from colonel Synnot, the governor, the general waited till he might have an explanation. In this view he corresponded with him by several papers. But finding that Synnot's whole intent was to protract time, while the earl of Castlehaven, with 500 men, came to his assistance, Cromwell applied himself to storming the castle. A small breach being made, commissioners were sent from the besieged, to treat of a surrender: but it was now too late; for no cessation having been agreed upon, the guns continued firing, the breach was made wider,

wider, the guard quitted the caftle, and fome of Cromwell's men entered it. The enemy obferving this, quitted their ftations in all parts; fo that the others getting over the walls, poffeffed themfelves of the town without any great oppofition. Here, as well as at Drogheda, none were fuffered to live that they found in arms. In this town great riches were taken, and fome fhips feized in the harbour, that had much interrupted the trade on that coaft; and the feverity here ufed had the fame effect as at Drogheda; the terror fpread to all the towns and forts along the coaft, as far as Dublin, which faved the general the trouble of fummoning them.

§. 5. The winter now coming on, and it being a very wet feafon, Cromwell's troops fuffered much from the weather, and the flux then raging amongft them. Many thought thefe reafons fhould have obliged him, for the prefent, to put a ftop to his conquefts; but he was of another mind, and more in the right than they. The difficulties the marquis of Ormond met with in bringing a new army into the field, the antient difagreement again breaking out between the popifh confederates and him, the fecret intelligence held by Cromwell in the province of Munfter, and the mighty affairs that called him back to England, were to him more powerful motives for continuing the war, than the winter was to interrupt his progrefs.

Being thus refolved, he marches towards Rofs, a ftrong town upon the Barrow. The lord Taaffe was governor of this place, who had a potent garrifon with him; and the better to fecure it, Ormond, Caftlehaven, and the lord Ardes, caufed 1500 men to be boated over to reinforce it; which was done in fight of Cromwell's army, who were not able to hinder it. However, the lord-general no fooner came before the town, but he fummoned the governor to furrender it to the parliament of England; declaring, that "he endeavoured, as much as poffible, to avoid the effufion of blood." No anfwer was at prefent returned, till the

great

great guns began to play; when the governor, being apprehensive of the same usage that other garrisons had met with, was willing to treat; which being allowed, they came to this agreement: " That the town be delivered up to the lord-general Cromwell, and they within march away with bag and baggage to Kilkenny." Fifteen hundred of them accordingly did so; but 600, being English, revolted to Cromwell. In the mean time Kinsale, Cork, Youghall, Bandonbridge, and other garrisons, voluntarily declared for the conqueror; which places proved of great use in the reduction of Munster, and of all Ireland. Sir Charles Coot and colonel Venables were very successful in the north; and lord Broghill and colonel Hewson, did good service in other places.

§. 6. Cromwell being master of Ross, laid a bridge of boats over the Barrow, and sat down before Duncannon: but this place being so well provided with necessaries, that he judged it would be losing time to tarry there, he quickly rose, and marched into the county of Kilkenny, where the marquis of Ormond, being joined by Inchequin, seemed resolved to give him battle. Ormond's army, both horse and foot, was superior to Cromwell's, which was much weakened by continual duty, difficult marches, the flux, and other diseases: notwithstanding which, the marquis, upon the approach of the enemy, drew off, without making any attempts, or striking one stroke. Hereupon Enistegoe, a little town five miles from Ross, was reduced by colonel Abbot; and colonel Reynolds coming before Carrick, divided his men into two parties, with one of which he entered a gate, while he amused the garrison with the other, and so took about a hundred prisoners without the loss of one man.

Cromwell, after this, took Passage-fort, and made an attempt upon Waterford: but the winter being far advanced, and the weather very bad, he thought proper to retire into quarters for a short time. In the mean while Passage-fort was attacked by a party of the enemy,

enemy, who were totally routed by colonel Zankey, and 350 of them taken prisoners. Several other skirmishes were maintained with the like success; but the loss of lieutenant-general Jones, who died at Wexford of a violent fever, struck a damp upon all, especially as it was followed by that of other brave commanders, and abundance of the common soldiers. Recruits, however, arrived daily from England; and some of the Irish under Ormond, as well as the English, revolted to the victorious Cromwell; who made great use of the animosities between them and Ormond, endeavouring in the mean time, by the most artful insinuations, to draw over the marquis himself to the interest of the parliament.

Even while the army was in winter-quarters, our vigilant general could not be inactive. He visited all the garrisons that were in his possession in Munster, and gave orders for affairs both civil and military. When the mayor of Kinsale delivered him the keys, he returned them not again, according to custom, but gave them to colonel Stubber the governor; his reason for which was, that the mayor being both a papist and an Irishman, he could not safely be trusted with such an important place.

§. 7. The parliament at this time being apprehensive of some designs carrying on in Scotland, which might require the lieutenant's presence, ordered the speaker to write for him over: but the letter not reaching him till the latter end of March, he had taken the field before, and proceeded far in the reduction of Ireland. Tho' he came not into winter-quarters till December, yet scarce was January over, but he divided his army into two bodies, the more to distress the marquis of Ormond. One party he commanded himself, and gave the other to Ireton; and these were to march into the enemy's quarters two several ways, and to meet near Kilkenny. Cromwell's rout was over the Blackwater, towards the counties of Limerick and Tipperary; and by the way he took in a castle called Kilkenny, Cloghern-house, and Raghill-castle.

Having

Having with difficulty paſſed the river Shewer, at ten one night he arrived before Feathard, a garriſon town under one Butler, and immediately ſent a trumpeter to ſummon it. But they ſhot at the trumpeter, and declared, that the night was not a fit time to ſend a ſummons in. Hereupon Cromwell prepared to ſtorm, which brought the governor to a treaty, and the next morning Feathard was ſurrendered upon articles.

Calan, a ſtrong place, defended by three caſtles, was next to be attacked. Here he was joined by Ireton, Reynolds, and Zankey, whoſe ſoldiers together made a conſiderable body. They ſtormed the caſtles one after another, and carried them all in the ſpace of one day: upon which the whole garriſon, except Butler's troops, who ſurrendered before the cannon were fired, were put to the ſword. After the ſoldiers had refreſhed themſelves in the town, they marched back to Feathard, by the way taking the caſtles of Onoctoter and Bullynard; which were ſoon followed by Kiltenon, Arſenon, Coher, and Dundrum, all very conſiderable places.

§. 8. Cromwell had now entirely ſubdued all the places of importance, except Limerick, Waterford, Clonmell, Galloway, and Kilkenny. Theſe were all towns of great ſtrength, and would neceſſarily take up ſome time. He reſolved, however, to attempt the laſt, and in that view, ſent orders to colonel Hewſon, the new governor of Dublin, to bring him all the forces he could draw out of the garriſons on that ſide. Accordingly Hewſon joined him near Gowram, a populous and ſtrong town, governed by one Hammond, who returned a very reſolute anſwer upon being ſummoned to ſurrender. The great guns upon this began to play, and did ſuch execution, as obliged Hammond to demand a parley: but the only terms he could now obtain were, "that the common ſoldiers ſhould have their lives, and the officers be diſpoſed of as the general thought fit." The place being thus delivered up, Hammond, and all the commiſſion officers but one, were the next day shot to death; and the popish priest, their chaplain, was hanged.

Proceeding now to Kilkenny (which, besides its ordinary garrison, had been reinforced from the neighbouring towns that surrendered) when he came within a mile of the walls, Cromwell summoned Sir Walter Butler the governor, and the corporation, to deliver up the city; which they refusing to do, he drew nearer, and erected a battery in the most convenient place, notwithstanding the opposition from within. With about 100 shot a breach was opened, at which the soldiers engaged the enemy, while colonel Ewer, with 1000 foot, gained another part of the city, called Irish-town. The besieged, however, were so desperate, that neither could Cromwell enter the breach, nor Ewer gain the bridge which led into the heart of the place. But a little consideration brought the governor to better measures, and after a day's debate, it was agreed, " that the castle and city should be delivered up to Cromwell, with all the arms, ammunition, and publick stores; that the inhabitants should be protected in their persons, goods, and estates, only paying two thousand pounds to Cromwell's army; and that the governor, officers, and soldiers, should march away with bag and baggage." Thus was Kilkenny, which had been the nursery of the late rebellion, and the residence of the supreme council, reduced to the parliament's obedience in less than a week, chiefly by the vigilance, activity, and indefatigable industry of the lord-general Cromwell, who frequently, on these desperate occasions, exposed himself to the most imminent dangers.

§. 9. Having settled the affairs of Kilkenny, Cromwell marched to Carrick, in order to proceed on further action. But first he wrote a letter to the speaker of the parliament, " giving an account of the taking of Kilkenny, and several other places; confessing that he had received many private intimations of the parliament's pleasure, as to his coming home; but that as he did not receive his honour's letter till the army was

Life of OLIVER CROMWELL. 45

d, and had not since heard any thing farther
liament's resolution, he thought himself ob-
/ait for a more clear expression of their will,
he was always ready to submit."
this time the marquis of Ormond, and his
appointed a meeting in West-meath, to con-
me way to support their cause, which was
most every where. The result of their confe-
, that they should molest the English in their
hereby to protract time, till they had an op-
of leaving the kingdom. But Cromwell,
reading their motions, sat down before Clon-
vhich was a garrison of 2000 foot; and 120
d as soon as the siege was formed, he de-
lonel Reynolds and Sir Theophilus Jones,
horse, foot and dragoons, to prevent Or-
esign. Sir Charles Coot also took the field
men, with the same intent. But the mar-
ng from place to place, to avoid fighting, co-
nolds, that his men might not remain idle,
'ecrogham. In the mean time the lord B:og-
another detachment, defeated the bishop of
) was marching with 5000 men to relieve
Many considerable persons were here taken,
g them the bishop himself, who was carried
kept by his own forces, and there hanged
walls, in sight of the garrison; which so
:d them, that they immediately surrendered
liament's forces. This bishop was used to
iere was no way of curing the English, but
g them."
dvantages were a spur to the soldiers that lay
>nmell, and made them resolute in the busi-
'ithstanding the vigorous resistance they met
he active Cromwell, having summoned O-
governor, to no purpose, proceeded to his
hod of storming. The great guns being
breach was soon opened, which the besie-
geously entered, and, in spite of the bravery
eged, kept their ground, till after four hours
fighting,

fighting, with doubtful fuccefs, they carried all before them. This was looked upon to be the hotteſt ſtorm, of ſo long continuance, that had ever been known. But the ſubduing of Clonmell, tho' with ſo much difficulty, occaſioned the ſurrender of ſeveral other garriſons.

§. 10. While the lord-general was thus victorious in one part of Ireland, his deputies, with the parties under them, were no lefs ſuccefsful in others: and his proceeding ſo profperouſly in his affairs, and obtaining thereby ſo great ſway, occaſioned a book to be diſperſed about this time, entitled, " The character of king Cromwell;" which, tho' ſuppreſſed as a libel, was received as a kind of prophecy. And indeed, by his good government in Ireland, both in civil and military affairs, and the great ſuccefs of it, Cromwell obtained a very great intereſt, both here and there, both in the officers of the army and the parliament: only the Scots and preſbyterians were generally no favourers of him. He was now preparing to take Waterford and Duncannon, and had actually blocked up Waterford, when about the middle of May, by a new order, or rather requeſt of the parliament, he was obliged to leave the finiſhing of his conqueſts to his ſon-in-law Ireton, whom, for that purpoſe, he conſtituted lord-deputy. And ſo fortunate was Ireton in his commiſſion, that tho' he died of the plague in a year and a half after, he took Waterford and Limerick, and left very few places in the hands of the enemy.

Cromwell was in Ireland about nine months, in which inconſiderable time, he performed more than any king or queen of England had been able to do in a much greater number of years. Before he left the kingdom, in order to weaken the Iriſh, he contrived means for tranſporting no lefs than 40,000 of them out of their country into foreign ſervice, few of whom ever returned again. He alſo ſettled the civil affairs, and procured a more ſummary way of adminiſtring juſtice than ever yet was known. After which

which he embarked for England, and failed home, as it were, in triumph. At Briftol, he was twice faluted by the great guns, and welcomed in with many other demonftrations of joy. On Hounflow-heath he was met by general Fairfax, many members of parliament and officers of the army, and multitudes of the common people. Coming to Hyde-park, the great guns were fired off, and colonel Barkftead's regiment, which was drawn up for that purpofe, gave him feveral vollies with their fmall arms. Thus in a triumphant manner he entered London, amidft a crowd of attendants, friends and citizens, and was received with the higheft acclamations. And having refumed his place in parliament, the fpeaker, in an elegant fpeech, returned him the thanks of the houfe for his great and faithful fervices in Ireland. After which, the lord-lieutenant gave them a particular account of the ftate and condition of that kingdom.

CHAP. IV.

CROMWELL's *war againft the Scots under king Charles the fecond, till he totally routs them at the battle of Worcefter.*

§. 1. THE laft war in which Cromwell was perfonally engaged, was againft the Scots, and other partizans of king Charles the fecond. In lefs than a month after his return from Ireland, he was employed in this new expedition, which took him up much time and labour, the Scots, upon the late king's death, had proclaimed his fon their fovereign, and fent commiffioners to the Hague, to acquaint his majefty on what terms they would receive him; the chief of which was, "that he fhould conform to both the covenants, and oblige others to do the fame." The treaty between

tween them was long on foot, his majesty, in the mean time, shifting from place to place for his security; till at last, by his granting a commission to the marquis of Montrose, who was hated by the kirk, the king had like to have spoiled all. But upon the execution of the marquis, and a fresh application from the covenanters, he consented in June, 1650, to all their demands, and arrived in Scotland on the 16th of that month, having signed the covenants before he set foot on shore.

The parliament of Scotland, hereupon began to raise forces for the king's service, with which, it was supposed, they intended to invade England. While these preparations were carrying on in Scotland, the commonwealth here were providing for their own security; and it was with a view to this, that they had sent for Cromwell from Ireland. He, as soon as he arrived, persuaded the council not to be behind-hand with the enemy, but to prevent the Scots invasion of England, by carrying the war directly into Scotland. Some scrupulous men, however, and among them general Fairfax, objected to this, as being contrary to the covenant between the two nations. To which it was answered, "That the Scots had already broken the covenant, and that therefore it was not now binding on the one side, after it had been dissolved on the other." So that they came at length to this resolution, "That having a formed army, well provided and experienced, they would march it forthwith into Scotland, to prevent the Scots marching into England, and the miseries that might attend such an invasion." The lord-general Fairfax being again consulted herein, seemed at first to like the design; but having been afterwards persuaded by the presbyterian ministers, and his own lady, who was a great patroness of them, he declared, "That he was not satisfied, that there was a just ground for the parliament of England, to send their army to invade Scotland; but in case the Scots should invade England, then he was ready to engage against them in defence of his own country."

country." The council of state being somewhat troubled at the lord-general's scruples, appointed a committee to confer with him, in order to satisfy him of the justice and lawfulness of this undertaking. The chief members of this committee were Cromwell, Lambert, Harrison, St. John, and Whitelock, &c.

§. 2. Cromwell opened the conference; and after some previous discourse between the lord-general and the committee, his excellency acquainted them with the ground of his dissatisfaction, declaring, "That he did not see the Scots had given sufficient cause for this invasion of their country by the English." Upon which Cromwell proceeded thus: "I confess my lord, that if they had given no cause to invade them, it would not be justifiable for us to do it; and to make war upon them without a sufficient ground for it, will be contrary to that which in conscience we ought to do, and displeasing both to God and good men. But, my lord, if they have invaded us, as your lordship knows they have done since the national league and covenant, and contrary to it, in that action of duke Hamilton, which was by order and authority from the parliament of that kingdom, and so the act of the whole nation by their representatives; and if they now give us too much cause of suspicion, that they intend another invasion upon us, joining with their king, with whom they have made a full agreement, without the assent or privity of this commonwealth; and are very busy at this present in raising forces and money to carry on their design: If these things are not a sufficient ground and cause for us to endeavour to provide for the safety of our own country, and to prevent the miseries which an invasion of the Scots would bring upon us, I humbly submit to your excellency's judgment. That they have formerly invaded us, and brought a war into the bowels of our country, is known to all, wherein God was pleased to bless us with success against them: And that they now intend a new invasion upon us, I do as really believe, and have as good intelligence of it, as we can have of any thing that is not yet acted. Therefore I say, my lord, that upon thefe grounds, I think we have moft juft caufe to begin, or rather to return and requite their hoftility firft begun upon us; and thereby to free our country (if God fhall be pleafed to affift us, and I doubt not but he will) from the great mifery and calamity of having an army of Scots within our country. That there will be a war between us, I fear is unavoidable: Your excellency will foon determine, whether it be better to have this war in the bowels of another country, or of our own; and that it will be in one of them, I think is without fcruple." But no arguments could prevail on the general, who declared that his confcience was not fatisfy'd as to the juftice of this war; and therefore, that he might be no hindrance to the parliament's defigns, he defired to lay down his commiffion. Upon which Cromwell fpoke again, as follows:

"I am very forry your lordfhip fhould have thoughts of laying down your commiffion, by which God hath bleffed you in the performance of fo many eminent fervices for the parliament. I pray, my lord, confider all your faithful fervants us who are under you, and defire to ferve under no other general. It would be a great difcouragement to all of us, and a great difcouragement to the affairs of the parliament, for our noble general to entertain any thoughts of laying down his commiffion. I hope you lordfhip will never give fo great an advantage to the publick enemy, nor fo much difhearten your friends, as to think of laying down your commiffion." But all this would not do: The general ftill continued in the fame mind, and concluding thus: "What would you have me do? As far as my confcience will give way, I am willing to join with you ftill in the fervice of the parliament; but where the confcience is not fatisfied, none of you, I am fure, will engage in any fervice; and that is my condition in this, and therefore I muft defire to be excufed."

Cromwell and the other officers in this committee were moft earneft in perfuading the general to continue

his

his commission; and yet, 'tis said, there was cause enough to believe that they did not over-much desire it. Ludlow says, that Cromwell press'd the council of state, that notwithstanding the unwillingness of the lord Fairfax to command upon this occasion, they would yet continue him to be general of the army; professing for his own part, "that he would rather chuse to serve under him in his post than to command the greatest army in Europe." He also informs us, that the forementioned committee was appointed upon the motion of lieutenant general Cromwell, "who, says he, acted his part to the life, that I really thought him in earnest." * How far he was so, it is impossible to say with any certainty.

Thus Cromwell and his party carried it against the general, who thereupon laid down his commission; tho' he was seemingly much persuaded to the contrary. The parliament were at no loss for one to succeed in the great office; for having sufficiently experienced the valor, conduct and faithfulness of Cromwell, who had in fact been long at the head of the army, tho' only lieutenant-general in name, they soon voted, one and all, that he should be their general; † and so an act passed, "for constituting and appointing Oliver Cromwell, Esq; to be captain-general in chief of all the forces raised, and to be raised, by authority of parliament, within the commonwealth of England."

§. 3. Before his departure for Scotland, Cromwell moved the council that he might be eased of the affairs of Ireland. But he could only obtain to have five others joined with him in the commission for governing that kingdom, who were Ludlow, Ireton, colonel John Jones, major Salway, and one Mr. Weaver; any three of whom were to make a committee. And now the lord-general set out for the north, after the army, and received great demonstrations of respect as he

---

* Ludlow's Memoirs, vol. I. p. 315.
† Fairfax recommended Cromwell to this trust.

he paſſed along. At York he was attended, and magnificently entertained by the corporation; but ſtaid no longer than to order ſupplies for the army.

The committee of eſtates in Scotland, before this, ſeemed to be ſurpriſed at the news of an Engliſh army's marching northwards. They ſent a letter to the ſpeaker of the Engliſh parliament, "ſetting forth their conſternation, and declaring that the forces they were raiſing were only for their own defence? deſiring to know, whether the Engliſh army, now on the march, was to act on the offenſive or defenſive." They wrote alſo to Sir Arthur Haſlerigg, governor of Newcaſtle, major general Lambert, and the lord-general Cromwell, in much the ſame terms. On the other hand, the parliament of England publiſhed a declaration of the grounds and reaſons of their army's advance, "accuſing the Scots of acting contrary to agreement, and having invaded England before under duke Hamilton, and now preparing for another invaſion; in proclaiming Charles Stuart king of England and Ireland, though they had no authority in theſe kingdoms; and in declaring againſt the Engliſh parliament and army, as ſectaries, and ranking them with malignants and papiſts."

The Scots, perceiving that the parliament of England was not to be impoſed on, now laboured by all poſſible means to render their army odious; and ſo did they terrify the common people by miſrepreſentations of Cromwell's commiſſion, as if he was to deſtroy all he met with, that they were hardly ſatiſfied by a declaration of the lord-general and the army, "reminding them of the behaviour of the Engliſh forces when they were before in Scotland, and proteſting that none but thoſe who had endeavoured to engage foreign princes againſt the commonwealth of England, or had exerciſed actual hoſtility, ſhould have the leaſt violence offered to them, either in body or goods."

In the mean time leaving York, Cromwell came to Northallerton and Darlington, being ſaluted, as he paſſed by, with the ordnance. At Durham he was met with by Sir Arthur Haſlerigg, who conducted him to Newcastle, and there galantly entertained him. From Newcastle he haftened to Berwick, and caufed a general review of the army on Haggerton-moor, where he was received with great demonſtrations of joy, by a gallant body of 5000 horfe, and 11,000 foot. From Berwick he fent the army's declaration into Scotland, containing the grounds of their march into that kingdom. One copy hereof was conveyed to the Scotch general, another to the parliament, and a third to the committee of eſtates.

§. 4. While the lord-general was thus upon the verge of Scotland, he drew out the army upon a hill, within Berwick bounds, where they had a full profpect of the adjacent country, and made a fpeech to them, exhorting them to be faithful and courageous, and then not to doubt of a bleſſing from God, and all encouragement from himfelf." This fpeech was anfwered with loud and unanimous acclamations from the foldiers; who being ordered to march, entered Scotland with a fhout. That night they quartered near the lord Mordington's caſtle, where the general caufed proclamation to be made, " that none, on pain of death, fhould offer violence to the perfons or effects of any in Scotland not found in arms; and that none, on the fame penalty, fhould ſtraggle half a mile from their quarters, without fpecial licence."

The next day they arrived at Dunbar, where they were recruited with provifions, by fhips fent thither from England for that purpofe; the Scots having taken care, before-hand, that the country from Berwick to Edinburgh fhould afford them nothing. From Dunbar they marched to Haddington, within twelve miles of Edinburgh. And in all this march they did not fee one Scotchman under fixty years of age, nor any youth above fix, and but very few women and children; the Scotch miniſters having aſſured the people, " that the Engliſh would cut the throats of all the men between fixty and fixteen years of age, cut off the right-hands of all the youth between fixteen and fix, burn the womens breasts with hot irons, and destroy all before them."

§. 5. After the army's remove from Haddington, they understood that the enemy was disposed to give them battle on a heath called Gladsmoor. The English hereupon took care to possess themselves of the place before them: but the Scots did not think fit to appear, notwithstanding that the general did all that lay in his power to provoke them to it. Some skirmishes however happened, about the possession of a place called Arthur's-hill, which the English made themselves masters of.

As he could not draw the Scots to action, Cromwell intended to have begun with them; but was prevented by a great rain, and obliged to draw off his army towards Muscleborough. The enemy, upon his retreat, did all they could to distress his army, and put his rear guard into some confusion; but were soon repulsed by major-general Lambert, and colonel Whalley, the king standing all the while on a castle to see the encounter. Between three and four o'clock the next morning, the English were attacked in their quarters, at Muscleborough, with great fury, the enemy being animated by some of their ministers: but victory was still on their side, for they routed the Scots, and pursued them within half a league of Edinburgh, killing several, and taking many prisoners. Cromwell got much applause after this action, by sending the chief of the Scotch officers, who were wounded and taken, in his own coach to Edinburgh. This vindicated him, in a great measure, from the reports, that had been given out of his cruelty.

§. 6. Having marched again to Dunbar, to take in fresh supplies, the general gave away a great quantity of corn among the poor of the place, who were in extreme want. In the mean time the Scots ministers at Edinburgh, imagining he was quite retired, gave publick thanks to God, for putting terror into the

the hearts of the English sectaries: but his sudden return to Muscleborough made them ashamed of what they had done, and proved that general Lesley, who was not so confident to be off his guard, could judge better of events than his enthusiastical teachers.

An equivocal message now arriving from Lesley, concerning the state of the present difference, and full of insipid distinctions about the king and the cause; the English general gave him to understand, that he was not to be thus amused, but would take the intentions of the Scots from what they had continued to act; concluding, "That if Lesley was resolved to come to a battle, he had a fair opportunity of doing it; otherwise, to what purpose did they both wait?"

Finding he could not provoke the Scots to an engagement, Cromwell removed to Pencland-hills, and there pitched his tents within sight of Edinburgh. About the same time he executed a serjeant, for plundering a house contrary to his declaration. He also took in some small garrisons, and at the request of the Scots appointed a conference, in which he was assured, "that when opportunity served, it should be seen that they wanted not courage to give him battle." While he lay here, he advanced one day at the head of a party, in order to shew how ready he was to engage; when one of the Scots, who knew him, fired a carbine at him: upon which Cromwell called out with great composure, and told him, "that if he had been one of his soldiers, he should have been cashiered for firing so wide of the mark."

It would be tedious to recite all that passed between the two armies, before they actually came to an engagement. "Cromwell, says father * Orleans, whose interest it was to come soon to a battle, in a country where his army found nothing to subsist on, marched directly to the enemy, who lay encamped between Edinburgh and Leith, to cover those two places, and the heart of the country. The cunning Englishman

* Revolutions d'Angleterre.

tried all ways to draw Lesley to fight; but he understood his trade, and it being his interest to protract time, so to ruin the enemy's army, which had neither ammunition nor provisions, but what came from England at a great charge, he kept himself so strongly intrenched, that Cromwell durst not attack him. The English general used all baits and stratagems known in war to oblige the Scot to fight him; sometimes drawing him towards Dunbar, as if he would have besieged Edinburgh, and again moving to get between Sterling and him. But the Scot dexterously avoided those snares; and though the English army kept up close with him, he so ordered his motions, and posted himself so advantageously, that the whole month of August was spent in these counter-marches, so tedious to a man of Cromwell's spirit, who could never meet with an opportunity, either to fight in the open field, or attack his enemy in his camp.

§. 7. At last, on the 30th of August, Cromwell drew out his army from Muselcborough, and marched towards Haddington. The Scots observing the English army to retire, followed them close; and falling upon the rear-guard of horse in the night, having the advantage of a clear moon, beat them up to the rear-guard of foot. Which alarm, coming suddenly upon them, put them into some disorder. But the Scots wanting courage to prosecute the advantage, and withal, a cloud overshadowing the moon, gave the English an opportunity to secure themselves, and cover the main body. Being come to Haddington, where they were in continual danger of being assaulted by the enemy, the general ordered a strict watch to be kept, to prevent the worst. The Scots conceiving they had now more than ordinary advantage, about midnight attempted the English quarters on the west end of the town; but were soon repulsed and sent farther off. The next day, being the first of September, the Scots being drawn up at the west end of the town, in a very advantageous place, the English drew out on

the

Life of OLIVER CROMWELL.

the east into an open field, very fit for both armies to engage in; where having waited some hours for the coming of the Scots, and perceiving they would not fight but upon an advantage, they, pursuant to their former resolution, marched away to Dunbar.

The Scotch army followed at a convenient distance, being reinforced with the addition of three regiments; and seeing the English lodged in Dunbar, hovered about them upon the adjacent hills like a thick cloud, menacing nothing but ruin and destruction, and looking down upon them as their sure prey.

The lord general was now in great distress, and look'd on himself as undone. His army was in a very weak and sickly condition, and in great want of provisions, whereby their courage also was very much abated; while the Scots were stout and hearty, in their own country, and upon very advantageous ground. And besides, they more than doubled the English in number, being about twenty-seven thousand, whereas the others were but twelve thousand. Some say they had in their army about thirty thousand, horse and foot; and the English were reduced to ten thousand at most. General Cromwell, with this sickly company, was now hemmed in on every side by those greater numbers of his enemies; who, to make sure work, had also by a strong party secured Coberspath, the only pass between him and Berwick, thereby to hinder all provisions or relief from thence, and to cut off all retreat from the English army, who had not above three days forage for their horses. Thus were they reduced to the utmost straits *, so that they had now no way left, but either to give up themselves a prey to their insulting enemies, or to fight upon these

---

* Before the Battle of Dunbar, says Whitelock, the English were in a sad posture: very many of their men sick, and wanting provisions; the enemy having made up the passes before them: the whole Scots army on the right-hand, and the sea on the left; and the whole nation of Scotland behind them, p. 471.

these unequal terms, and under those great disadvantages.

In this extremity the lord-general, on the 2d of September, called a council of war, in which, after some debate, it was resolved to fall upon the enemy the next morning; about an hour before day; and accordingly the several regiments were ordered to their respective posts. Here we are told by bishop Burnet, that Cromwell, under these pressing difficulties, called his officers together to seek the lord, as they expressed it: after which, he bid all about him take heart, for God had certainly heard them, and would appear for them. Then walking in the earl of Roxburgh's gardens, that lay under the hill, and by prospective glasses discerning a great motion in the Scotch camp; Cromwell thereupon said, " God is delivering them into our hands, they are coming down to us." And the bishop says, that Cromwell loved to talk much of that matter all his life long afterwards.

The Scots, it seems, had now at last resolved to fight the English, and to that end were coming down the hill ? where, if they had continued, the English could not have gone up to engage them without very great disadvantage. This resolution was contrary to Lesley's opinion; who though he was in the chief command, had a commitee of states to give him his orders, among whom Wariftoun was one. These being weary of lying in the fields, thought that Lesley did not make haste enough to destroy the army of the sectaries, as they called them. Lesley, on the other hand, told them, that by lying there all was sure, but that by engaging in action with brave and desperate men, all might be lost; and yet they still pressed him to fall on. Many have imagined that there was treachery in all this; but the fore-mentioned author says, he was persuaded there was no treachery in it; only Wariftoun was too hot, and Lesley was too cold, and yielded too easily to their humours, which he should not have done. This resolution of the Scots to fall upon the English was some time retarded by the
unseasonable-

unseasonableness of the weather; and in the mean while, as we have already observed, Cromwell resolved to fall upon them.

§. 8. The night before the battle proving dreadfully rainy and tempestuous, the lord-general took more than ordinary care of himself and his army. He refreshed his men in the town, and above all things secured his match-locks against the weather, whilst his enemies neglected theirs. The Scots were all the night employed in coming down the hill; and early in the morning, being Tuesday the third of September, before they were put in order, general Cromwell drew out a strong party of horse, and falling upon the horse-guards, made them retire *. Then immediately his bodies both of horse and foot advancing, the fight soon grew hot on all sides; 'till after about an hour's dispute, the whole numerous army of the Scots was totally routed. Two regiments stood their ground, and were almost all killed in their ranks. The rest fled, and were pursued as far as Haddington with great execution. About four thousand were slain on the place and in the pursuit, and ten thousand taken prisoners, many of whom were desperately wounded. Fifteen thousand arms, all the artillery and ammunition, with above two hundred colours, were taken; and all with the loss of scarce three hundred English. Prisoners of note were Sir James Lumsdale lieutenant-general of the foot, the lord Libberton (who soon after died of his wounds) adjutant-general Bickerton, scout-master Campbell, Sir William Douglas, the lord Grandison, and colonel Gordon; besides twelve lieutenants-colonels, six majors, forty-two captains, and seventy-five lieutenants. The two Lesleys escaped to Edinburgh, which upon

---

* Rapin says, the Scots cavalry on the right wing performed very well at first; but were at last drove back, and put to flight. The left wing fled without sustaining one charge.

the news of this defeat was immediately quitted by his garrison, and Leith resolved to admit the conquerors, being not able to keep them out.

Thus this formidable army, which had so lately triumphed in a confident assurance of victory, was totally defeated and overthrown by one not half so numerous, which at the same time was reduced almost to the last extremity. But this extremity making them fix upon a firm resolution either to conquer or die, and withal, their falling so suddenly upon the Scots, when they so little expected them, but designed first to fall upon them, seem to be the true occasion of this wonderful turn of affairs. The lord-general himself drew up a narrative of this memorable victory, and sent it by a courier to the council of state, who ordered it to be read in all the churches of London, with solemn thanksgiving: and the colours taken in this battle being sent up to the parliament, were by their order hung up as trophies in Westminster-hall.

§. 9. This great action (the most critical one that ever Cromwell was engaged in, and which for that reason we have related more particularly than many others) being thus happily ended, the English soldiers were inspired with new courage. The lord-general, soon after this battle was over, sent Lambert to attempt Edinburgh, the capital, and secure Leith, that the English ships might the more conveniently supply the army. Lambert took possession of both on the same day, they having been deserted by the Scots, and found there several pieces of ordnance, many arms, and a considerable quantity of provisions. But though the English were masters of the town, Edinburgh-castle still remained in the hands of the enemy: yet this, though judged impregnable, was at last reduced by our victorious general.

Several things passed, however, before the siege of that fortress was undertaken. Cromwell invited the Edinburgh ministers in the castle to return to their cures;

cures; which they obstinately refused, pretending they had no security for their persons. On this occasion several letters passed between the general, the governor, and these ministers; who still persisting in their stiff-necked way, the general caused English ministers to officiate in their places. The chief magistrates of Edinburgh, the committees of the church and state, and the remains of the army from Dunbar, all retired to Sterling, in order to recover their shattered strength. But all the methods they could use signified little; for the Scots were divided among themselves, and split into many parties and factions, which Cromwell, no doubt, knew how to manage to his advantage, while the motions of his army round about Edinburgh kept the whole country in awe. Several places, in the mean time, were taken in by his deputies, and a considerable victory was gained by Lambert over colonel Ker, at Hamilton; whereby the power of the remonstrators, one of the most violent parties then subsisting, was entirely ruined.

§. 10. The taking of Edinburgh castle soon followed. This is the most considerable strong-hold in Scotland, having all the requisite advantages both of nature and art. It is seated upon a high abrupt rock, has but one entrance, and that steep, and by which only two or three can go a-breast. Besides, it overlooks and commands all the places about it; so that Cromwell's men were often galled by the cannon from thence, in their quarters at Edinburgh.

When Cromwell came first before this strong place, which was not long after the defeat at Dunbar, he summoned the governor, colonel Dundass, to deliver it up to him; which having no effect, he began to consult how to reduce it by force. Nothing encouraged the attempting it by storm; and all probable ways being debated, it was at last resolved to force it by mines. In order for this work, miners were sent for, and towards the latter end of September, the galleries were begun in the night; which the besieged no sooner saw, but they fell to firing upon them. But this proved no impediment to the English, who, with indefatigable labour, wrought through the earth till they came to the main rock. This put them to a stand, but did not make them give over; for having made holes in the rock, they filled them full of powder, and endeavoured to make it fly by firing.

But this mining work going but slowly on, the lord-general, fearing he should not be able to blow the castle into the air, endeavoured now to level it with the ground; and to that end, he raised a battery fortified with gabions and other contrivances, designing to play incessantly from thence with cannons and mortars. The governor was very much amazed at this, and began to think it a vain thing to endeavour to withstand the English industry; though he did his utmost to answer the expectations of those by whom he was intrusted. The battery being raised to a convenient height, 4 mortar-pieces and 6 battering guns were forthwith mounted against the castle. But before the word of command was given, the lord-general thought fit once more to summon the governor, in the following terms; "That he being resolved to use such means as were put into his hands, for the reducing of the castle, did, for preventing further misery, demand the rendering of the place to him upon fit conditions." To this the governor returned this answer, " That being intrusted by the estates of Scotland, for the keeping of the castle, he could not deliver it up without leave from them: and therefore he desired ten days time to send to them, and receive their answer." But the lord-general knowing his time was precious, made this sudden reply, " That it concerned him not to know the obligations of them that trusted him; but that he might have honourable terms for himself, and those that were with him: but he could not give liberty to him to consult with the committee of estates."

'Twas

'Twas defigned that this parley fhould continue two days; but fome great fhot flying from the caftle before, order was given to try the mortar-pieces, three with fhells, and the fourth with ftones. Which being done accordingly, the governor returned an anfwer to the general's laft meffage; in which "he adjured him that liberty might be granted to him to fend to the committee of eftates: and faid, that he would be very willing to receive information from thofe of his countrymen whom he could truft." To this the general replied, "That whoever he would appoint to come to him, fhould have liberty for one hour; but to fend to the committee of the eftates he could not grant." The governor took no notice of this, till the mortar-pieces and great guns had for fome fmall time play'd againft the caftle. This moved him to fend forth a drum, defiring a conference with the provoft of Aberdeen, and one more then in Edinburgh; to which the general readily confented. But they knowing it to be an affair of the utmoft importance, refufed to concern themfelves in it, leaving the governor to take his own courfe. Hereupon Dundafs was in great perplexity, till having refolved the matter in his mind, he at laft came to this refult, to acquit himfelf manfully in the defence of the place. Accordingly a red enfign was immediately hung out in defiance, and the great guns began to roar from the battlements of the wall. Upon this, the lord general fent in upon them fuch continual fhowers of fhot, that the governor in a fhort time offered to furrender, if his former requeft, of fending to the committee, might be granted. But this being ftill refufed, Dundafs thought it not good to hold out any longer againft fuch violent affaults; and fo entering upon a treaty with the lord-general, came to an agreement; Firft, that the caftle, the cannon, arms, and ammunition, and furniture of war, be delivered up to Cromwell: Secondly, that the Scots have liberty to carry away their publick regifters, publick moveables, private evidences and writs: Thirdly, that thofe goods in the caftle castle belonging to any person, the owners should have restored to them: Fourthly, that the governor, and all military officers, and soldiers, might depart without molestation, to Bruntisland in Fife.

According to these articles, this strong castle, which gloried in its virginity, as having never before yielded to any conqueror, was, after a siege of three months, delivered up to Cromwell on the 24th day of December; whereby there also fell into his hands fifty-three pieces of ordnance, some of them remarkable both for size and beauty, 8,000 arms, fourscore barrels of powder, and all the king's hangings, tapestry and jewels. The subduing of this place was so unexpected by several, that the Scots cried out, "That Cromwell took it only by silver bullets." But what appeared most strange to others, and which made well on Cromwell's side, was, that the Scotch army, which lay not very far off, should never attempt the relief of this most important place.

§. 11. The Scots were now intent upon the coronation of their king, which had been long delayed, that he might "humble himself for his father's sins, and his own transgressions." But the vigorous proceedings of the English put them upon hastening what of themselves they were backward enough in; so on the first of January this solemnity was performed at Scone, his majesty first subscribing both the covenants. And now, in order to raise a powerful army, all persons were promiscuously admitted, and great numbers of honorary volunteers flocked to the king's standard at Aberdeen. From thence he marched for Sterling, where having mustered his army, he made duke Hamilton lieutenant-general, Lesley major-general, Middleton major-general of horse, and Massey general of the English troops.

Cromwell, who observed these proceedings, was little concerned at them. He endeavoured, however, to secure all the garrisons south of Firth: to which end he ordered colonel Fenwick to reduce Hume castle.

castle. Fenwick immediately applied himself to the work, and having drawn up his men before the place, sent a summons to the governor to surrender. But the governor, one Cockburn, being a man of fancy, returned only a quibbling answer. However, he did not continue long in this merry humour: for Fenwick having planted a battery, and made a breach in the castle, was invited to a parley just as he was about to enter. But he would allow only quarters for life; which being accepted, the garrison marched out, and captain Collinson took possession of it for the parliament. About the same time colonel Monk reduced Tantallon castle, after a vigorous defence.

The king and his party were now very active, and had got together an army of 20,000 men. But the earl of Eglington, with some other commanders, going into the west to raise recruits, were seized by Lilburn, and sent prisoners to Edinburgh.

§. 12. The English parliament, all this while, had a special regard to their army in Scotland. So careful were they to furnish them with men, money, and provisions, that as no army could better deserve it, so no army ever had more encouragement. Yet both parliament and army suffered a great affliction in the sickness of their general, who was now wholly confined to his chamber: and his not acting in person made the Scots believe, and confidently report, that he was certainly dead. To convince them however of their mistake, he ordered a Scotch trumpeter, who was sent to the English on a particular affair, to be brought before him, being then on the mending hand. But he relapsed soon after, and was in more danger than ever: yet the goodness of his constitution overcame his distemper, with the help of two eminent physicians that were sent him by the parliament; so that he did not think fit to accept of the parliament's offer, of returning into England before his business was done.

No sooner was he able to stir abroad, but he consulted with his chief officers about carrying on the war. He encamped again on Pencland-hills, a place well known to the English army. From Pencland hills he marched to Newbridge, and from Newbridge to Lithgow, where from the battlements of the castle, he could discern the Scotch army, as it lay encamped at Torwood, near Sterling, all guarded round with regular fortifications. Though the English could not possibly drive them out of this fastness, yet the-lord-general, to provoke them to fight, marched his army in battalia before them, and stood in that posture eight hours. But finding all this ineffectual, he drew off to Glasgow, in order to refresh his men; which being done, he again pursued the Scotch army, who had now removed their camp, and in their sight stormed and took Calendar-house, a place of considerable strength, and resolutely defended.

§. 13. Finding he could by no means bring the Scots to a battle, Cromwell sent colonel Overton, with near 2000 foot and horse, to make an attempt on Fife, in order to cut off all supplies from the enemy. Overton crossed the Forth, and landed his army at North-Ferry, in spite of the showers of shot that were poured on him from the shore. He was followed by Lambert and Okey, with two regiments of horse, and two of foot. The king now sent 4000 men, under major-general Brown, and colonel Holborn, to drive the English back again over the Forth: but they were entirely defeated by Oliver's party, 2000 of them being killed on the spot, and most of the rest taken prisoners. Among the latter was major-general Brown himself, who died soon after, for grief, as it was thought, of this misfortune.

The English now took in garrisons almost as fast as they approached them. That of Innesgary was so terrified at the late defeat, that they surrendered on the first summons to Lambert, leaving behind them all their provisions, ammunition, and arms, except their

swords

swords only." The king himself and his whole army were in such consternation, that they suddenly decamped from Torwood, and marched into Sterling-park. Cromwell followed them at their heels, and passing over the ground where they so lately lay, he found there all their sick men, and a considerable quantity of military stores, which shewed in what a panick they left the place.

§. 14. Cromwell's attempts were still in vain; for the Scots would not come to an engagement. Hereupon he marched away to Lithgow, and sent the greatest part of his men over the Forth, in order to carry on the war in Fife. At Leith, whither he retired in person to provide for the supply of his soldiers, he received the welcome news of the surrender of Bruntisland to Lambert; which place was of great advantage to the English, being a commodious harbour for the landing of stores.

Soon after he crossed the Forth himself, and drawing the greatest part of his army from Bruntisland, with the train of artillery, he went to St. John's-town, the taking of which, he knew, would prevent the Highlanders from sending any supplies, either of men or provisions, to Sterling. But, contrary to his expectation, the messenger whom he sent to summon it, was denied admittance, and returned back with this short answer from the townsmen, "that they were not in a condition to receive letters." The reason of this was, as it afterwards appeared, that the lord Duffus had the day before entered the town, with 1300 men. But the lord-general Cromwell, upon the refusal of a new summons which he sent, immediately drained the water out of the moats about the town, and falling to batter the walls, obliged the lord Duffus to surrender in one day's time.

§. 15. These wonderful successes of Cromwell in Scotland, threw the king into great perplexity, and put him upon making an irruption into England. His fate depended upon the fuccefs of one battle, and being much nearer to England than Cromwell, who could not overtake him till feveral days, he was in hopes to ftrengthen himfelf greatly, by the coming in of the well-affected in the north. The thing being refolved, his majefty fent expreffes to all his friends, that they might be ready to receive him, and on the 6th of Auguft entered England by the way of Carlifle, with about 16,000 men. This fudden invafion alarmed the whole Britifh nation, efpecially the parliament, who were now ready to cenfure the conduct of their general. But he affured them by letter, "that he would overtake the enemy, and give a good account of them, before they came near London." Accordingly he ordered Lambert to follow the king immediately with 7 or 800 horfe, and to draw as many others as he could from the country militia; and to moleft the king's march as much as poffible, by being near, and obliging him to march clofe; not engaging his own party in any fharp action, without a manifeft advantage, but keeping himfelf entire till the army came up.

The militia of moft counties was now drawn into the field, in order to obftruct the king's march. An act was publifhed, declaring, " that no perfon fhould hold any correfpondence with Charles Stuart, or his party, or give them encouragement or affiftance, under pain of high-treafon." And now Cromwell, having fettled the affairs of Scotland, and left Monk with a ftrong party, to fecure that kingdom, entered England with the remainder of the army; and on the 12th of Auguft croffed the Tine, upon the banks of which river he gave the foldiers fome repofe: the corporation of Newcaftle, in the mean time, bringing them plenty of provifions.

§. 16. The king's army marched through Lancafhire, where at the head of it he was proclaimed, as he paffed along, in all the market towns. But he met not with that encouragement which he expected;
for

Life of Oliver Cromwell. 69

for besides that the Scots daily deserted him, the countries did not come in as he believed they would, being continually obstructed by the forces of the commonwealth. The passage of Warrington-bridge, in Cheshire, was sharply contested with him by Lambert; but at last his majesty carried it, and continuing on his march with great expedition, on the 23d of August he came to Worcester, which he entered after some opposition; and looking upon it as a convenient place he determined to settle there with his army, and wait the coming of the enemy. And that he might not be wanting in any thing that might tend to the preservation of his forces, he ordered works to be raised for better security. Then he sent a summons to Mackworth, governor of Shrewsbury, inviting him to yield up that garrison; to which the governor returned a peremptory denial. He also sent letters to Sir Thomas Middleton, to raise forces for him in Montgomeryshire; but Sir Thomas detained the messenger prisoner, and sent up the letter to the parliament. A day or two after the king had taken up his quarters in Worcester, he received the melancholy news of the defeat of the earl of Derby. This brave man was the only person, who made any considerable attempt to support the king. He got together a body of 1500 horse; but before he could join the king's army, colonel Lilburn set upon him near Wiggan, and entirely routed him. The earl himself, being wounded, retreated into Cheshire with about eighty horse, and from thence to the king at Worcester.

In the mean time general Cromwell having refresh'd his soldiers near Newcastle, immediately marched away by Rippon, Ferrybridge, Doncaster, Mansfield, and Coventry; and at Keinton joined with the rest of the parliament's forces, under lieutenant-general Fleetwood, major-general Desborough, the lord Grey of Groby, major-general Lambert, and major-general Harrison; making in all 30,000 men. The commonwealth had indeed, by their new levies, increased their forces to a prodigious number; and England never before

fore produced so many soldiers in so short a time: for the standing army, with those other forces raised upon this occasion, are said to have amounted to above 60,000 men.

§. 17. The lord-general being come up, and having observed the posture of the enemy's army, began with an attempt upon Upton-bridge, seven miles from Worcester; designing there, if possible, to pass over his army. Lambert was appointed to manage this affair, who immediately detached a small party of horse and dragoons, to see how feasible the enterprise might be. This party coming to the bridge, found it broken down, all but one plank. Over this these daring fellows pass'd, who finding the Scots took the alarm, presently betook themselves to a church for security. Hereupon Massey, who lay at Upton with about 60 dragoons, and 200 horse, gave a camisado on the church; but major-general Lambert, having passed over a new supply of horse, fell furiously upon the enemy's party, and over-powering them, forced them to a retreat; which Massey supported with so much bravery, that sometimes facing, then fighting, and so falling off, himself brought up the rear, and never quitted his station, till he arrived with his men at Worcester. The bridge being thus gain'd, all possible industry was used to make it up; so that Fleetwood's army quickly passed over; which still marching forward, they laid a bridge over the Teame, which falls into the Severn, about a mile beneath Worcester: and the general, in the mean time, caused a bridge of boats to be laid over the Severn on his side, for the better conjunction of the army, and that the enemy might be the more straightened.

The Scots drawing out to oppose Fleetwood's passage, the lord-general resolved to divert their design, or to oblige them to fight on great disadvantage: to which end, himself in person led over the river two regiments of foot, colonel Hacker's horse, and his own life-guard, on that side of Worcester which he
designed

designed to attack. Whilst this was doing, lieutenant-general Fleetwood, assisted by two regiments of foot, maintained a brave fight from hedge to hedge, which the Scots had lined thick with musqueteers. And indeed they stoutly maintained their ground, till colonel Blake's, Gibbons's, and Marsh's regiments came in, and joined with the others against them; upon which they retreated to Powick-bridge, where they were again engaged by the colonels Haines, Cobbet, and Matthews; and perceiving they were not able to prevail, they thought fit at last to secure themselves by flying into Worcester.

§. 18. Presently after, the king calling a council of war, it was resolved to engage Cromwell himself. Accordingly, they on a sudden sally'd out against him with so much fury, that his invincible life-guard could not sustain the shock, but was forced to retire in some disorder; and his cannon likewise were for some time in the power of the king's party. But multitudes of fresh forces coming in, at last turned the scale on Cromwell's side. The battle continued for three or four hours with great fierceness and various success, till the Scots, being overpowered by Cromwell's superior force, were totally routed, flying away in great confusion to secure themselves. The horse made as fast as they could back again, towards the north; but the foot ran into the city, being closely pursued by some of the conquerors, who furiously flew through all the streets, doing such terrible execution, that there was nothing to be seen for some time but blood and slaughter.

As soon as the lord-general had forced his way through Sudbury-gate, whilst his party were killing and slaying all they met with, he with some regiments ran up to the Fort-royal, commanded by colonel Drummond; and being just about to storm, he first ventured through whole showers of shot, to offer the Scots quarter, if they would presently submit, and deliver up the fort; which they refusing, he soon reduced

ced it by force, and without mercy put them all to the sword, to the number of 1500 men. In the mean time very considerable parties were sent after the flying enemy, and the country every where rose upon them.

The slain in this battle were reckoned about 4000, and the prisoners taken in the fight, and in the pursuit, amounted to about 10,000; so that near all were lost. The chief of the prisoners were duke Hamilton (brother of the late duke) who died soon after of his wounds; the earl of Derby, who not long after was sentenced to death, and lost his head at Bolton; the earls of Lauderdale, Carnwarth, Rothes, and Kelly; lord Sinclair, Sir John Packington, Sir Charles Cunningham, Sir Ralph Clare, major-general Montgomery, major-general Piscotty, Mr. Richard Fanshaw, secretary to the king, the general of the ordnance, the adjutant-general of the foot; besides several colonels, and other inferior officers. There were also taken all their artillery and baggage, 158 colours, the king's standard, his coach and horses, and several other things of great value. The king escaped, and having wandered some time in disguise about England, he at last found means to embark, and landed safely at Diepe in France. This great victory, which was justly looked upon as the decision of the grand cause between the king and the commonwealth, was obtained by general Cromwell on the 3d of September, the same day twelve-month that the Scots had such a defeat given them by his forces at Dunbar, as lost them their kingdom *.

§. 19.

* The next day after this victory, the lord-general sent a letter to the parliament; which was as follows:

" I am not able yet to give you an exact account of the great things which the Lord hath done for this commonwealth, and for his people; and yet I am unwilling to be silent, but according to my duty I shall represent it to you, as it comes to hand. This battle

§. 19. Cromwell, having given this deadly blow to all the king's party, staid no longer at Worcester, than

battle was fought with various success for some hours, but still hopeful on your part, and in the end became an absolute victory, and so full an one, as proved a total defeat and ruin of the enemy's army, and possession of the town. Our men entering at the enemy's heels, and fighting with them in the streets with very great courage, took all their baggage and artillery. What the slain are, I can given you no account, because we have not taken an exact view; but they are very many, and must needs be so, because the dispute was long, and very near at hand, and often at push of pike, and from one defence to another. There are about six or seven thousand prisoners taken here, and many officers and noblemen of quality; duke Hamilton, the earl of Rothes, and divers other noblemen : I hear, the earl of Lauderdale, many officers of great quality, and some that will be fit objects of your justice. We have sent very considerable parties after the flying enemy : I hear they have taken considerable numbers of prisoners, and are very close in the pursuit. Indeed, I hear, the country riseth upon them every where; and I believe, the forces that lay through providence at Bewdley, and in Shropshire and Staffordshire, and those with colonel Lilburne, were in a condition, as if this had been foreseen, to intercept what should return. A more particular account than this will be prepared for you, as we are able. I heard they had not many more than a thousand horse in their body that fled, and I believe we have near four thousand forces following and interposing between them and home. Their army was about sixteen thousand strong, and fought ours on Worcester side Severn, almost with their whole, whilst we had engaged half our army on the other side, but with parties of theirs. Indeed it was a stiff business; yet I do not think we have lost two hundred men. Your new rais'd forces did perform

than to see the walls of it levelled with the ground, and the dikes filled with earth; thereby to curb the disaffection of the inhabitants. This done, he marched up in a triumphant manner to London, driving 4 or 5000 prisoners before him. Beyond Aylesbury, he was met by four commissioners from the parliament, whom they sent to pay him all the marks of honour and esteem. When he came to Acton, he was solemnly met by the speaker, and the rest of the members

form singular good service, for which they deserve a very high estimation and acknowledgement; as also for their willingness thereunto, forasmuch as the same hath added so much to the reputation of your affairs: They are all dispatched home again; which, I hope, will be much for the ease and satisfaction of the country, which is a great fruit of the successes.

The dimensions of this mercy are above my thoughts; it is, for ought I know, a crowning mercy; surely, if it be not, such a one we shall have, if this provoke those that are concerned in it to thankfulness, and the parliament to do the will of him, who hath done his will for it, and for the nation; whose good pleasure is, to establish the nation, and the change of the government, by making the people so willing to the defence thereof, and so signally to bless the endeavours of your servants in this late great work. I am bold, humbly to beg, that all thoughts may tend to the promoting of his honour, who hath wrought so great salvation, and that the fatness of these continued mercies may not occasion pride and wantonness, as formerly the like hath done to a chosen people. But that the fear of the Lord, even for his mercies, may keep an authority, and the people so prospered, and blessed, and witnessed to, humble and faithful; that justice and righteousness, mercy and truth may flow from you, as a thankful return to our glorious God: This shall be the prayer of, Sir, your most humble and obedient servant,

O. CROMWELL.

bers and council of state; and soon after by the lord-mayor, aldermen and sheriffs, and many persons of quality, with the militia, and multitudes of people; who welcomed him with loud shouts and acclamations, and several vollies of great and small shot. Whitelock says, he carried himself with great affability, and seeming humility; and in all his discourses about the business of Worcester, would seldom mention any thing of himself, but the galantry of the officers and soldiers, and gave all the glory of the action unto God.

After some small repose, on the 16th of September, he took his place in parliament, where the speaker made a speech to him, congratulating his return after so many atchievements, and giving him the thanks of the house for his services to the commonwealth. On the same day, he with his chief officers, was feasted in the city, with all possible state and pomp: and soon after two acts were drawn up, that were much to his honour; one for a solemn thanksgiving-day, and the other for a yearly observation of the 3d of September, in all the three kingdoms. The parliament likewise settled 4000 l. a year upon him, out of the duke of Buckingham and the marquis of Worcester, besides 2,500 l. per Annum formerly granted.

§. 20. Soon after the battle of Worcester, the Isle of Man, bravely defended by the heroick countess of Derby, and the isle of Jersey, that had been long maintained by Sir George Carteret, were both reduced to the parliament's obedience. They had long since been masters of Guernsey, except the chief fort, called Cornet-castle, which had been a great while defended by Roger Burges, but was about the latter end of October surrendered by him upon very good articles. And the Scilly isles, which had been the chief harbour for the king's men of war, were some time before reduced by a part of the parliament's fleet.

Major-general Monk, whom the lord-general had left in Scotland, to perfect the reduction of that kingdom, proceeded in his work with very good success. Before the fight of Worcester, he took Sterling, the chief strength of the Scots; as also Dundee, with as terrible an execution as Cromwell had before used at Tredagh; and surprised a convention of the Scotch nobility, among whom was old general Lesley, and sent them prisoners to London. The example that was made of Dundee, occasioned such a terror, that St. Andrews, Aberdeen, Dunbarton, and Dunnoter castles, with other towns, castles, and strong-holds, either voluntarily declared for the conquerors, or surrendered upon summons. Notwithstanding this, the Scots made one attempt more, under Middleton, Huntley, Glencarne, and others in the Highlands: but they were soon suppressed and dispersed by colonel Morgan: so that the English extended their conquests through all parts of the kingdom, even as far as the isles of Orkney and Shetland, which now submitted to them. After this, there was no more work for our general in the field; who therefore continued about London most of the remainder of his days.

And here I shall dismiss the affairs of Scotland with the remarks that bishop Burnet makes on the state of that kingdom, after their absolute reduction of it under the power of the English. "After this, says he, the country was kept in great order: some castles in the Highlands had garrisons put into them, that were so careful in their discipline, and so exact to their rules, that in no time the Highlands were kept in better order, than during the usurpation. There was a considerable force of about seven or eight thousand men kept in Scotland: these were paid exactly, and strictly disciplined. The pay of the army brought so much money into the kingdom, that it continued all that while in a very flourishing state. Cromwell built three citadels, at Leith, Air, and Inverness, besides many little forts. There was good justice done, and vice was suppressed and punished; so that we always

ways reckon those eight years of usurpation, a time of great peace and prosperity. There was also a sort of union of the three kingdoms in one parliament, where Scotland had its representatives. The marquis of Argyle went up one of our commissioners."

§. 21. Thus have we gone through Cromwell's military life, and with as much brevity as possible, except in two or three of the principal actions, which I have taken more at large from the historians of the time. His next conquest was over the parliament who employed him, by another sort of warfare, in which he was no less expert and successful than in the open field. But that will be the subject of another chapter. I would only observe at the end of this, that with whomsoever of the great captains of antiquity we compare him, Cromwell is in no danger of losing by the comparison*. Like Lucullus, he came to the field unexperienced, and shone out at once an accomplished general. For the rapidity of his conquests he might vie with Alexander, or, whom he more nearly resembled, with Julius Cæsar. That an army of veteran Greeks, though fewer in number, should triumph over the effeminate Asians, was what might well enough be expected: but where Roman was opposed to Roman, and Briton to Briton, it seems but an act of justice to ascribe it to the generals, that one of these parties was for ever victorious; especially if the party which prevailed, as in Cromwell's case, appeared at first under many disadvantages.

Those who conclude, from the severity used at Tredagh, and a few other places, that Cromwell in his temper was savage and cruel, are certainly much mistaken, We find him excusing those actions himself from the necessity of affairs, which has always been taken for a sufficient reason in matters of this

* See the panegyrick in the appendix.

nature. And if we confider the barbarities which the Irifh, for fome years before, had been practifing on the poor Englifh proteftants, efpecially in the horrid maffacre of 1641, we fhould have no reafon to wonder if a fpirit of vengeance had prevailed in the Englifh army, when they had it in their power to make retaliation. We fee nothing however of this kind breaking out among them, which doubtlefs was owing, in a great meafure, to the good conduct of the general, and the ftrict difcipline for which he was fo remarkable.

CHAP. V.

A view of CROMWELL's *conduct towards king* Charles I. *with a vindication of him in many particulars.*

§. 1. IT cannot be denied that Cromwell, in a multitude of inftances, appears to have been a great mafter of diffimulation: and if the old maxim be true, "that he who knows not how to diffemble, knows not how to reign," we fhall find it was neceffary for him to be fo. This puts us under a difficulty, however, with regard to many of his actions, to find what were his real motives and views. But if we may judge from a feries of the moft probable circumftances, we have no reafon to think that he had at firft, or even for a long time after he arrived at great power, any fettled defign againft the king's life. It was owing to him *, indeed, that the king

was

* The animofities between the parliament and army ftill continuing and increafing, the agitators feared the parliament would now, for their own fecurity, receive the king upon any terms, or rather

put

was seized at Holmby-house, contrary to the sense, and without the knowledge of the parliament: but this put themselves under his protection, that they might the better subdue the army, and reduce them to obedience. Wherefore, being instigated thereto by Cromwell, they, on the 4th of June, sent cornet Joyce, one of their body, with a party of horse, to take him out of the hands of the parliament-commissioners, and bring him away to the army. Accordingly, Joyce about midnight drew up his horse in order before Holmby-house, demanding entrance. Colonel Greaves, and major-general Brown, who being alarm'd, had doubled the guards, enquiring his name and business, he said his name was Joyce, a cornet in colonel Whalley's regiment, and his business was to speak with the king. Being asked from whom, he said, " From myself; my errand is to the king, I must and I will speak with him." Greaves and Brown commanded their men within to stand to their arms; but they, seeing them to be their fellow-soldiers of the same army, open'd the gates, and shook hands with them as old friends. The cornet placed his centinels at the commissioners chamber-doors, and went himself, by the back-stairs, directly to the king's bed-chamber. The grooms being much surprised, desired him to lay aside his arms, and assured him, that in the morning he should speak with the king: but he, with sword and pistol, insisted to have the door opened, and made so much noise that it waked his majesty, who sent him out word, " that he would not rise nor speak with him till the morning: upon which the cornet retir'd in a huff. The king getting up early in the morning, sent for him, who with great boldness told his majesty, he was commanded to remove him. Whereupon the king desired the commissioners might be called; but Joyce said, " they had nothing to do but to return back to the parliament." Being ask'd for a sight of his instructions,

this was done with no other view than to get his majesty structions, he told his majesty, " he should see them presently;" so drawing up his troop in the inner court, " These, Sir, said he, are my instructions." The king having took a good view of them, and finding them to be proper men, well mounted and arm'd, told the cornet with a smile, " his instructions were in fair characters, legible without spelling." Joyce then pressing the king to go along with him, his majesty refused, unless the commissioners might attend him; to which the cornet reply'd, " he was very indifferent, they might go if they would." So the king, being attended by the commissioners of the parliament, went along with Joyce, and was that night conducted by him to colonel Montague's house at Hinchingbrook, and the next night to Sir John Cut's at Childersley near Cambridge. Here Fairfax, Cromwell, Ireton, Skippon, and many other officers came to wait upon the king, and some of them kissed his hand. 'Tis said, that Joyce being told, that the general was displeased with him, for taking the king from Holmby, he answered, " that lieutenant-general Cromwell had given him orders at London to do all that he had done;" and indeed Fairfax now resigned himself entirely to Cromwell's judgment, who led and governed him as he pleased. And though he was at first dissatisfied with this proceeding of Joyce, yet Cromwell soon appeased him by representing to him, " that nothing could have been done of greater advantage to the army and their generals, to the church and state, than what Joyce had been doing: that the king was on the point of making an accommodation with the parliament, who had determined to send colonel Greaves to fetch him; and if Joyce had not fetch'd him, there would have been an end of both officers and army, and all the pains they had taken for the publick good, would not only have been useless, but criminal." Life of Oliver Cromwell, in 8vo.

jesty into the hands of the army, who were jealous of the parliament, as the parliament were of them.

For when the royal power was quite broken, and the royal person made a prisoner, misunderstandings began to arise among the victors, from the soldiers arrogating more to themselves than their masters were willing to allow. On this account it was imagined, that they who could secure the king's person, might play him off against the other party, and restore him upon their own terms, without any provision for the others. It was even suspected at this time, that the parliament had actually a design of restoring the king's authority, in order to make use of it to ruin their own army. But the chief officers were more tenacious of the power they had acquired, and in particular Cromwell, who was a member of parliament as well as a general, than thus to resign it without any security to themselves. It was thought necessary, therefore, in order to lessen the parliament's authority, and increase their own, to take this otherwise unwarrantable step; of which Cromwell was the chief adviser, as appears from the testimony of Joyce, who acted in the affair.

§. 2. Cromwell's grand design, we are assured, was to hinder any conjunction between the king and the presbyterians, the army's greatest enemies; and having now got him into his hands, he spirited up an address from the army, containing a charge of high treason against * eleven members of the house of commons, who were the heads of the presbyterian party. This had the desired effect; for knowing this charge was rather to hinder their influencing the house, than with a view of proceeding capitally

---

* These members were, Mr. Denzil Hollis, Sir Philip Stapleton, Sir John Clotworthy, Serjeant Glyn, Mr. Anthony Nichols, Mr. Walter Long, Sir William Lewis, colonel Edward Harley, Sir William Waller, colonel Massey, and Sir John Maynard.

against them, they determined to withdraw themselves voluntarily, and leave the sway of the house, in the hands of the opposite party; who, though called independants, were made up of men of different persuasions, that were in general friends to the army. There was also a moderate party in the house, who usually voted on the side of liberty, till they found what lengths they were like to be led.

Having proceeded thus far, Cromwell's next intentions were to restore the king by means of the independants, now the predominant party; thinking that liberty of conscience would thereby be better secured, than it could be under a presbyterian hierarchy. And the king himself began to think his condition altered for the better, and to look upon the independant interest as more consistent with episcopacy than the presbyterian, because it might subsist under any form, which the other could not do. He was also much more civilly treated since his being in the army, than he was before while the parliament's prisoner: for though he was obliged to attend the motion of the camp, he was every where allowed to appear in state and lustre, with his nobility about him, his chaplains in waiting, and all his servants in their proper places. His majesty received also an address from the army, full of protestations of duty: which was set on foot by Cromwell and Ireton; though, to prevent the parliament's jealousy of them, they were at first somewhat reserved in their own behaviour; and even desired to be excused from seeing his majesty often, and waved the ceremony of kissing his hand when before him, notwithstanding all the address which his majesty made use of, as to persons he knew could do him service.

After some time, however, Cromwell's behaviour was more open and free; he visited the king frequently, and had long conferences with him. Once in particular he is said to have promised his majesty, "that if he and his party would sit still, and neither act nor declare against the army, he would restore him,

him, and make him the greatest prince in Christendom." Though in private, among his friends, he boasted, "that now he had got the king into his hands, he had got the parliament in his pocket." His majesty knew that Cromwell bore the greatest sway in the army, and finding him not averse to his interest, was so indiscreet as to say to general Fairfax, upon his offering him his service, "Sir, I have as good interest in the army as you." Which expression was taken very ill by the general, and did the king no service.

§. 3. But notwithstanding the king's indiscretion, Cromwell was certainly in earnest as to his design of a restoration, though he durst not openly avow it. This was evident from his message to Sir John Berkeley, who was sent over by the queen and the prince to promote an agreement between the king and the army. Sir Allen Appesley, the messenger, was ordered to inform Sir John, that "Cromwell well remembered what he had once heard him say, concerning the difficulty of introducing a popular government, against the king, the nobility and gentry, the presbyterians, and the genius of the nation; and that therefore it would be well for the independants to do what the presbyterians had only pretended to, and restore the king and people to their just and antient rights; this being the only way to obtain trust and power for themselves, as much as subjects are capable of: whereas, if they aimed at more, it would be attended with a great hatred, and their own destruction. That though Cromwell, when Sir John held this discourse, only gave him the hearing, yet he had since found by experience, that all, or the greatest part of it was reasonable, and he was resolved to act accordingly, as might be perceived by what had already pass'd; desiring that the queen and the prince would not condemn his party, but suspend their opinion of them, and their intentions, till their future carriage should make full proof of their integrity,

grity, of which they had already given some testimony."

And when after leave obtained from Cromwell, Sir John came to wait on the king, Cromwell confirmed with his own mouth all that Sir Allen had reported; with this addition, " that he thought no man could enjoy his life and estate quietly, unless the king had his right; which, says he, we have already declared to the world in general terms, and will more particularly very soon, when we shall comprize the several interests of the royalists, presbyterians, and independants, as far as they are consistent with one another." And some time after Sir John meeting him at Reading, as he was coming from the king at Caversham, Cromwell told him, " that he had lately seen the tenderest sight that ever his eyes beheld, which was the interview between the king and his children." He even wept while he mentioned it; and added, " that never was man so abused as himself in the sinister opinion he had of the king, whom he now thought the most upright and conscientious man of the three kingdoms:" Concluding with this wish, " that God would be pleased to look upon him, according to the sincerity of his heart towards the king."

§, 4. Indeed the army in general, as well as Cromwell, appeared at this time very zealous for the king's interest; and yet they seemed to suspect the reality of one another's intentions. Some of the principal agitators whispered their suspicions of the lieutenant-general to Berkeley, but they appeared to be suspicions only; every one confessing, that if Cromwell and Ireton were not hearty for the king, they were complete dissemblers. And what room could there be to imagine this, when proposals were actually drawn up by Ireton for a reconciliation, by which episcopacy was not to be abolished, nor the militia taken from the crown?·when they both pressed the king to consent to them without delay, there being no assurance of

the

the army, who had changed more than once? Cromwell, in particular, was so earnest in the affair, that he blamed Ireton's slowness in perfecting the proposals, and his backwardness in coming up to his majesty's sense; telling Sir John Berkeley on the other hand, "that he wished he would act more frankly, and not tie himself up to narrow principles; because there was great room to think, that the army would not persist in their good intentions towards the king."

About the same time arrived Mr. Ashburnham, upon the like message as Sir John Berkeley. This gentleman soon got familiar with colonel Whalley, who commanded the guard that attended the king; and also with Cromwell and Ireton, who seemed greatly to come into his measures, so as even to raise a jealousy in the army of their carrying on a separate treaty. But all these promising circumstances were soon defeated, merely by the imprudence of his majesty, and those about him; as we shall see by what follows.

§. 5. The parliament feared nothing so much, as a conjunction between the king and the army: and now there was such an appearance of it, many of the king's friends, through an intemperate zeal, made it the subject of their triumph. Hereupon the two houses sent a committee to his majesty, with an address of another strain than they had lately used, making many protestations of duty, and declaring, "that if he was not in all respects treated as he ought to be, and as he desired, it was not their fault, who were desirous he might be at full liberty, and do what he would." The army, at the same time, was not without jealousy, that the king hearkened to some secret propositions from the presbyterian party, and designed to make an absolute breach between the parliament and the army; which occasioned Ireton to say to him, "Sir, you have an intention to be arbitrator between the parliament and us, and we mean to be so between you and the parliament." In the mean time the king,
finding

finding himself courted on all hands, was so confident of his own importance, that he imagined himself able to turn the scale on which side he pleased.

This high consideration of himself, which was one of king Charles's greatest foibles, was the occasion that when the proposals were brought him from the army, and his concurrence to them humbly desired, he entertained their commissioners with haughty and disobliging language; declaring, " that no man should suffer for his sake, (there being justice required on some of his evil advisers) and that he repented of nothing so much, as that he passed the bill against the earl of Strafford: also, that he would have the church of England established by the proposals;" there being nothing in them concerning church-government. These proposals however, were much more moderate than those sent to him from the parliament: but he unhappily thought, that they proceeded only from the necessity they had of him; and in discoursing with the commissioners, would frequently use such expressions as these, " You cannot do without me; you will fall to ruin, unless I sustain you." This kind of proceeding greatly astonish'd his own party, as well as the deputies from the army; whereupon he began to soften his discourse, but it was too late: for colonel Rainsborough, who seemed least of all to desire an accommodation, had retired from the conference, and going immediately to the army, had given them to understand what treatment their commissioners and proposals had met with.

It may not be amiss, on this occasion, to introduce part of Dr. Wellwood's character of this unhappy prince, in which he seems to have had some view to the present affair. After telling us, " that if king Charles had any personal faults, they were much over weighed by his virtues; but that an immoderate desire of power, beyond what our constitution allow'd of, was the rock he split upon;" the doctor adds, " there was another error that run through the whole management of his affairs, both domestick and pub-
- lick,

lick, and which occafioned a great part of his misfortunes: he appeared many times ftiff and pofitive in denying at firft what he granted afterwards out of time, and too late to give fatisfaction; which encouraged interefted perfons to afk more than they thought of at firft, and loft him the fruits of his former conceffions: fo that in the whole conduct of his life he verified this maxim, that errors in government have ruined more princes than their perfonal vices."

§. 6. To proceed with our hiftory: There happened, about the time we are now upon, an infurrection in the city of London, occafioned by the parliament's voting the city militia, through Cromwell's influence, into other hands than their own. The mob that was got down to Weftminfter, on this occafion, not only obliged both houfes to revoke their ordinance, but forced them to pafs a vote, " that the king fhould come forthwith to London, and be invited thither with honour, freedom, and fafety." This violence put upon them, occafioned feveral of the members, and in particular the fpeakers of both houfes, to repair with fpeed to the army, and offer up their complaints. The army could not have defired a greater advantage than this gave them, who therefore received the members with all the appearances of refpect, profeffed their fubmiffion to the parliament, and declared, " that they would re-eftablifh them in their full power, or perifh in the attempt." Nor did they fail of their promife; for though the houfes had chofen new fpeakers, and paffed feveral * votes

* Thefe votes were, " Firft, That the king fhould come to London. Secondly, That the militia of London fhould be authorized to raife forces for the defence of the city. Thirdly, That power be given to the fame militia to chufe a general. Fourthly, That the eleven members impeached by the army, fhould refume their feats in parliament."

The

votes according to the mind of the citizens, yet all thofe proceedings were difannull'd upon the army's coming

The citizens, armed with thefe powers, proceed to raife forces under the command of Waller, Maffey, and Pointz; but they were very much difcouraged in their proceedings by the news of the general rendezvous of the army on Hounflow-heath, where the two fpeakers appeared with their maces, and fuch members as accompanied them, viz. the earls of Northumberland, Salifbury, and Kent, the lord Grey of Werke, the lord Howard, the lord Wharton, the earl of Mulgrave, and the lord Say, and fix lords more, with the earl of Manchefter, their fpeaker; and about a hundred members of the houfe of commons, with their fpeaker, Mr. Lenthall. Befides, the borough of Southwark was generally for the army, which was now marching towards London, to reftore the members who fled to them, to their places and authorities. Part of the army feized upon the block-houfe at Gravefend, and blocked up the city by water towards the eaft, and the general with the reft of the army towards the weft. Upon this, the aldermen and common-council of the city deferted their three generals, and fent to Fairfax for a pacification; which he granted them upon thefe conditions. "Firft, That they fhould defert the parliament then fitting, and the eleven members. Secondly, That they fhould recal their late declaration. Thirdly, That they fhould relinquifh their prefent militia. Fourthly, That they fhould deliver up to the general all their forts, and the tower of London. Fifthly, That they fhould difband all the forces they had lately raifed, and do all things elfe, which were neceffary for the publick tranquillity."

The next day, Cromwell marched to Weftminfter, and placed guards in the court, in the hall, and even at the doors of the two houfes: and a little after, general Fairfax conducted the feveral members who had fled

coming to London; the members were restored, and every thing settled again as the officers, or rather as Cromwell, who governed all the rest, would have it.

§. 7. But the city being subdued, and the parliament and army seemingly united, there arose differences in the army itself. The agitators, whose rise we shall mention elsewhere, were no longer inclined to an agreement with the king, and declared their discontent at the intimacy kept up by Cromwell and Ireton with his majesty's agents. The doors of these commanders, they said, were open to the royalists, and shut to their own soldiers. Cromwell was very uneasy at these discourses, and informed the king's party of them, speaking thus to Ashburnham and Berkeley: "If I am an honest man, I have said enough of the sincerity of my intentions; and if I am not, nothing is enough: therefore I conjure you, as you tender the king's service, not to come so frequently to my quarters, but to send your business in private; the suspicion of me being grown so great, that I am afraid to be in them myself." Thus the agitators, who were set up at first by Cromwell, to oppose the parliament's design of disbanding, began now to be very troublesome to him, and at last obliged him to abandon the king's interest, in order to make his peace with them.

fled to the army, to their seats in parliament; where they annulled all the acts and orders, which had passed since the 26th of July. Two days after, the army marched, as it were, in triumph through the city, the general leading the avant-guard, major-general Skippon the main body, and Cromwell the rear-guard; and all the soldiers having laurel branches in their hats. After this pompous march, the army was distributed into quarters, in Kent, Surrey, and Essex; and thus they surrounded the city. Life of Cromwell, p. 58.

For

For the parliament having addreſſed themſelves again to the king, Cromwell found means to prevent his treating with them, and got it inſinuated, "that if the king would aſſent to their propoſals, lower than thoſe of the parliament, the army would ſettle him again on his throne." His majeſty, upon this, inſtead of liſtening to the parliament, deſired a perſonal treaty on the propoſals of the army. With this the officers were well pleaſed; and Cromwell and Ireton, with others of their party, preſſed his majeſty's deſires in the houſe with great earneſtneſs. But ſo far were they from ſucceeding, that they met with a vigorous oppoſition, and loſt moſt of their friends in the parliament, where they were now looked upon as betrayers of the cauſe. The army likewiſe, which then lay about Putney, were no leſs diſſatisfy'd with their proceedings; ſo that the agitators complained openly in council, both of the king and the malignants, about declaring, "that ſince the king had rejected their propoſals, they were no farther engaged to him, but were now to conſult their own ſafety, and the publick good; and having the power devolved upon them by deciſion of the ſword, and being convinced that monarchy was inconſiſtent with the good of the nation, they reſolved to uſe their endeavours to reduce England to a commonwealth." They alſo deſigned to have ſeized Aſhburnham and Berkeley, the king's agents, and to wreſt the king out of the hands of the two traitors, as they called Cromwell and Ireton.

§. 8. Cromwell was ſo terrify'd with theſe things, that he thought it neceſſary to bring the army to a general rendezvous; knowing that moſt of the great officers were ſtill well affected to the king, and diſliked theſe proceedings of the agitators, whoſe power he hoped by that means to ſuppreſs. The agitators, in the mean time, endeavoured to prevent the rendezvous, and to get the king into their own hands. But Cromwell was too hard for them all: for finding

how

how matters were like to go, he acquainted the king with his danger, and assuring him of his real service, advised him to escape where he might be more secure. His majesty took the general's counsel *, and leaving Hampton court, where he then resided, made away for the isle of Wight, accompanied by Berkeley, Ashburnham, and some others. They were well received by colonel Hammond, the governor, who met the king at Titchfield, and conducted him forwards in his own person. Cromwell soon received letters of the king's arrival, which he communicated to the parliament, and thereby removed the consternation they were before in, on account of his escape. And lord Clarendon remarks, that he made the relation of this matter with so unusual a gaity, that all men concluded, his majesty was where Cromwell desired he should be.

The agitators now declared openly against the king, and against the continuance of the present par-

---

* Milton endeavours to vindicate Cromwell from being the adviser of this flight. " I admire those cavaliers, says he, who never stick to affirm so often, that Charles was one of the most prudent persons living, and yet that the same man was hardly ever at his own disposal: that, whether with his enemy or his friend, in the court, or in the camp, he was almost always in the power of another; now of his wife, then of the bishops; now of the peers, then of the soldiery; and last, of his enemies; that, for the most part, he followed the worser counsels, and, almost always, of the worser men. Charles is persuaded; Charles is imposed on; Charles is deceived; fear is impressed on him; vain hope is set before him! Charles is carried and fetched about as if he was the common prey of all, both friends and enemies! But let them either blot these things out of their writings, or else give over trumpeting up the sagacity of Charles." *Defensio secundo populi Anglicani*, Mr. Peck's translation.

liament; requiring that a new one might be elected, by a more equal diftribution of the counties, cities, and boroughs. A great part of the army came over to them, who were diftinguifhed by the name of levellers: and at the general rendezvous, they that were of this party wore every one a paper in his hat, with thefe words written upon it, "The rights of England, and the confent of the people." And tho' Cromwell, by his fingular addrefs and extraordinary courage, did for the prefent quell this fpirit in the army; yet fo apprehenfive was he of the fecret remains of it, and the confequences that might hence enfue, and fo weary was he of treating with the king to the purpofe, that he foon altered his conduct to both parties, and reconciled himfelf to the one, by abandoning the other.

§. 9. To vindicate Cromwell, as much as poffible, in the affair of leaving the king, I fhall infert the fubftance of what is collected on this head, by the anonymous author of Cromwell's life. He tells us from Ludlow, that colonel Hammond and Mr. Afhburnham had frequent conferences with the king, who made fuch promifes to Hammond, that he exprefs'd his earneft defire that the army might refume their power, and rid themfelves of the agitators, whofe authority, he faid, he never liked. To this end he fent one Mr. Traughton, his Chaplain, to the army, to advife them to make ufe of their late fuccefs againft the agitators; and foon after he prefs'd the king to fend fome of thofe who attended on him, to the army, with letters of compliment to Fairfax, and others of greater confidence to Cromwell and Ireton. He alfo wrote to them himfelf, " conjuring them by their engagements, their honour and confcience, to come to a fpeedy agreement with the king, and not to expofe themfelves to the fantaftick giddinefs of the agitators." Sir John Berkeley was appointed by the king, in purfuance of Hammond's advice, to go to the army; who taking with him Mr. Henry Berkeley his coufin,

went

went over with a pafs from the Governor of Cowes. Being on his way towards the army, he met Mr. Traughton on his return between Bagfhot and Windfor, who inform'd him, that he had no good news to carry back to his majefty, the army having enter'd into new refolutions concerning his perfon. He was not gone much farther, before he was met by cornet Joyce, who told him, " that he was aftonifhed at his defign of going to the army, for it had been debated amongft the agitators, whether, in juftification of themfelves, the king fhould be brought to a trial;" of which opinion he declared himfelf to be. Sir John however refolved to go to the army, and being arrived at Windfor, went to general Fairfax's quarters, where the officers were affembled. Being admitted, he delivered his letters to the general, who receiving them, ordered him to withdraw. Having waited about half an hour, he was called in, when the general, with fome feverity in his looks, told him, that they were the parliament's army, and therefore could fay nothing to the king's motion about peace, but muft refer thofe matters, and the king's letters, to their confideration. Sir John then looked upon Cromwell, Ireton, and the reft of his acquaintance; but they faluted him very coldly, and fhewing him colonel Hammond's letter to them, fmiled with difdain upon it.

Finding himfelf thus difappointed, Berkeley went to his lodging; where having ftaid two hours without any company, he at laft ordered his fervant to go out, and fee if he could find any of his acquaintance. The fervant going out, met with one who was a general officer, who bid him tell his mafter, that he would meet him at fuch a place at midnight. They being accordingly met, the officer acquainted Berkeley in general, that he had no good news to tell him; and then proceeding to particulars, faid, " You know, that I and my friends engaged ourfelves to you; that we were zealous for an agreement, and if the reft were not fo, we were abus'd: that fince the tumults in the army, we did miftruft Cromwell and Ireton; whereof

I informed

I informed you. I come now to tell you, that we miftruft neither, and that we are refolved, notwithftanding our engagement, to deftroy the king and his pofterity; to which purpofe Ireton has made two propofitions this afternoon; one, that you fhould be fent prifoner to London; the other, that none fhould fpeak with you upon pain of death; and I do now hazard my life by doing it. The way defigned to ruin his majefty, is to fend 800 of the moft difaffected in the army to fecure his perfon, and then to bring him to a trial; and I dare think no farther. This will be done in ten days; and therefore, if the king can efcape, let him do it as he loves his life."

Sir John being exceedingly troubled at this relation, afk'd his friend the reafon of this change, feeing the king had done all things in compliance with the army, and the officers were become fuperior fince the laft rendezvous. Whereupon he gave him this account. "That though one of the mutineers was fhot * to death, eleven more imprifon'd, and the reft in appearance over-awed; yet they were fo far from being fo in reality, that two-thirds of the army had been fince with Cromwell and Ireton, to let them know, that though they were fure to perifh in the enterprize, they fhould leave nothing unattempted to bring the whole army to their fenfe; and if all failed, they would make a divifion in the army, and unite with any who would affift them in the deftruction of their oppofers. That Cromwell and Ireton reafoned thus with themfelves, " if the army divide, the greateft part will join with the prefbyterians, and will moft probably prevail to our ruin; or we fhall be obliged in fuch a manner to apply ourfelves to the king, as rather to beg than offer any affiftance: which if the king fhall give, and be fo fortunate as to prevail; if he fhall then pardon us, it will be all we can expect, and more than we can affure ourfelves of:" and thereupon concluded, that if they could not bring the army to their fenfe, it

* See the chapter next following, §. 7.

mply with them, a division being ut-
e to both.
e therefore of this resolution, Cromwell
his thoughts and endeavours to make
the party that was most set against the
ɔ sent comfortable messages to the pri-
seiz'd at the late rendezvous, assuring
hing should be done to their prejudice;
and the like arts, he perfected his recon-
the levelling party.

eley returning to his lodging, dis-
usin the Isle of Wight with two let-
olonel Hammond, giving a general ac-
ubtful judgment of affairs in the army;
pher, with a particular relation of the
had with the fore-mentioned officer,
tion to his majesty, to think of nothing
liate escape. The next morning he sent
to Cromwell, to acquaint him that he
d instructions to him from the king:
returned him answer by the messenger,
st not see him, it being very dangerous
" assuring him, " that he would serve
ing as he could do it without his own
red, that it might not be expected that
ish for his sake."

ave seen the motives that prevailed on
eneral to abandon the king's interest.
e same account is given by Salmonet,
at all be suspected of being partial to
ɔ that if he hitherto acted sincerely in
erve the king, as is most probable, they,
m with having contrived his ruin from
of the civil wars, ascribe to him more
ws than he really had. He was indeed
ugh, and as good as any man at the
ation: but certainly nothing hinders,
issembler may sometimes be in earnest;
ion might be gratify'd by the private
was supposed to be carried on between
him

him and the king, by ſtipulating ſuch honours and advancements for himſelf and family, as reſtoring the king to his throne might reaſonably lay claim to.

§. 19. And here we cannot omit another account, that is given by ſome, of Cromwell's falling off from the king, and deſerting his intereſt. They tell us, there was a report, that Cromwell made a private article with the king, that if his majeſty cloſed with the army's propoſals, he ſhould be made Earl of Eſſex, knight of the garter, and fir███████ of the horſe-guards; and Ireton was t█████ lieutenant of Ireland. Other honours and █████ments were likewiſe ſtipulated for Cromwell's ██ily and friends. But the king was ſo uxorious, that he would do nothing without the ad███ of his queen, who not liking the propoſal, he ſent a letter to acquaint her, " that tho' he aſſented to the army's pro██als, yet if by ſo doing he could procure peace, it would be eaſier then to take off Cromwell, than now he was the head that governed the army." Cromwell, who had his ſpies upon every motion of the king, intercepted this letter, and thereupon reſolved never to truſt the king more. This is ſaid to have happened before the king left Hampton court: for upon this, they tell us, Cromwell fearing he could not manage his deſigns, if the king was ſo near the parliament at Hampton-court, gave him private information, that he was in no ſafety there, by reaſon of the hatred which the agitators bore him; and that he would be more ſecure in the iſle of Wight. Hereupon the king, whilſt the parliament and the Scotch commiſſioners were debating on his anſwer to their propoſitions, made his eſcape as before related.

We leave the reader to judge of this ſtory as he thinks fit. Only thus much we may obſerve, that father Orleans ſays, 'twas believed in France, that the king had deceived Cromwell; though he makes this to be purely the effect of Cromwell's artifice. And the lord Clarendon ſpeaks of Cromwell's complaining

that

that the king could not be trusted, though he makes his whole carriage towards his majesty to be nothing but hypocrisy and dissimulation, in order to bring about his own designs. "Ashburnham and Berkeley, says he, received many advertisements (but a little while before the king's escape) from some officers with whom he most conversed, and who would have been glad that the king might have been restor'd by the army, for the preferments which they expected might fall to their share, that Cromwell and Ireton resolved never to trust the king, or do any thing towards his restoration." And a little after he says, "that Cromwell himself expostulated with Mr. Ashburnham, and complained, that the king could not be trusted, and that he had no affection or confidence in the army, but was jealous of them, and of all the officers; that he had intrigues in the parliament, and treaties with the presbyterians of the city, to raise new troubles; that he had a treaty concluded with the Scotch commissioners, to engage the nation again in blood: and therefore he would not be answerable, if any thing fell out amiss and contrary to expectation."

§. 11. Agreeable enough to this account is the relation given by the author of the memoirs of the lord Broghill, of a conversation that passed between the said lord and Cromwell, whilst he was in Ireland, in 1650. He informs us, that the lord Broghill being in discourse with Cromwell and Ireton, fell upon the subject of the king's death. Cromwell said, that if the king had followed his own mind, and had had trusty servants about him, he had fooled them all: adding, "we had once an inclination to have come to terms with him, but something that happened drew us off from it." The lord Broghill seeing they were both in a good humour, asked them, why, if they were inclined to close with him, they had not done it; Upon which Cromwell frankly told him, "The reason of our inclination to come to terms with him, was

was, we found the Scots and presbyterians began to be more powerful than we, and were strenuously endeavouring to strike up an agreement with the king, and leave us in the lurch; wherefore we thought to prevent them by offering more reasonable conditions. But while we were busied with these thoughts, there came a letter to us from one of our spies, who was of the king's bed-chamber, acquainting us, that our final doom was decreed that day: what it was he could not tell, but a letter was gone to the queen with the contents of it, which letter was sewed up in the skirt of a saddle, and the bearer of it would come with a saddle upon his head, about ten o'clock the following night, to the Blue-boar inn in Holborn, where he was to take horse for Dover. The messenger knew nothing of the letter in the saddle, but some one in Dover did. We were then at Windsor; and immediately upon the receipt of the letter from our spy, Ireton and I resolved to take a trusty fellow with us, and in troopers habits to go to the inn; which accordingly we did, and set our men at the gate of the inn to watch. The gate was shut, but the wicket was open, and our men staid to give us notice when any one came with a saddle upon his head. Ireton and I sat in a box near the wicket, and called for a can of beer, and then another, drinking in that disguise till ten o'clock, when our centinel gave us notice that the man with a saddle was come: upon which we immediately rose; and when the man was leading out his horse saddled we came up to him with our swords drawn, and told him, we were to search all who went in and out there; but as he looked like an honest fellow, we would only search his saddle; which we did, and found the letter we looked for; and opening it; read the contents, in which the king acquainted the queen, that he was now courted by both the factions, the Scots presbyterians, and the army; that which of them bid fairest for him should have him; that he thought he could close sooner with the Scots than the other. Upon which we speeded to
Windsor,

Windsor, and finding we were not likely to have any tolerable terms from the king, we immediately resolved to ruin him."

For a conclusion, I shall set down what Dr. Wellwood in his memoirs, observes concerning this matter. " As every thing, says he, did contribute to the fall of king Charles I. so did every thing contribute to the rise of Cromwell, and as there was no design at first against the king's life, so it is probable that Cromwell had no thoughts, for a long time, of ever arriving at what he afterwards was. It is known, he was once in treaty with the king, after the army had carried his majesty away from Holmby-house, to have restored him to the throne; which probably he would have done, if the secret had not been like to take vent, by the indiscretion of some about the king; which pushed Cromwell on to prevent his own, by the ruin of the king."

§. 12. However it was (for these things must still remain under some confusion) it is certain, that a few days after the king's departure from Hampton-court, and after it was known he was in the isle of Wight, there was a meeting of the general officers of the army at Windsor, where Cromwell and Ireton were present, to consider what should now be done with the king: and it was resolved, that he should be prosecuted for his life as a criminal person. This resolution, however, was a great secret, whereof the parliament had not the least notice or suspicion; but was, as it had been, to be led on by degrees to what it never design'd.

It is very well known, that, after this time, Cromwell was no more a friend to the king. For when his majesty refused to sign the four famous bills, that were sent him by the parliament, as preliminary to a treaty, there was nobody in the house that turned this refusal more to his disadvantage than Cromwell; who declared, " that the king was a man of great understanding; but withal so great a dissembler, and so false a man, that he was not to be trusted." And to confirm what he said, he rehearsed several particulars of the king's behaviour whilst he was in the army: concluding, " that they might trouble themselves no farther with sending propositions to the king, but enter into those counsels that were necessary towards the settlement of the kingdom." Which motion being seconded by those of his party, produced that memorable vote, " that no more addresses or applications should be made to the king, nor any message received from him, under the penalty of high-treason." And some writers go so far as to assert, that Cromwell and Ireton were so bold in this debate, as to threaten not only the king, but even the parliament, if they gave the army any farther grounds of jealousy: and that Cromwell, at the end of his speech, clapp'd his hand upon his sword.

§. 13. But the second civil war breaking out soon after, Cromwell and the army were obliged to remove from London, and the presbyterians began again to prevail in the house. The vote of no addresses was repealed, and a personal treaty was resolved on with the king. Cromwell * wrote to his friends about these proceedings,

* Cromwell had written to his friends, " that it would be such a perpetual ignominy to the parliament, that nobody abroad or at home would ever give credit to them, if they should recede from their former vote and declaration of no more addresses to the king; conjuring them to continue firm in that resolution." But the parliament had made too great a step to go back from what they were now upon; and since the first motion for a treaty, many absent members resorted to the house, and promoted the design; so that they were much more numerous than those who laboured to obstruct it. And so, notwithstanding all opposition, it was declared, "That the votes of no addresses should stand repealed; that the treaty should be at
Newport;

ings, but to no purpose; which made him use all expedition to finish his business in the north, that he might return to the parliament, and restrain the presbyterian party. But while the treaty was on foot, the main army under Fairfax presented their large remonstrance * to the parliament, advising them to resume the

Newport; and that his majesty should be there with the same freedom, as when he was at Hampton-court: that the instructions given to colonel Hammond, for the more strict confining him, should be recalled; and that all whom the king had named, should have liberty to repair to him, and remain with him undisturbed." Then they nominated five lords and ten of the house of commons to be their commissioners to treat with the king, and ordered them to hasten the treaty with all possible expedition: but Sir Henry Vane being one of them, us'd all his arts to delay it, as he had done before with the parliament, in hopes that Cromwell would finish matters in Scotland time enough to return, and use more effectual means to obstruct it, than he was furnished with. Cromwell was very well appriz'd of these proceedings, which made him think, that his presence at the parliament was so necessary to restrain the presbyterians who ceased not to vex him at any distance, that he would not be prevail'd with to tarry and finish that only difficult work which remained, viz. the reducing Pomfret-castle; but leaving it to Lambert, continued his march for London. Vide life of Cromwell, in 8vo. p. 99.

* They desired, " that the parliament would lay aside all further proceedings in this treaty, and return to their votes of no addresses: that the king might come no more to government, but be brought to justice, as the capital cause of all the evils in the kingdom: that a day might be set for the prince and the duke of York, to appear and answer to such things as might be laid to their charge; and if they failed herein, they might be declared traitors;

the affair of no addresses, and to fix a time for their own dissolution, that a new representative might be chosen. This put the house into great confusion, especially as the king, about the same time, was removed from colonel Hammond, and committed to colonel Ewer at Hurst-castle. They voted that this action was without their consent, and should be enquired into; and some resolute members moved, "that the army, which was now at Windsor, might be declared traitors, if they presumed to march nearer London than they were at present; and that an impeachment of high-treason might be drawn up against the principal officers of it." Hereupon the general marched directly to London, and quartered at Whitehall, placing the other chief men in the great houses thereabouts, in order to terrify the parliament.

But the commons, notwithstanding this, carried it by a majority upon the question, "that his majesty's concessions were a sufficient ground to proceed upon, for the settlement of the peace of the kingdom;" and appointed a committee to treat with the general. Fairfax, however, instead of holding a conference, ordered some regiments down to Westminster, who set guards upon all the avenues to the parliament-house, seized one and forty of the members as they were entering, and denied entrance to a hundred more; whereupon the rest of the presbyterians declining to come, the house was left in possession of about an hundred and fifty. And the night after this interruption,

traitors; that an end might be put to this parliament, and new representatives of the people chosen, for the governing and preserving the whole body of the nation: that no king might be hereafter admitted, but upon election of, and in trust for the people, &c." In conclusion, they press these things "as good for this and other kingdoms, and hope it will not be taken ill, because from an army, and so servants, when their masters are servants, and trustees for the kingdom."

interruption, Cromwell arrived in town, and the next day took his place in parliament *.

It is generally fuppofed that Cromwell, though abfent, influenced the late proceedings, and that it was by his advice and direction that the remonftrance of the army was drawn up, and prefented to the houfe. 'Tis certain that both he and Ireton could manage the general, in whatever they pleafed. However Cromwell, upon his arrival declared, that " he had not been acquainted with the defign of purging the houfe; but that fince it was done, he was very glad of it, and would maintain it."

§. 14. The remnant of the houfe immediately renewed their votes of non-addreffes, and annull'd all thofe that introduced and fucceeded the treaty; and particularly refolved, that the king's anfwer to their propofitions was not fatisfactory. Soon after which a motion was made, to proceed capitally againft the king; when Cromwell ftood up and declared, " that if any man moved this upon defign he fhould think him the greateft traitor in the world; but fince providence and neceffity had caft them upon it, he would pray to God to blefs their counfels, though he was not prepared to give them advice. †"   I fhall

* The army having thus purged the houfe from all they either knew or fufpected to be enemies to their defigns, lieutenant-colonel Axtel came in, and prefented to the remaining members the propofals of the army, fetting forth, " That they had for a long while fadly beheld, and tafted in their proceedings, the miferable effects of counfels divided and corrupted by faction, and perfonal intereft; and defiring, that all faithful members would acquit themfelves by a proteftation of their not concurring in the late proceedings, and would then fpeedily and vigoroufly proceed to take orders for the execution of juftice."

† On December 16th, a party of horfe was fent over to Hurft-caftle, to bring the king to Windfor;

I shall pass over all the affair of the king's trial, as a matter commonly known; but must not omit what bishop Burnet relates, that commissioners were sent from Scotland, to protest against putting the king to death. They laid indeed a great load upon the king; but by a clause in the covenant, to which they had sworn, by the terms upon which Scotland had engaged in the war, and by the solemn declarations that they had so often published to the world, they were obliged, they said, to be faithful in the preservation of his majesty's person. Cromwell undertook to answer them, by shewing, " that a breach of trust in a king ought to be punished more than any other crime whatever: that they had sworn to the preservation of the king's person, only in the defence of the true

who lay at Farnham on the 22d, and was delivered up at Windsor-castle the day following, colonel Harrison commanded the guards about him. Soon after, the council of war was ordered, " that nothing should be done upon the knee to the king; that all ceremonies of state used to him should be left off, and his attendance should be with fewer persons and at less charge." Next day the committee of the commons, which had been appointed to draw up a charge against the king, reported an ordinance " for impeaching Charles Stuart king of England of high-treason; and for trying him by commissioners to be nominated in the said ordinance; which being agreed to by the commons, was, on January 2d, carried up to the lords, for their concurrence. But upon their rejecting it, the commons passed these remarkable votes. " First, That the people are, under God, the original of all just power. Secondly, That the commons of England, being chosen by the people, are the supreme power of the nation. Thirdly, That whatever is enacted or declared by them, has the force of law, without the consent of the house of peers." It was on these votes that all their subsequent proceedings were founded.

true religion; but that when the true religion was obstructed by the king, their oath was no farther obligatory: that the covenant did bind them to bring all malignants, incendiaries, and enemies to the cause, to condign punishment; and that those to whom publick justice had been done, as in the matter of Montrose, were in comparison but small offenders; they acted by commission from the king, who was therefore the principal, and so the most guilty." Thus Cromwell had manifestly the better of them, upon their own principles.

Another attempt, in favour of the king, was made upon the lieutenant-general by his own kinsman, colonel John Cromwell, who came to town with credential letters from the states of Holland, whereto was added a blank, with signets both of the king and the prince, for Cromwell to set down his own conditions, if he would now save his life. The colonel used a great deal of freedom, and even reproached him warmly for turning the king's enemy, after having protested so much in his favour. But the general answered, "that it was not he, but the army, and that times were altered since he had engaged for the king." And at last when he could no longer bear his cousin's importunity, he desired he might have till night to consider of it, and that the colonel would wait at his inn till then. But about one in the morning, a messenger came, to inform the colonel that he might go to bed; for the council of officers had resolved, that the king must die.

This resolution was accordingly executed; and king Charles, as bishop Burnet observes, " died greater than he had lived, shewing, what has often been remarked of the family of the Stuarts, that they bore misfortunes better than prosperity." He was a prince of great devotion and piety, remarkable for his temperance and chastity, being an utter enemy to all debauchery. But his reign, both in peace and war, was a continual series of errors; so that his judgment could hardly be good. He was out of measure

sure set upon following his own humour, but was unreasonably feeble to those he trusted, especially the queen. His notion of regal power was carried too high, and every opposition to it he thought rebellion.

§ 15. Thus, says the anonymous author before quoted, have we got over this dark scene, in which our lieutenant-general is commonly supposed to be chiefly concerned. But as it is not strange he should, if the story of the king's dealing deceitfully with him be true; so it may more reasonably be concluded, that his son-in-law Ireton, rather than he, was the person who chiefly influenced in these proceedings. I know Ireton is supposed all along to have acted by Cromwell's directions; but whether he did or no, may, I think, in many cases be questioned. Ireton was certainly a zealous commonwealth's-man, which party was always averse to any treaty with the king; and though he with Cromwell was in such a treaty, he never really intended to close with the king; but only to lay his party asleep, whilst they were contesting with the presbyterian interest in parliament: but he says no such thing of Cromwell, whom he seems all along to be angry with, for his design of making an agreement with the king, being himself utterly averse to it, and supposing Cromwell's main end was to gratify his own ambition; which is not unlikely; and yet he might have been in earnest in the treaty, and also have designed the publick good. Cromwell was certainly no commonwealth's-man, though he was forced to humour, and in many things actually to comply with the party: and as the agitators, and their offspring the levellers, who were no other than the commonwealth's-men in the army, and whom it is likely Cromwell at first might make use of to bring about some of his designs, were the original contrivers and chief actors in the king's death; so whatever hand Cromwell had in it, seems to be chiefly owing to their fury and desperate resolutions, which
made

made him apprehensive of the greatest danger, if he did not comply with their designs; though at the same time, the contradictions that appeared in the king's conduct, might the more easily incline him to join purposes with them.

In short, what with the danger that threaten'd his person, if he had persisted to oppose the design of the levellers; and what with the consideration of the king's past mis-government, which had been the original cause of all the evils the nation had suffered, and the fear of the like happening for the future, if he should be restored; he having discovered himself to be of a very inconstant and wavering, not to say equivocating, temper; Cromwell was at lengh so wrought upon, as to think it necessary, and so lawful, to take off the king; in which towards the last he seemed to be pretty active, though always in some doubt about it. We are expresly told, he at first shewed some repugnance to so black an undertaking, as my author calls it, and seemed to shew an abhorrence of it, and not to surmount it, as he said himself, but only because he saw that the providence of God, and the necessity of the times, had inspired the army to make so terrible a sacrifice; but that that sacrifice, after all, was the only one that could save the state and religion. And I cannot here omit what bishop Burnet says of this matter: he tells us, that Ireton was the person that drove on the king's trial and death, and that Cromwell was all the while in some suspense about it. " Ireton, says he, had the principles and the temper of a Cassius in him: he stuck at nothing that might have turned England to a commonwealth; and he found out Cooke and Bradshaw, two bold lawyers, as proper instruments for managing it." And we are informed by others, that Ireton was the person who wrought upon Fairfax, and managing the affair of the army's remonstrance, and purging the parliament.

§. 16.

§. 16. To conclude, it is apparent in general, that the king's behaviour during the whole courfe of his troubles, was enough to deftroy that confidence which might otherwife have been repofed in him, and to alienate the hearts of thofe who were inclined to his intereft. Whatever conceffions he at any time made, through the neceffity of his affairs, upon the leaft advantage appearing on his fide, he was ready to revoke them all. And we find, by the letters to his queen, that were taken at the battle of Nafeby, how little regard he had for the parliament, and for the rights of the people, about which they were then contending. In one of them he declares "his intention to make peace with the Irifh, and to have 40,000 of them over in England to profecute the war here;" and in another he complains, " that he could not prevail with his mongrel parliament at Oxford, to vote that the houfes at Weftminfter were not a lawful parliament." So little thanks, as * one obferves, who was no enemy to his majefty, had thofe noble lords and gentlemen, for expofing their lives and fortunes in defence of the king in his adverfity. What then might they expect, if he fhould prevail by conqueft? In thofe letters alfo, he tells the queen, " that he would not make a peace with the rebels without her approbation, nor go one jot from the paper fhe fent him: that in the treaty at Uxbridge, he did not pofitively own the parliament; it being otherwife to be conftrued, though they were fo fimple as not to find it out: and that it was recorded in the notes of the king's council, that he did not acknowledge them a parliament."

§. 17. Concerning the defeat of this treaty at Uxbridge, Dr. Wellwood gives us the following account. " Many endeavours, fays he, were ufed from time to time, to bring matters to an accommodation by way of treaty; but ftill fome one unlucky accident or

* Coke.

other render'd them abortive. At the treaty of Uxbridge, though the parliament's demands were high, and the king shewed a more than ordinary averfion to comply with them; yet the ill pofture of the king's affairs at that time, and the fatal confequences they feared would follow upon breaking off of the treaty, obliged a great many of the king's friends, and more particularly that noble perfon the earl of Southampton, who had gone poft from Uxbridge to Oxford for that purpofe, to prefs the king again and again upon their knees, to yield to the neceffity of the times; and by giving his affent to fome of the moft material propofitions that were fent him, to fettle a lafting peace with his people. The king was at laft prevailed with to follow their counfel; and the next morning was appointed for figning a warrant to his commiffioners to that effect. And fo fure were they of a happy end of all differences, that the king at fupper complaining his wine was not good, one told him merrily, " he hoped that his majefty would drink better before a week was over at Guildhall with the lord-mayor." But fo it was, that when they came early the next morning to wait upon him with the warrant that had been agreed upon over-night, they found his majefty had changed his refolution, and was become inflexible in thefe points.

The unhappy occafion of this alteration has lain hitherto a fecret in hiftory, and might have continued fuch ftill, if a letter from the marquis of Montrofe in Scotland, whereof I have feen a copy under the duke of Richmond's hand, did not give a fufficient light into it. To make the matter better underftood, it is neceffary to fay fomething of Montrofe and his actions in Scotland.

This nobleman had been at firft very active and zealous for the liberties of his country; and was the firft man that paffed the River Tweed at the head of five hundred horfe, upon the Scots firft expedition into England; but being afterwards difobliged,

obliged, or, as some say, repenting of his former error, he left that side, and came in to the king at the breaking out of the war between him and the parliament. When the Scots came into England the second time to assist the parliament, Montrose applied himself to the king for a commission to levy war against his rebel subjects, as they were called, of Scotland; assuring his majesty, that he was able, with the assistance of his friends, and concurrence of the rest of the royal party, to make at least a very considerable diversion, if not to reduce the whole country to his majesty's obedience. Accordingly the marquis was made governor of Scotland; where, in the space of five months, with a handful of raw undisciplined men, and those not half-armed, he did over-run a great part of the country, and gain three very considerable battles; the last of which was that of Inverlochy, fought the second of February 1644, according to the English, and 1645, according to the Scotch account. In this battle the Earl of Argyle was entirely defeated, and the prime of the noble family of the Campbells cut off, with inconsiderable loss, on Montrose's side; who next day dispatched an express to the king with the news of this and the two former victories: and in his letter expressed his " utter aversion to all treaties with his rebel parliament in England," as he calls them: tells the king, " he is heartily sorry to hear that his majesty had consented to treat; and hopes it is not true: advises him not to enter into terms with his rebellious subjects, as being a thing unworthy of a king: and assures him that he himself was now so much master of Scotland, that he doubted not but to be able within a few months to march into England to his majesty's assistance, with a brave army." And concludes with this odd expression, " when I have conquered from Dan to Beersheba, as I doubt not I shall very quickly, I hope I may then have leave to say, as David's general said to his master, Come thou, lest this country be called by my name."

This

This letter, writ with such an air of assurance, and by a person that was thought capable to make good his promises, and the matter contained in it suiting but too well with the king's inclinations, was unluckily delivered to the king but a few hours before he was to have signed the warrant beforementioned; and had as ill effects as the worst of king Charles's enemies could have wished: for it dashed out in a moment all the impressions his best friends had been making upon him for a considerable time, towards a full settlement with his people.

It looked, says my author, as if there was some secret fatality in this whole matter; for it could hardly have been imagined, that a letter writ the third of February, in the furthermost north corner of Britain, should come so soon to Oxford, considering the length of the journey, the badness of the roads at that time of the year, especially through the mountainous part of Scotland, together with the parliament's and Scotch armies and garrisons that were posted all along the road: and yet certain it is, it came through all these dangers and inconveniencies in very few days: for it's indors'd upon the copy I have seen, that it was delivered to the king during the treaty of Uxbridge; which every body knows began the 30th of January, and ended the 22d of February. And further, it must have been delivered before the 19th of February, because king Charles takes notice of it in a letter to the queen of that date, found among others at Naseby; where he says, " though I leave news to others, yet I cannot but tell thee, that even now I have received certain intelligence of a great defeat given by Montrose to Argyle, who upon surprize totally routed these rebels, and killed 1500 upon the place." And it's remarkable that in the same letter to the queen, immediately after the mentioning Montrose's victory, the king adds, that as for trusting the rebels, either by going to London, or disbanding my army before a peace, do no ways fear my hazarding so cheaply or foolishly: for I esteem the interest thou hast in me at a far dearer rate; and

pretend

pretend to have a little more wit (at least by the sympathy that is betwixt us) than to put myself into the reverence of perfidious rebels." Which words being compared with Montrose's letter *, it will be found the one is a commentary upon the other.

Dr. Wellwood concludes with this observation, "that considering the time when this letter of Montrose was writ, this critical minute, it was delivered, with the sad consequences that attended it; it makes the axiom true, That oftentimes the fate of princes and states is chiefly owing to very minute and unforeseen accidents." But may we not add from his own relation, that king Charles's fluctuating and vain temper, which easily received every flattering impression, and could be trusted only in proportion to the restraint it was under, was what in reality ruined his cause, more than any fatality or accident that appeared in this affair?

* See this letter in the appendix.

CHAP. VI.

CROMWELL's *management towards the parliament, the army, and the parties he had to deal with, till he assumed the sovereignty.*

§. 1. AS there is nothing more essential in the character of a prince, or a great minister, than the art of governing parties, and reconciling different interests, so as to make them concur in the advancement of his own designs; so there is no art more difficult than this to attain, or that requires more extraordinary qualifications in the person who attempts to practise it. But never was there a greater master in this art than Cromwell; never was there a man who practised it so succesfully, with so little assistance,

and

and so few advantages. His whole publick life was one continued instance of his address and dexterity, either in circumventing and distressing others, or in evading and breaking the snares that were laid for himself.

His first care, from the beginning, was to secure himself a party in the house of commons; which he effected by his zeal for the public good, and his vigilance in prosecuting all the measures that were entered into by the parliament. Hence it was that the earls of Essex and Manchester, tho' the former was general in chief, and the other Cromwell's superior, were not able to prejudice him, after he had established his reputation by the victory of Marston-moor. When the Scotch chancellor * accused him of being an incendiary, and a publick

---

* The chancellor's speech against him was in the following terms.

"Mr. Maynard and Mr. Whitelock, I can assure you of the great opinion, both my brethren and self have of your worth and abilities; else we should not have desir'd this meeting with you: and since it is his excellency's pleasure, that I should acquaint you with the matter upon whilk your counsel is desir'd, I shall obey his command, and briefly recite the business to you.

You ken vary weele, that lieutenant-general Cromwell is no friend of ours; and since the advance of our army into England, he has used all underhand and cunning means to tak off from our honour, and merit of this kingdom, an evil requital of our hazards and services; but so it is, and we are nevertheless fully satisfy'd of the affections and gratitude of the gude people of the nation in general.

It is thought requisite for us, and for carrying on the cause of the twa kingdoms, that this obstacle or remora be removed out of the way, whom

we

lick enemy of his country, with a view to remove him out of Essex's way; Mr. Whitelock informed that minister, " that he looked upon Cromwell to be a gentleman of quick and subtle parts, and who had a great interest in both houses of parliament, and that it would be needful to collect such particular passages concerning him, as might be sufficient to prove him an incendiary, before they could expect the parliament should proceed against him." And though some gentlemen present, in particular Mr. Hollis and Sir Philip Stapleton, attempted to mention such particular passages, and to maintain that Cromwell had not

we foresee will be no small impediment to us in the gude design we have undertaken.

He not only is no friend to us, and the government of our church, but he is also no well-willer to his excellency, whom you and we have all cause to love and honour; and if he be permitted to go on this way, it may, I fear, endanger the whole business; therefore we are to advise of some course to be taken for prevention of this mischief.

You ken vary weele the accord betwixt the twa nations, and the union by the Solemn League and Covenant; and if any be an incendiary between the twa nations, how he is to be proceeded against. Now the matter is, wherein we desire your opinions, what you tak the meaning of the word incendiary to be, and whether the lieutenant-general be not sick an incendiary, as is meant thereby; and whilk way wud be best to tak to proceed against him, if he proved sick an incendiary, that we may clepe his wings from soaring to the prejudice of our cause.

Now you may ken, that by our law in Scotland, we clepe him an incendiary wha kindleth coals of contention and raiseth differences in the state, to the publick damage; and he is *tanquam publicus hostis patriæ*. Whether your law be the same or not, you ken best, who are mickle learned therein, and therefore we desire your judgments in these points.

suck

such interest in the parliament as was pretended, yet the whole process came to nothing, and the lieutenant-general escaped.

While he was thus put to it to secure himself, who would have thought that he should have accused another, and even that very general to whom he was lieutenant? Yet this was the case between him and Manchester, whom he charged * with betraying the parliament, and speaking disrespectfully of their cause. And though the earl recriminated, and affirmed that Cromwell had once said to him, My lord, if you will stick firm to honest men, you will find an army at your command, that will give law to king and parliament;"

---

* About four months after the fight at Marstonmoor happened the second battle of Newbury, where Cromwell is said to have endanger'd the king's person, had not the earl of Cleveland interpos'd, and bore off the pursuit. This battle was the occasion of an irreconcilable breach between him and the earl of Manchester. Cromwell accus'd the earl of cowardly betraying the parliament, for that he might very easily have defeated the king's army, when he drew off his cannon, if he would have suffer'd him with his own brigade to have charged them in their retreat; but that the earl obstinately oppos'd all advice and importunity, giving no other reason, than " That if he did overthrow the king's army, the king would always have another to keep up the war; but if his army should be overthrown at that nice juncture, they should be all rebels and traitors, and executed and forfeited by the law." This last expression was heinously taken by the parliament, as if the earl believed the law was against them, after they had so often declar'd, that the law was on their side. The earl acknowledg'd, that he had in effect said, " That they would be treated as traitors if their army was defeated," when he dislik'd the lieutenant-general's advice, in exposing the army to an unseasonable hazard. Vide Life of Cromwell, p. 17.

parliament;" yet Cromwell had visibly the advantage in this contest, and soon after succeeded Manchester in his post, who was laid aside by his masters.

§. 2. It is not to be thought that a man who had raised himself in the army, could be in earnest about laying down his commission, when he appeared so vigorous about the self-denying ordinance. But Cromwell was certain of carrying his own point in the house, provided he could get his superiors, and those who were jealous of him, removed from the service. He ran little risk therefore in proffering to lay down his own commission, while he moved that an ordinance might be prepared, " to make it unlawful for any member of either house to hold any office in the army, or any place in the state." And when he hinted at the people's jealousy, that while members of the parliament were in chief command, they found too much interest in continuing the war to suffer them to be earnest in endeavouring to end it; he gave a thorough blow to my lord Manchester, whom he had before accused of labouring to protract the present confusion *.

Cromwell

* Cromwell's speech in the house in favour of this ordinance, was to the following purpose; viz. "That there were many things upon which he never reflected before; yet upon reconsideration, he could not but own that all was very true; and till there was a perfect reformation in those particulars recommended to them, nothing they took in hand would prosper: That the parliament had done wisely in the beginning of the war, to engage many of their members in the most dangerous parts of it, that the nation might see they design'd not to embark others in perils, whilst themselves sat securely out of gun-shot, but would march with them where the danger most threaten'd; and those honourable persons who had thus exposed themselves, had

Cromwell pretended indeed, when the army was new modelled upon this motion, and all the old officers removed, to go among the reſt and take his leave of Sir Thomas Fairfax the new general, who was then at Windſor: but how much ſoever he might ſeem to be ſurprized, there is no room to queſtion but he knew of the committee's recommendation of him to Sir Thomas, as the moſt proper perſon for an enterprize then projected, that of interrupting the correſpondence between
the

had merited ſo much of their country, that their memories would be held in perpetual veneration: and whatever ſhould be well done after them, would be imputed to their example. But now God had ſo bleſſed their army, that there had grown up with it many excellent officers, who were fitter for much greater charges than they now enjoy'd; therefore he deſir'd them not to be terrified with an imagination, that they ſhould want able men to fill the greateſt vacancy; for beſides that it was not good to put ſo much truſt in any arm of fleſh, as to think that ſuch a cauſe as this depended upon any one man, ſo he aſſur'd them, that they had officers in their army, who were fit to be generals in any enterprize in Chriſtendom." He added, "He thought nothing ſo neceſſary as to vindicate the parliament from partiality towards their own members; proffer'd to lay down his own commiſſion in the army, and deſir'd, that an ordinance might be prepared, to make it unlawful for any member of either houſe to hold any office in the army, or any place in the ſtate;" and ſo concluded with an enlargement upon the vices and corruptions crept into the army, and freely told them, "That till the whole army were new modell'd, and brought under ſtricter diſcipline, they muſt not expect any remarkable ſucceſs in any undertaking." In concluſion, a committee was appointed to prepare an ordinance for the excluſion of all members from the fore-mention'd truſts; which took up much time, and was long debated; but in the end paſs'd, and was call'd the ſelf-denying ordinance.

the king and prince Rupert. This was only a prelude to what foon followed, when his perfonal fervice in the houfe was difpenfed with, and his commiffion continued from time to time, till he was conftituted lieutenant-general of the horfe, with the fame full powers that Manchefter had before enjoyed.

§. 3. But when the firft civil war was over, Cromwell had yet a more difficult part to act. Diffenfions broke out between the parliament, which was chiefly prefbyterians, and the army, which inclined to indepency. Thefe differences were heightened by the citizens of London, who addreffed the parliament againft the independants, and complained particularly of the army, where many, they faid, who were neither learned or ordained, took upon them to preach and expound the fcripture. Cromwell, for a long-time, had feemed to favour prefbytery; but having got many of his friends into power, and finding the army on his fide, he now efpoufed the independant party. Hereupon the parliament grew particularly jealous of him, and were for taking meafures to difmifs him and his partizans from their military pofts. Cromwell was no lefs jealous of them, and being aware of what they defigned, refolved to be even with them. Accordingly he took care to whifper fufpicions of the parliament, and made a ftrong party for military power *.

There

---

* Ludlow tells us, that as he was walking with him one morning in Sir Robert Cotton's garden, he inveigh'd bitterly againft the parliament, and faid familiarly to him, "If thy father were alive, he would let fome of them hear what they deferve;" adding farther, "That it was a miferable thing to ferve a parliament, to whom let a man be never fo faithful, if one pragmatical fellow amongft them rife up and afperfe him, he fhall never wipe it off; whereas, when one ferves under a general, he may do as much fervice, and yet be free from all blame and envy."

Life of Oliver Cromwell.   119

There was actually a design on foot, to break some of the independant regiments, and send the others to Ireland: of which Cromwell getting timely notice, he and Ireton got it insinuated thro' all the army, that the parliament intended to disband them without paying their arrears, or else to consume them in Ireland with sickness and famine. This so exasperated the soldiers, that when the orders came for disbanding some, and transporting others, they refused to comply with them. When the parliament heard this, they were highly offended, and threatening expressions came from some of the members; which occasioned Cromwell, then in the house, to whisper Ludlow, who stood by, saying, "these men will never leave, till the army pull them out by the ears."

§. 4. A spirit of opposition being thus raised in the army, they began now professedly to enter into competition with the parliament, and to claim a share with them in settling the kingdom: and that they might be upon a nearer level with them, they made choice of a number of such officers as they approv'd, which was called the general's council of officers, and was to resemble the house of peers; and three or four out of each regiment, mostly corporals or serjeants, were chosen by the common soldiers, and called agitators, who were to answer to the house of commons. These two bodies met separately, and examined all the acts and orders of the parliament towards settling the kingdom, and reforming, dividing or disbanding the army: and after some consultations, they unanimously declared, "that they would not be divided or disbanded till their full arrears were paid, and till full provision was made for liberty of conscience, which hitherto had been little secured." They added, "that as they had voluntarily taken up arms, for the liberty and defence of the nation, of which they were a part; before they laid down those arms, they would see all those ends provided for." This declaration was delivered at the bar

bar of the houfe of commons, by three or four perfons of the army's council *.

This contrivance for keeping the army together, and fetting them up againſt the parliament, was a maſter ſtroke of Cromwell's. It not only faved him at prefent, but proved the foundation of all his future greatnefs. For the army continued refolute in their defign, and grew more haughty in their expreffions, till the difference feemed almoſt irreconcilable. Fairfax the general indeed was a prefbyterian; but then Cromwell had fo much the afcendant over him, as well as over the army, that he was prevailed with

to

---

* Soon after this declaration, the foldiers drew up a vindication of their proceedings, directing it to their general; wherein they complained of a defign to difband, and new-model the army; which, they faid, " was a plot contrived by fome men, who had lately taſted of fovereignty, and being rais'd above the ordinary fphere of fervants, would fain become mafters, and were degenerated into tyrants." For which reafon they declared, " that they would neither be employed for the fervice of Ireland, nor fuffer themfelves to be difbanded, till their defires were obtained, and the fubjects rights and liberties fhould be vindicated and fecur'd." This paper being fign'd by many inferior officers, the parliament declar'd them enemies of the ſtate, impriſoning fome of them who talk'd loudeſt: Whereupon they drew up another addrefs to the general, complaining, " how difdainfully they were ufed by the parliament, for whom they had ventured their lives, and fpilt their blood; that the privileges due to them as foldiers, and as fubjects, were taken from them; and when they complained of the injuries done to them, they were abus'd, beaten, and impriſon'd."

to write a letter to back the army's petitions *. These proceedings grievously troubled the parliament; but resolving not to submit to those who lived on their pay, they declared, "that whosoever should refuse, being commanded, to engage in the service of Ireland, should be disbanded." The army, however, would not recede from their resolutions, and falling into direct mutiny, called for the arrears that were due to them, "which they knew where, and how to levy for themselves." Nor would they be pacified till the declaration against them was erased out of the journal-book, and a month's pay sent to them. Nay, they still gave out, "that they knew how to make themselves as considerable as the parliament, and where to have their service better esteemed and requited." Which so startled the parliament, that they sent a committee of both houses, to treat with a committee of officers, upon the best means for composing these differences. And thus the army, by a concession of the parliament's, seemed to be put upon a level with it: which disposed Fairfax to a greater concurrence with the humour of the soldiers, as he saw it so much complied with, and submitted to.

§. 5. Cromwell hitherto thought it necessary to keep fair with the parliament; and, through his choice knack at dissimulation, he would seem highly displeased with the insolence of the soldiers, and inveighed bitterly against their presumption in the house of commons, when any of their addresses were presented. He also proposed, that the general might be

* In this letter he took notice of several petitions, which were prepared in the city of London, and other places, against the army; adding, "that it was look'd upon as strange, that the officers of the army might not be permitted to petition, when so many petitions were received against them; and that he much doubted, that the army might draw to a rendezvous, and think of taking some other course for their own vindication."

sent down to the army; who, he said, would soon conjure down this mutinous spirit. Himself, by these means, was once or twice sent, to reduce them to order; when, after staying two or three days, he returned again to the parliament, with heavy complaints of the great licence that was got into the army; declaring, " that for his own part, he was rendered so odious to them by the artifice of his enemies, that they had designed to kill him, if he had not timely escaped out of their hands." But he was greatly suspected by some, notwithstanding this, of having under-hand encouraged the army's proceedings; and the most active officers and agitators were believed to be his own creatures, who would do nothing without his directions: so that it was privately resolved by the chief members of the house of commons, that when he came the next day to the house, which he seldom failed to do, they would send him to the Tower.

This design could not be managed so secretly, but Cromwell got intelligence of it. The next day, when the house expected every minute to see him come in, they were informed he was met out of town by break of day, with only one servant, posting away to the army. Here he ordered a rendezvous of some regiments of horse, and then dispatched a letter to the house of commons, to acquaint them, " that the jealousy the troops had conceived of him was much abated, and he had therefore been invited by the officers to his own regiment, in order to reclaim them by his advice; in which view he made all possible haste to the army." He also advised a general rendezvous of the troops, and that general Fairfax might be sent down with all expedition.

§. 6. It was during this quarrel between the house of commons and the army, that Cromwell gave the world that specimen of his deep artifice, which was related by Sir Harbottle Grimston to bishop Burnet. In a meeting of officers it was proposed to purge the army better, in order to know whom they might depend on. Cromwell said, " he was sure of the army; but there was another body, naming the house of commons, that wanted more to be purged, and the army could only do that." This was reported to the house by Grimston, and witnesses attested it at the bar. Whereupon Cromwell, who was present, fell down upon his knees, and made a solemn prayer to God, attesting his innocence, and great zeal for the service of the house. This he did with great vehemence, and many tears: after which he made a long speech, justifying himself, and the rest of the officers, except a few, who seemed inclinable to return back to Egypt, as he phrased it. And so was the house wrought upon by these means, that what the witnesses said was little believed; and Grimston was of opinion, that had the motion been made, both he and they would have been sent to the Tower. Cromwell however no sooner got out of the house, but he resolved not to trust himself there again: so hastening to the army, he in a few days brought them to town, and did in effect purge the house of many members, which enabled him to treat the rest just as he pleased.

There is another story of Mr. Locke's, in his memoirs of Anthony Ashley Cooper, the first earl of Shaftsbury, which deserves to be here inserted. He tells us, that Sir Anthony Ashley Cooper (for he was not a lord till after the restoration) calling upon Mr. Holles, in his way to the house, found him in a great heat against Cromwell, saying, he was resolved to bring him to punishment. Cooper shewed him how dangerous such an attempt might be, earnestly dissuaded him from it, and told him it would be enough to send him with a command into Ireland; which, as things stood, he would be glad to accept. But this would not satisfy Holles, who, when he came to the house, brought the matter to a debate, wherein it was moved, that Cromwell, and those guilty with him, should be punished. Cromwell being then in the house, immediately stole out, took horse, and hastened away to the army, which was at Triploe-heath, where he

informed

informed them of what was now doing in the houfe by the prefbyterian party, and made fuch ufe of it, that the army united under him, who forthwith led them to London, giving out fuch menaces againft Holles and his party, that they were fain to abfent themfelves, whereby the independant party became the ftrongeft. Soon after meeting Sir Anthony Afhley Cooper, Cromwell said unto him, "I am beholden to you for your kindnefs to me; for you, I hear, were for letting me go without punifhment; but your friend, God be thanked, was not wife enough to take your advice."

§. 7. The feizing of the king at Holmby through Cromwell's initigation, and the ufe that was made of him by the army againft the parliament, are particulars that have been elfewhere mentioned. There is no queftion but Cromwell had herein a view to his own intereft, and to the keeping the parliament under; though I have made it very manifeft, that his good intentions towards the king were real, provided he could have fecured himfelf and the liberties of the people by a reftoration, and had not his majefty dealt unfairly with him. I fhall not repeat any of the intrigues on that fcore; but muft not omit an action of Cromwell, while they were on foot, that fhews more prefence of mind and perfonal courage, as well as deep penetration, than almoft any other paffage that is to be met with in hiftory.

It was the defign of the levellers, who were now a great part of the army, not only to abolifh monarchy, but alfo the houfe of peers, and to eftablifh a pure democracy *. This was what colonel Rainfborough, one

---

* They prefented a writing to the general, and afterwards to the parliament, declaring;

1. "That the people being unequally diftributed by counties, cities and boroughs, for election of their deputies in parliament, ought to be more indifferently proportioned according to the number of inhabitants.

2 That

Life of Oliver Cromwell. 125

one of their leaders, affifted by others, went about foliciting from one regiment to another; ftirring up the foldiers againft Fairfax, Cromwell, and the other general officers, who were fufpected of being for an accommodation. But Cromwell was refolved to endeavour the fuppreffion of this licence, which he thought could be effected only by fome extraordinary act of authority. Being accompanied therefore with divers officers, he with a wonderful brifknefs

2. That the prefent parliament be diffolved by the laft day of September next.

3. That the people do of courfe chufe themfelves a parliament once in every two years.

4. That the power of this, and all other future reprefentatives, is inferior only to theirs who chufe them, and extends, without the confent of any other perfon, to the enacting, altering, and repealing of laws; to the erecting and abolifhing of offices and courts; to the appointing, removing, and calling to account, magiftrates and officers of all degrees; to the making war and peace; to the treating with foreign ftates; and generally to whatfoever is not referved by thofe reprefented to themfelves." And here they declare, " That impreffing or conftraining any to ferve in the war, is againft freedom, and not allowed to the reprefentatives.

5. That in all laws every perfon be bound alike; and that tenure, eftates, charter, degree, birth or place, do not confer any exception from the ordinary courfe of legal proceedings whereunto others are fubjected. And,

6. That the laws muft be equal and good, and not deftructive to the fafety and well being of the people."

Thefe they declared to be their native rights, which they were refolved to maintain, and not to depend, for the fettlement of their peace and freedom, upon him that intended their bondage [meaning the king] and brought a cruel war upon them.

briskeness rode up to one of the regiments, which wore the distinguishing marks *, and commanded them to take them out of their hats; which they refusing to do, he caused several of them to be seized, and knocked down two or three with his own hand; and the others hearts failing, they submitted to him. He ordered one of those whom he had seized to be shot dead on the place, and delivered the rest into the hands of the marshal: then writing up an account of what he had done to the parliament, they returned him the thanks of the house.

He suppressed them in like manner some time after when upon abolishing the council of agitators, they were once more exasperated. There being a rendezvous at Ware, several regiments, among whom was Cromwell's own, in pursuance of a petition they had presented Fairfax, and in order to distinguish themselves, wore white in their hats, as they had done before. Cromwell having notice of the design, ordered two regiments of horse from distant quarters, who knew nothing of this combination, to appear there likewise. Being all drawn up, Cromwell with an angry and down look walks round, and on a sudden commands one of those two regiments to encompass a regiment of foot. This being done accordingly, he called four men by their names out of the body, and with his own hands committed them to the marshal; and immediately calling a council of war, (whilst the rest of the confederates slunk their white colours into their pockets, and trembled at the boldness of Cromwell) tried and condemned them. But they had the favour of casting lots for their lives; and the two whose lot it was to die, were presently shot to death by the other two, in sight of the army.

* At the general rendezvous, they who were of this party, to distinguish themselves, appear'd every one with a paper in his hat, with these words written upon it, " The rights of England, and the consent of the people."

§. 8. The

§. 8. The parliament and army being united * againſt the king, upon his majeſty's refuſing to ſign
the

* The commiſſioners of the parliament being come back from the iſle of Wight with the king's anſwer, which imported, "That he had refuſed to paſs the four bills, 1. For veſting the militia in the two houſes. 2. For revoking all declarations againſt the parliament. 3. For vacating all titles of honour conferred ſince his leaving the parliament. 4. That the houſes ſhould adjourn themſelves as they thought fit; or to make a compoſure in that way; but had barely made a perſonal treaty;" there followed a long debate in the houſe, and many ſevere and bitter ſpeeches were made againſt the king. Ireton, according to ſome, was the firſt that ſpoke with warmth, and Cromwell ſeconded him; and from the king's refuſing to ſign the four acts, they inferr'd, "That he had ſufficiently declared himſelf for arbitrary government:" and alledging, "That he was no longer the protector, but the tyrant of his people; and conſequently, that they were no longer his ſubjects; and that they ought to govern without him; that their long patience had availed nothing; and that it was expected, from their zeal to their country, that they ſhould take ſuch reſolutions, as were worthy of an aſſembly with whom the nation had intruſted their ſafety." And as thoſe two perſons were not only members of the houſe, but alſo chiefs in the army; after they had firſt ſpoken under the former character, they ſpake again in the other, to this effect: "That they were well perſuaded of the parliament's good intentions, and were aſſured, that without ſuffering themſelves to be amuſed any longer, they would defend the nation by their own proper authority, and by the courage of thoſe valiant men, that were enroll'd under their banners, who by their mouths gave them aſſurances of their fidelity, which nothing could ſhake. But have a care, ſaid they, that you do not give the army

the four preliminary bills, and colonel Rainsborough appointed admiral of the fleet, tumults and discontents began to renew among the people. In the mean time Cromwell appointed a meeting of several leading men of the presbyterian and independant parties, both members of parliament and ministers, in order to promote a reconciliation between the two interests. He could not indeed effect it, on account of these inveterate animosities; but the attempt shewed how indefatigable he always was, and how fruitful in schemes for the service of the cause.

A like conference was held by his contrivance, between the grandees of the house and army, of whom himself was one, and the commonwealth's-men. The grandees here delivered themselves with some uncertainty, as to the form of government they should prefer; but the commonwealth's-men declared absolutely against monarchy, and recommended the establishment of an equal commonwealth. Cromwell, very artfully, seemed unresolved at present; but informed Ludlow afterwards, that he was inclined to be of his opinion, as to the expediency of a popular government, and from that time seemed to close with the republicans. But this was artifice only, in order to secure himself, in these times of danger, under the shelter of that powerful party: which Ludlow suspecting, he freely told him, "You know how to cajole and give us good words, when you have occasion to make use of us." Cromwell, however, tho' always suspected by one side or the other, and sometimes

army, who sacrifice themselves for the liberty of the nation, any grounds to suspect you of betraying them; and do not oblige them to look for their own safety, and that of the nation, in their own strength, which they desire to owe to nothing, but the steadiness and vigour of your resolutions." This was that famous debate before-mentioned, in which Cromwell is said to have put his hand to his sword. Vide chap. 5. §, 12.

times by all parties together, yet still preserved his footing, either by making himself necessary to the publick in general, or by falling in with the reigning faction, or by setting up another faction that might over-balance the former.

One of his most effectual engines in these enthusiastical times, was his continual pretensions of humility and devotion, ascribing the glory of all his actions to the providence of God, smiling on the justice of the parliament's cause. And how little soever such a behaviour would take at present, it was then the only way of becoming popular; as popularity, especially in the army, was the only infallible way to power; so that though hypocrisy, in matters of religion, is undoubtedly very odious, yet as much may be here said to extenuate the crime of it, as in any other instance I know. One may even venture to say, that if Cromwell's dissimulation be any disadvantage to his character, we may from the same principle condemn most of the great men in all ages, who have conformed with popular prejudices to serve the ends of ambition: for whether the point be religion or policy (if indeed there be any difference between these two among the great and mighty ones of the earth) the deception is just the same, and the laws of truth are equally infringed.

§. 9. Soon after the death of the king, the commons voted the house of peers to be useless and dangerous; and an act was accordingly pass'd for abolishing it, though Cromwell is said to have appeared in their behalf. And to remove all that stood in the way of their intended commonwealth, they resolved and declared, "That it had been found by experience, that the office of a king in this nation, was unnecessary, burthensome, and dangerous to the liberty, safety, and publick interest of the nation; and therefore it should be utterly abolished." Then the form of government was declared to be a commonwealth; and a council of state was appointed, confifting of forty perfons *, whereof Cromwell was one; to whom power was given, to command and fettle the militia of England and Ireland, to order the fleet, and fet forth fuch a naval power, as they fhould think fit; to appoint magazines and ftores for England and Ireland, and to difpofe of them for the fervice of both nations, as they thought proper. And they were to fit and execute thefe powers for the fpace of one whole year. From this time all writs, formerly running in the king's name, were to be iffued out in the names of the keepers of the liberty of England. And a new oath, or engagement, was prepared, " to be true and faithful to the government eftablifhed without king or houfe of peers: all who refufed to take it, uncapable of holding any place or office in church or ftate. It was during the exiftence of this commonwealth, in which Cromwell had the chief fway, that the lord Capels petition, which his lady delivered, was read in the houfe. That nobleman was condemned for high-treafon, together with

* If the reader is curious of knowing what perfons compofed the council of ftate for this firft year, they were as follows: John Bradfhaw, Efq; prefident, earl of Denbigh, earl of Mulgrave, earl of Pembroke, earl of Salifbury, lord Grey, lord Grey of Groby, lord Fairfax, John Lifle, Efq;——Rolles, Efq; Oliver St. John, Efq; John Wild, Efq; Bulftrode Whitelock, Efq; lieutenant general Cromwell, major-general Skippon, Sir Gilbert Pickering, Sir William Maffum, Sir Arthur Haflerigg, Sir James Harrington, Sir Henry Vane, jun. Sir John Danvers, Sir William Armine, Sir Henry Mildmay, Sir William Conftable, Alexander Popham, William Purefoy, Ifaac Pennington, Rowland Wilfon, Edmund Ludlow, William Heveningham, Robert Wallop, Henry Marten, Anthony Stapely, John Hutchinfon, Valentine Walton, Thomas Scot, Dennis Bond, Luke Robinfon, John Jones, Cornelius Holland, Efquires.

with duke Hamilton, the earls of Holland and Norwich, and Sir John Owen. Many fpoke in his favour, and faid, that he had never deceived or betrayed them, but had always freely and refolutely declared for the king: and Cromwell, who knew him very well, fpoke fo many things to his honour, and profeffed fo much refpect for him, that all believed he was fafe, till he concluded, "That his affection for the publick fo out-weighed his private friendfhip, that he could not but tell them, that the queftion was now, Whether they would preferve the moft bitter and moft implacable enemy they had? That he knew well, that the lord Capel would be the laft man in England, that would abandon the royal intereft; that he had great courage, induftry, and generofity; that he had many friends who would always adhere to him, and that as long as he liv'd, what condition foever he was in, he would be a thorn in their fides: and therefore for the good of the commonwealth, he fhould give his vote againft the petition." By this fpeech he prevented the lenity of the houfe, which every one thought would have taken place.

About this time feveral things were declared by the parliament to be high-treafon, and among the reft, " for any foldier of the army to contrive the death of their general, or lieutenant-general; or endeavour to raife mutinies in the army." The extending of this to the lieutenant-general by name, plainly fhews what power Cromwell had acquired under that title; and there is good reafon to think, that this act was made purely for the fecurity of his perfon.

§. 10. The wars being all over, as well in Scotland, Ireland, and the reft of the Britifh Ifles, as in England itfelf, Cromwell, who with the title of lord-general was now poffeffed of fupreme authority, defired a meeting with feveral members of parliament, and fome of the principal officers of the army, at the fpeaker's houfe. This was very foon after the battle of Worcester. Whitelock, who was one of the number, gives a remarkable account of the conference here held. Cromwell proposed, that some method might be fixed on for settling the liberties of the nation, both civil and spiritual: and upon Whitelock's offering in the first place, to consider whether an absolute republick, or with any mixture of monarchy, were to be preferred; Cromwell added, that Whitelock had hit upon the right point. " It is my meaning, says he, that we should consider, whether a republick, or a mix'd monarchical government, will be best to be settled; and if any thing monarchical, then in whom that power shall be placed." Sir Thomas Widdringhton, lord chief justice St. John, Lenthall the speaker, and Whitelock, were all of them for monarchy; because any other form of government, they said, would make too great an alteration in the proceedings of our law. Fleetwood was in doubt which to prefer: Desborough and Whalley, both noted republicans, were not for having any mixture of monarchical power. But as to a proper person, in case such a power were admitted, no body was nominated but one of the late king's sons. Whereupon Cromwell told them, " that this would be a matter of more then ordinary difficulty; but he really thought, if it might be done with safety, and preservation of our rights, that a settlement with something of monarchical power in it would be very effectual." *

It appeared in general, from the discourse that passed, that the soldiers were for a pure republick, the lawyers for a mix'd monarchy, and many for the duke of Gloucester to be made king: but Cromwell still put off that debate to some other point. Hence it seems evident, that having now entertain'd thoughts of setting up for himself, his only design in this conference, was to discover the inclinations of the persons present, that he might make a proper use thereof

* See the appendix, No. II.

of in profecuting the ends of his own ambition, which was much heightened by the finifhing ftroke that was given to his fucceffes, in the late glorious victory at Worcefter.

He had already, indeed, a power little lefs than fovereign. His commiffion for Ireland expiring, though the parliament did not renew it in the fame form, yet they made him general and commander in chief of all the forces in that kingdom, by virtue of which commiffion he appointed Fleetwood his deputy: in fhort, the whole military power was in his hands, and the civil adminiftration almoft entirely under his influence; but his ambition afcended yet higher, and the confufed ftate of the legiflature, while it appeared like a body without a head, gave him at leaft a plaufible excufe for pufhing on, and affuming that authority to himfelf, which was vifibly wanting.

§. 11. In a converfation with Whitelock alone, foon after the conference above-mentioned, he opened himfelf more fully than he had hitherto done *. He complained that the officers of the army were inclined to factions and murmurings, and fpread the fame fpirit among the private foldiers: that the members of the parliament were proud, ambitious, partial, covetous, and many of them fcandalous in their lives: that it would be impoffible to prevent the ruin of the nation, unlefs fome authority were fet up that might reftrain and keep things in better order. Whitelock confeffed the danger they were in from fuch extravagancies as thefe; but faid, his excellency had power to reftrain the foldiers, which as he had hitherto done, fo he might do it ftill: and as to the members of parliament, though fome of them were to blame, yet better things might be hoped for the reft. And upon Cromwell's intimating that he could not hope for much good from them, Whitelock infifted, that as they

* See this conference alfo at large in the appendix, No. III. as extracted from Whitelock's own account, in his memoirs.

they had been acknowledged the fupreme power, and all commiffions taken out in their name, it would now be very difficult for thofe who acted under them to curb their authority.

The general finding he did not come to the point, put this fhort queftion, "What if a man fhould take upon him to be king?" Whitelock faid, "He thought that the remedy would be worfe than the difeafe:" and gave this reafon as to Cromwell in particular, that as he had already the full kingly power, the title would only bring with it envy and danger equal to the pomp. Cromwell then argued on the * legality of a king by election, and urged the ftatute of king Henry VII. which makes it fafer for the people to act under a king, let his title be what it will, than under any other power. The legality Whitelock owned, but much doubted the expediency of it: and being afked, "What danger he apprehended in taking this title?" he anfwered, "That it would entirely alter the ftate of the controverfy between them and their adverfaries: for as the difpute had hitherto been, whether the government fhould be in a monarchy, or in a free commonwealth; the only queftion then would be, whether Cromwell or Stuart fhould be monarch; and thus all who were for a commonwealth, being a very confiderable party, finding

* We find Whitelock, and the other members of the committee, in the conference fome years after, when the parliament requefted Cromwell to affume the title of king, making ufe of the very fame arguments that Cromwell himfelf here ufes, and the general giving much the fame anfwers againft himfelf as Whitelock here gives againft him. But Whitelock and the reft had then learned what was the real aim of this afpiring commander, and fo gave him an opportunity to fave appearances, by refufing that crown when offered him, which he had before fo openly confeffed himfelf defirous of wearing. See that conference in the appendix.

finding their hopes fruſtrated, would be intirely againſt the eſtabliſhment.

Cromwell acknowledged the reaſon of what the commiſſioner had ſaid, and demanded, " what other expedient he could propound, that might obviate the preſent dangers and difficulties." But the other wav'd giving an anſwer, until Cromwell had aſſured him that no harm ſhould come of it: then he ſet forth the hazard the general would run from his ſecret enemies, and even from the officers of the army, who would be ſpirited up by many members of parliament and others: and upon the general thanking him for his care, and encouraging him to proceed, he propoſed the bringing in of the king of Scots, meaning Charles the Second, under ſuch reſtrictions as might ſecure the liberty of the ſubject, and with ample proviſions for Cromwell himſelf, and all his friends. Which advice ſeemed not very agreeable; for though Cromwell owned the reaſon of it, he put off the farther conſideration of the affair, and went away with ſome diſpleaſure in his countenance. After this, his carriage towards Whitelock was more cold than formerly, and he ſoon found out an occaſion, by an honourable employment *, to ſend him out of the nation. This behaviour, as well as another converſation he had with the † city divines,
plainly

* An embaſſy to Sweden.

† Harry Nevill, who was then one of the council of ſtate, us'd to tell it as a ſtory of his own knowledge, " that Cromwell upon this great occaſion ſent for ſome of the chief city divines, as if he had made it a matter of conſcience to be determined by their advice. Among theſe was the leading Mr. Calamy, who very boldly oppos'd the project of Cromwell's ſingle government, and offered to prove it both unlawful and impracticable. Cromwell anſwered readily upon the firſt head of unlawful, and appeal'd to the ſafety of the nation being the ſupreme law: But, ſays he, pray, Mr. Calamy, why impracticable? Calamy reply'd,

plainly indicated that the general's intentions, at this time, were no lefs than to bring the crown upon his own head.

§. 12. The concurrence of leading men not being to be procured, a cry was immediately promoted in the army againſt the long parliament, accompanied with warm declarations for right and juſtice, and publick liberty, which was ſaid to be now wanting, while the members were all kings, and ordered things as they pleaſed. If the parliament would not diſſolve themſelves, it was ſaid, and ſuffer a new repreſentative to be choſen, the army and people muſt do it for them. And that no obſtacle might be in the way of the intended government, means were found to ſet the young duke of Glouceſter at liberty, who had been confined here ever ſince the king's death, and ſend him out of the kingdom.

While this clamour was kept up in the army, and backed every day with petitions, addreſſes, and remonſtrances, demanding the payment of their arrears, and the diſſolution of the parliament. Some of the officers profeſſed againſt them, and one major Streater was ſo bold as to declare, "that the general deſigned to ſet up for himſelf:" upon which Harriſon, a fifth monarchy man, ſaying he believed the contrary, and that the general's aim was only to make way for the kingdom of Jeſus; the major replied, "Unleſs Jeſus comes very ſuddenly, he will come too late *."

During

ply'd, Oh, 'tis againſt the voice of the nation; there will be nine in ten againſt you. Very well, ſays Cromwell; but what if I ſhould diſarm the nine, and put the ſword in the tenth man's hand, would not that do the buſineſs?"

* About this time Cromwell ſent a letter to the cardinal de Retz in France; which the ſaid cardinal thus relates in his memoirs: " 'Tis remarkable that the ſame night, as I was going home, (viz. after he had

During these transactions abroad, a dissolution was moved for in the house itself, by some of Cromwell's friends: but the only effect it had, was to procure a vote for filling up the house, and to declare it high-treason for any one to propose a change in the present government. Hereupon Cromwell held a consultation with some officers and members whom he knew to be in his interest, to consider of some expedient for carrying on the government, and putting an end to the parliament. But at their second meeting, news being brought that the parliament were then sitting, and it was hoped would dissolve themselves, the conference was broke off, and the members present left Cromwell, to go and strengthen his interest in the house: when, contrary to their expectation, they found a motion under debate, for continuing the present parliament above a year and a half longer. The news of this was carried to Cromwell, who went directly to Westminster.

Having brought with him a party of soldiers, to the number of three hundred, he placed some of them at the doors, some in the lobby, and others on the stairs. Then entering the house, he told his friend St. John, "that he came to do that which griev'd

had been to carry some money he had borrowed for king Charles, who was now at Paris) I met one Tilney, an Englishman, whom I had formerly known at Rome, who told me that Vere, a great parliamentarian, and a favourite of Cromwell, was arriv'd at Paris, and had orders to see me. I was a little perplex'd: however, I thought it would be improper to refuse him an interview. He gave me a letter from Cromwell in the nature of credentials, importing, that the sentiments I had discover'd in the defence of publick liberty, added to my reputation, had induced him to enter into the strictest friendship with me. It was a most civil complaisant letter, and I answer'd it with a great deal of respect; but in such a manner as became a true catholick and an honest Frenchman."

griev'd him to the soul; but there was a necessity laid upon him therein, in order to the glory of God, and the good of the nation." He then sat down for some time, and heard the debates on the forementioned act; making an offer to put his design in execution, but was dissuaded from it by Harrison. At last, when the question for passing the act was put, he said to Harrison, " This is the time, I must do it." And so standing up on a sudden, he bade the speaker leave the chair, and told the house, " they had sat long enough, unless they had done more good." Then charging several particulars with their private vices, he told them in general, that they had not a heart to do any thing for the publick good, but only an intention to perpetuate themselves in power." And when some of them began to speak, he stepped into the midst of the house, and said, " Come, come, I will put an end to your prating. Then, walking up and down the house, he cried out, " You are no parliament, I say you are no parliament;" and stamping with his feet, he bade them " be gone and give place to honester men." Upon this signal, the soldiers entered, and he said to one of them, " take away that fool's bauble," meaning the mace; and Harrison taking the speaker by the arm, he came down from the chair. After this addressing himself to the members, the general told him, "they had forced him to do this:" So seizing on all their papers, he ordered the soldiers to clear the house of the members; and having caused the doors to be locked up, he returned to Whitehall *. In the afternoon he did the

---

* Whitelock has the following remark on this transaction. " Thus it pleased God, that this assembly, famous throughout the world for its undertakings, actions, and successes, having subdued all their enemies, were themselves overthrown and ruin'd by their servants; and those whom they had raised, now pulled down their masters. An example never to

the same thing by the council of state, where he was boldly opposed by serjeant Bradshaw *. But nothing could stop him in the execution of his design.

* As he enter'd the council, he spoke thus to them; "Gentlemen, if you are met here as private persons, you shall not be disturbed; but if as a council of state, this is no place for you: and since you cannot but know what was done at the house in the morning, so take notice that the parliament is dissolv'd." Serjeant Bradshaw boldly answered; "Sir, we have heard what you did at the house in the morning, and before many hours all England will hear it: but, Sir, you are mistaken, to think that the parliament is dissolv'd; for no power under heaven can dissolve them but themselves; therefore take you notice of that." Some others also spoke to the same purpose: but the council finding themselves to be under the same force, they all quietly departed.

to be forgotten, and scarce to be parallel'd in any story! By which all persons may be instructed, how uncertain and subject to change all worldly affairs are; how apt to fall when we think them highest."

CHAP. VII.

A view of CROMWELL'*s civil government, from his dissolving the long parliament till his death.*

§. 1. WE are to consider the government of England, under the remnant of the long parliament, as a kind of anarchy. Many of the ablest members, either through compulsion or of choice, had no longer seats in the house of commons: and those who remained, at least the majority of them, if we may judge of what would be by what was, were

degenerating

degenerating apace from thofe noble principles that had at firft diftinguifhed them; and having tafted the fweets of power, were endeavouring to eftablifh themfelves in the full and lafting poffeffion of it, to the utter exclufion of their fellow-fubjects, who upon the principles now avow'd, had an equal right to it with themfelves. What would this have been, but the erecting of a tyranny worfe than that they complained of, the tyranny of the many inftead of an arbitrary monarchy?

While affairs were thus running on, if there was any member of the commonwealth who had fufficient power to ftop the courfe of them, and turn the conftitution, which had been thus diverted, into its old and natural channel, that of monarchy, was it not his duty, was it not for the general good of the nation that he fhould do this; Oliver Cromwell had fuch a power; he faw the neceffity of exerting it, and, by an act of heroifm that is hardly to be parallel'd, he undertook and went through with the work in his own perfon; while his timorous friends diffuaded him from the attempt, and looked on trembling for the event. It ended fuccefsfully both to himfelf and his friends, as well as to the nation in general, whofe laws he maintained, whofe honour he afferted, whofe reputation he raifed, more than any fovereign had done for a long time before *.

It

---

* Cromwell's panegyrift addreffes him thus on the diffolution of the parliament. "That which you acted unfriendly againft the enemy, you have acted friendly towards your friends Not that they yet attempted any thing againft their country, but left they fhould go back from the government appointed with their country. They ftudied the affair of an ariftocracy, you of a democracy: they to act the nobles, you to elect the fenators: they to contract the commonwealth to themfelves, you to extend it to the people: they to rule the publick after their own will,

you

It is manifest from many instances, that there are such crises in governments, as well as in arts and sciences, when

you to direct every thing by the common assent. Not that they had already offended, but least they should create a suspicion of offence. You have consulted for their credit, you have preserved their honour; nor have you done them any injury, but only taken away the matter of envy. You have not so much reproached their counsels, as you have been ready to fetch them back to better. You truly understand the free nature of the English nation, which will not bear even the shadow of servitude; like that of the Romans, which even in their deliverer, would not endure the empty sound of a name favouring of tyranny. The English senate suffer on this side the hurt, what Collatinus did beyond the injury. Let this then be granted to liberty, that, in defending herself, she may exceed the mean. There is nothing over-much faulty in the defence of liberty. Cromwell is no more to be blamed for taking away the senate, than Brutus for banishing his friend and companion Collatinus the consul. You, Cromwell, who had stood up an advocate for liberty, had before constituted a commonwealth: it was your duty then to support what you had constituted. The commonwealth desired to have you for her faithful and ready guardian: for that truly she had given you arms. You therefore, thus set in a watch-tower, had bound yourself to be vigilant. You perceived the people to be moved; to require the faith plighted to them; to wish that nothing might be done save what was agreeable to the constitution. You saw the army, who had made themselves, after a certain manner, the security and pledges of the publick faith, to be out of patience. You flew; you made yourself wings of your weapons, that you might comply with the desires of the people. You neither appeared at your own fancy; nor acted by your own judgment; nor changed any thing thro' your

when a matter-genius may exert itself, and by deviating from the common rules, effect that in a few bold and licentious ftrokes, which a regular procefs could never reach! I may venture to add, that fuch a genius as this is fometimes neceffary, and what alone can reftore the ruins of a decayed conftitution, and repair the devaftations of the unfkilful many. The dictatorfhip of Cæfar, however obtained, was better for Rome than the times that preceded it, when the emulation

your own fenfe. You undertook, you affected all things at the defire of the people, who are the fountain and origin of empire. Nor have you been fo much obedient to them, as to that reafon and faith which governs in them. You have ftood forth a defender of the common right; nor, fave only to defend it, would you have ever taken up thofe innoxious quiet arms, the pure pledges of your faith, devoted to the commonwealth, engaged to your country.

But if you have diffolved the fenate, you have employed the office of a cenfor: you have brought in the Roman magiftrate to London. The cenfor removed the fenators from their places at Rome; you, cenfor like, have ejected the fenators out of their feats at London. Yet you have retained the fenate, you have preferved the common dignity, and not hurt the majefty of the office or degree in the perfons. That private authority, which was ready to fall, hath been taken away: that common authority, which fhould laft a year only, hath been removed. Increafe, O Cromwell, in judgment; increafe in prudence: increafe in faithfulnefs; increafe in integrity! Brave before the commonwealth was freed; renowned before it was conftituted; but glorious now it is changed." Vide the fecond panegyric, affirmed to be written by a certain Jefuit, the Portuguefe ambaffador's chaplain, but compofed as the editor (Mr. Peck) thinks, by Milton. I fhall give a new tranflation of the greateft part of this piece in the appendix, having here tranfcribed from that of the editor.

Life of Oliver Cromwell. 143

emulation of her great men were a continual source of contention: and the protectorship of Cromwell, tho' not conferr'd in the most legal manner, was more glorious to England, than the reigns of her two preceding monarchs, or any the confused usurpation of her new-fangled commonwealth. If either the Roman or the Briton had played the tyrant, it had been but as one in the room of many: but history has freed Cæsar from all imputations of this kind, except in such cases where his own security, and the temper of the times, obliged him to it: and that Cromwell's severity never went farther than this, is what even his enemies, amidst their invectives, are obliged to allow.

§. 2. Cromwell had three assemblies during his whole administration, that met under the name of parliaments. Considering all circumstances, it could hardly be expected, that the first of these, before he knew the temper of the nation, should be left to the choice of those very electors, whose representatives he had forcibly dissolved. But it was soon manifest, that this dissolution was very grateful and acceptable to the majority of the people: for when he and his council of officers published a declaration *, setting forth

---

* This declaration was to the following effect: "That after God was pleased marvelously to appear for his people, in reducing Ireland and Scotland to so great a degree of peace, and England to perfect quiet; whereby the parliament had opportunity to give the people the harvest of all their labour, blood and treasure, and to settle a due liberty in reference to civil and spiritual things; whereunto they were obliged by their duty, engagements, and those great and wonderful things God had wrought for them: they notwithstanding made so little progress therein, that it was matter of much grief to the good people of the land; who thereupon applied themselves to the army, expecting redress by their means; who (tho' unwilling

forth the reasons of this arbitrary proceeding, it was answered by addresses and congratulations from the fleet,

unwilling to meddle with the civil authority) agreed that such officers, as were members of parliament, should move them to proceed vigorously in reforming what was amiss in the commonwealth, and in settling it upon a foundation of justice and righteousness; which being done, it was hoped the parliament would have answered their expectations. But finding the contrary, they renewed their desires by an humble petition in Aug. 1652. Which produced no considerable effect, nor was any such progress made therein, as might imply their real intentions to accomplish what was petitioned for, but rather an averseness to the things themselves, with much bitterness and opposition to the people of God, and his spirit acting in them; insomuch that the godly party in parliament were rendered of no farther use than to countenance the end of a corrupt party, for effecting their designs of perpetuating themselves in the supreme government. For obviating these evils, the officers of the army obtained several meetings with some of the parliament, to consider what remedy might be applied to prevent the same: but such endeavours proving ineffectual, it became evident, that this parliament, through the corruption of some, the jealousy of others, and the non-attendance of many, would never answer those ends, which God, his people, and the whole nation expected from them; but that this cause, which God had so greatly bless'd, must needs languish under their hand, and by degrees be lost; and the lives, liberties, and comforts of his people be deliver'd into their enemies hands. All which being sadly and seriously considered by the honest people of the nation, as well as by the army, it seemed a duty incumbent upon us, who had seen so much of the power and presence of God, to consider of some effectual means, whereby to establish righteousness and peace in these nations.

And

fleet, the army, and the corporations, who acknowledged the Juſtice of the action, and promiſed to ſtand by

And after much debate, it was judged neceſſary, that the ſupreme government ſhould be by the parliament devolv'd upon known perſons fearing God, and of approv'd integrity, for a time, as the moſt hopeful way to countenance all God's people, reform the law, and adminiſter juſtice impartially; hoping thereby the people might forget monarchy, and underſtand their true intereſt in the election of ſucceſſive parliaments; that ſo the government might be ſettled upon a right baſis, without hazard to this glorious cauſe, or neceſſitating to keep up armies for the defence of the ſame. And being ſtill reſolved to uſe all means poſſible to avoid extraordinary courſes, we prevailed with about twenty members of parliament to give us a conference; with whom we plainly debated the neceſſity and juſtice of our propoſals; the which found no acceptance, but inſtead thereof it was offered, That the way was to continue ſtill this parliament, as being that from which we might probably expect all good things. This being vehemently inſiſted on, did much confirm us in our apprehenſions, that not any love to a repreſentative, but the making uſe thereof to recruit, and ſo to perpetuate themſelves, was their aim in the act they had then under conſideration. For preventing the conſummating whereof, and all the ſad conſequences, which upon the grounds aforeſaid muſt have enſued, and whereby at one blow the intereſt of all honeſt men, and of this glorious cauſe, had been endangered to be laid in the duſt, and theſe nations embroil'd in new troubles, at a time when our enemies abroad were watching all advantages againſt, and ſome of them actually engag'd in war with us; we have been neceſſitated (tho' with much reluctancy) to put an end to this parliament." Then they promiſed, to put the government into the hands of perſons of approved fidelity and honeſty; and at laſt declar'd,

by the present government. And this very affair gave rise to the practice of addressing, which hath since been so common under all our monarchs.

Under this convention, chosen by summons directed to particular persons *, it appeared that so far was Cromwell

clar'd, " That all magistrates and officers whatsoever shall proceed in their respective places and offices, and obedience shall be paid to them as fully, as when the parliament was sitting."

This declaration was subscribed by the lord- general, and his council of officers, Whitehall, April 22d, 1653. Which council of officers, and some others, were soon after formed into a council of state, which was composed of the thirty persons following; Cromwell, Fleetwood, Lambert, Lisle, Harrison, Desborough, Pickering, Wollesley, Ashley Cooper, Hope, Hewson, Norton, Montague, Bennet, Stapeley, Sydenham, Tomlinson, Jones, Tichburn, Strickland, Carew, Howard, Broughton, Lawrence, Holister, Courtney, Major, St. Nicholas, Moyer, and Williams.

* The form of this summons was as follows :
" Forasmuch as upon the dissolution of the late parliament, it became necessary that the peace, safety, and good government of this commonwealth should be provided for; and in order thereunto, divers persons fearing God, and of approved fidelity and honesty, are by myself, with the advice of my council of officers, nominated, to whom the great charge and trust of so weighty affairs is to be committed; and having good assurance of your love to, and courage for God, and the interest of this cause, and of the good people of this commonwealth; I OLIVER CROMWELL, captain-general and commander in chief of all the armies and forces raised and to be raised within this commonwealth, do hereby summon and require you, being one of the persons nominated, personally to appear at the council-chamber at Whitehall within

Cromwell from defigning to take away the freedom of parliaments, that in the inftrument of government then paffed, which conftituted him lord-protector, provifion was made for carrying on the elections in a more equitable manner, and with lefs poffibility of corruption and minifterial influence, than ever had been known under the beft monarchs; and this by confining the choice to the counties, cities, and great boroughs, according to their number of people, and their real intereft in the lands, wealth, and trade of the kingdom. He alfo united the three kingdoms in one common intereft, by allowing Scotland and Ireland to fend reprefentatives to the parliament at Weftminfter. All this will appear in the inftrument itfelf, which was paffed on the 12th of December, 1653, and confifted of forty-two articles, the fubftance of which here follows.

" That the fupreme legiflative authority be and refide in a fingle perfon, and the people in parliament; the ftyle of which perfon to be lord-protector of the commonwealth of England, Scotland, and Ireland. The executive power to be in the protector, with the advice of his council; the number whereof not to exceed twenty-one, nor be lefs than thirteen. All proceedings to run in the name and ftile of the lord-protector; and all honours, offices, and titles to be derived from him; and that he may pardon all offences but treafon and murder. The militia, in time of parliament, to be in his and their hands; but in the intervals only in his and his council's. He and his

within the city of Weftminfter, upon the fourth day of July, next enfuing the date hereof, then and there to take upon you the faid truft, unto which you are hereby called, and appointed to ferve as a member of the county of———And hereof you are not to fail. Given under my hand this eighth day of June, 1653.

O. CROMWELL."

his council to make war and peace with foreign princes. Not to make new laws, or abrogate old ones, without confent of parliament. A parliament to be fummoned to meet at Weftminſter, upon the third day of September, 1654, and afterwards every third year, and, if need be, oftner, which the protector ſhall not diſſolve without confent in parliament, till after five months. The parliament to confiſt of four hundred Engliſh, to be chofen according to the propofitions and numbers hereafter expreſſed, that is to ſay, For the county of Bedford, fix ; viz. for the town of Bedford, one ; for the county of Bedford, five. For the county of Berks, feven ; viz. for the borough of Abington, one ; for the borough of Reading, one ; for the county of Berks, five, &c. The members for Cornwall were in this inſtrument reduced to twelve ; thoſe for Eſſex were enlarged to fixteen ; and the city of London was to chuſe fix *. The members for Scotland were to be thirty, and the fame number for Ireland. The fummoning the parliament to pafs under the feal of the commonwealth to the ſheriffs ; and if the protector omit or deny that, then the commiſſioner of the feal to be held under pain of treafon to iſſue out fuch writs ; and in cafe of failure in him, the high-ſheriffs. Such as are elected, to be returned into the chancery by the chief magiſtrates (ſheriffs, mayors, or bailiffs) within twenty days after the election. If either the ſheriff, mayor, or bailiff make a falfe return, or any ways procure an undue election, let him be fined two thouſand pounds. Thoſe who have borne arms againſt the parliament to be uncapable of being elected, or giving their vote for any members to ſerve in the next parliament or in the three preceding triennial parliaments ; and the Iriſh rebels and papiſts to be for ever uncapable. None to be elected under the age of twenty-one years,

nor

* See this liſt at large in the appendix, No. IV. every one that reads it will be apt to wiſh that this part of the inſtrument of government had been kept in force.

nor unlefs he be a man of good converfation. None to have votes in elections, but such as are worth 200 l. Sixty to make a quorum. Bills prefented to the protector, if not affented to by him within twenty days, to pafs into laws notwithftanding; provided they contain nothing contrary to this inftrument. A competent revenue to be fettled for the maintenance of 10,000 horfe and dragoons, and 20,000 foot, in England, Scotland, and Ireland, and for a convenient number of fhips to guard the feas; and upon abating any of the forces by land or fea, the monies to be brought to the exchequer to ferve fudden occafions. The raifing of money for defraying the charge of the prefent extraordinary forces both at land and fea, to be by confent in parliament, and not otherwife; fave only that the protector, with the advice of his council, fhall have power, until the meeting of the firft parliament, to raife money for the purpofes aforefaid, and alfo to make laws and ordinances for the peace and welfare of thefe nations; which fhall be in force, till the parliament fhall take order concerning the fame. All forfeited lands unfold to belong to the protector. The protectorate to be elective, but the royal family to be excluded; and no protector after the prefent to be general of the army. Oliver Cromwell to be the prefent protector. All the great officers of the commonwealth, fuch as chancellor, keeper of the feal, treafurer, admiral, governors of Ireland, Scotland, &c. if they become void in time of parliament, to be fupplied with their approbation, and in intervals of parliament with the approbation of the council. The chriftian religion, as contained in the holy fcriptures, to be the publick profeffion of thefe nations; and thofe that adminifter it, to be maintained by the publick, but by fome way more convenient and lefs liable to envy than tithes. None to be compelled to confent to the publick profeffion by fine, or any punifhment whatever, but only by perfuafion and arguments. None that profefs faith in Chrift, however otherwife they differ, to be reſtrained from, but to be protected in the exerciſe of their religion, ſo they do not quarrel with and diſturb others: this liberty, however, not to extend to popery or prelacy. All ſales of parliament to ſtand good. Articles of peace to be kept. The protectors ſucceſſively, upon entering on their charge, to ſwear to procure by all means the peace, quiet, and welfare of the commonwealth; to obſerve theſe articles, and to adminiſter all things (to their power) according to the laws, ſtatutes, and cuſtoms."

§. 3. The protector having been inſtall'd and ſworn *, in a very pompous and ſolemn manner, proceeded

* This was the form of his oath. " Whereas the major part of the laſt parliament (judging that their ſitting any longer, as then conſtituted, would not be for the good of the commonwealth) did diſſolve the ſame, and by a writing under their hands, dated the 12th day of this inſtant December, reſigned unto me their powers and authorities; and whereas it was neceſſary thereupon, that ſome ſpeedy courſe ſhould be taken for the ſettlement of theſe nations upon ſuch a baſis and foundation, as, by the bleſſing of God, might be laſting, ſecure property, and anſwer thoſe ends of religion and liberty, ſo long contended for; and upon full and mature conſideration had of the form of government hereunto annexed, being ſatisfied that the ſame, through divine aſſiſtance, may anſwer the end aforementioned; and having alſo been deſired and adviſed, as well by ſeveral perſons of intereſt and fidelity in the commonwealth, as the officers of the army, to take upon me the protection and government of theſe nations, in the manner expreſſed in the ſaid form of government; I have accepted thereof, and do hereby declare my acceptance accordingly: and do promiſe in the preſence of God, that I will not violate or infringe the matters and things contained therein; but to my power obſerve
the

proceeded to the exercife of his authority; which he ufed at home with great moderation and equity, but fo effectually afferted at all foreign courts, that he foon made the greateft figure in Europe, and received marks of refpect from all the fovereigns in Chriftendom, who trembled at his power, and courted his friendfhip, at the fame time that they hated his perfon.

At the time appointed he fummoned his fecond parliament, according to the tenor of the recited inftrument: and the 3d of September being his fortunate day, though it happened to be Sunday, he refolved to open the feffion. This he did with all the folemnity of our kings, in the Painted-chamber at Whitehall. And the next day riding in ftate to Weftminfter, he there heard a fermon: after which, in a long and artful fpeech to the parliament, he took a view of the ftate of the nation, and the advantages that had been procured under the prefent government. Some of the paragraphs are as follows.

He told them " the danger of the levelling principles, and of the fifth-monarchy opinions, that the two pretenfions, liberty of the fubject, and liberty of confcience, were brought in to patronize thofe evils. Nay the fame, and caufe them to be obferved; and fhall in all other things, to the beft of my underftanding, govern thefe nations according to the laws, ftatutes, and cuftoms, feeking their peace, and caufing juftice and law to be equally adminiftered."

After taking this oath, he fat down in the chair cover'd; and the commiffioners delivered up the great feal to him, and the lord-mayor his fword and cap of maintenance; which the protector immediately returned to them again. The ceremony being over, the foldiers with a fhout cried out, " God blefs the lord-protector of the commonwealth of England, Scotland, and Ireland." And fo they went back to Whitehall, the lord-mayor covered, carrying the fword before his highnefs.

Nay these abominations swelled to that height, that the ax was laid to the root of the ministry; and as the extremity was great before, so that no man, tho' well approved, might preach, if not ordained; so now, on the other hand, they will have ordination a nullity upon the calling.

I conceive in my soul, said he, that many of the fifth-monarchy opinion have good meanings; and I hope this parliament will pluck some out of the fire, and save others with fear: the danger of that spirit being not in the notion, but in its proceeding to a civil transgression.

Whilst these things were in the midst of us, and the nation rent and torn from one end to the other; family against family, parent against child, and nothing in the hearts and minds of men, but overturn, overturn; that common enemy in the mean time sleeps not; swarms of jesuits come over, and have their consistories abroad, to rule all the affairs of England, and the dependencies thereof: in the mean time visible endeavours were used to hinder the work in Ireland, to obstruct the work in Scotland; correspondencies and intelligencies were held to encourage the war in those places.

And withal, we were deeply engaged in a war with Portugal, whereby our trade ceased; and not only so, but a war with Holland, which consumed our treasure, as much as the assessment came to. At the same time we fell into a war with France, or rather we were in it: and all this fomented by the divisions amongst us; which begat a confidence, that we could not hold out long; and the calculation had not been ill, if the Lord had not been gracious to us. Besides, strangers increased in the manufacture, the great staple commodity of this nation.

In such a heap of confusion was this poor nation; and that it might not sink into a confusion from the premises, a remedy must be applied: a remedy hath been applied, This government. A thing that is seen and read of all, and which (let men say what they will,

will, I can fpeak with comfort before a greater than you all, as to my intention ; and let men judge out of the thing itfelf) for the interest of the people alone, and for their good, without refpect had to any other intereft.

I may, with humblenefs towards God, and modefty before you, fay fomething in the behalf of it.

It hath endeavoured to reform the laws, and for that end hath join'd perfons (without reflection upon any) of as great integrity and ability as any other, to confider how the laws might be made plain, fhort, and eafy ; which may in due time be tendered.

It hath taken care to put into feats of juftice, men of the moft known integrity and ability.

The chancery hath been reformed, and I hope to the juft fatisfaction of all good men.

It hath put a ftop to that heady way, for every man that will to make himfelf a preacher, having endeavoured to fettle a way for approbation of men of piety and fitnefs for the work, and the bufinefs committed to perfons both of the prefbyterian and independant judgment ; men of as known ability and integrity, as any the nation hath.

It hath taken care to expunge men unfit for that work, who have been the common fcorn and reproach to that adminiftration.

One thing more : it hath been inftrumental to call a free parliament ; bleffed be God, we fee here this day a free parliament ; and that it may continue fo, I hope, is in the heart of every good man of England : for my own part, as I defir'd it above my life, fo to keep it free, I fhall value it above my life.

A peace is made with Sweden, wherein an honourable perfon [meaning Whitelock] was inftrumental ; it being of much importance to have a good underftanding with our proteftant neighbours.

A peace is alfo made with the Danes, and a peace there that is honourable, and to the fatisfaction of the merchants.

The Sound is open to us, from whence, as from a fountain, our naval provisions are supplied.

A peace is made with the Dutch, which is so well known in the consequences of it, and the great advantages of a good understanding with protestant states.

I beg that it may be in your hearts to be zealous of the protestant interest abroad, which if ever it be like to come under a condition of suffering, it is now; many being banished, and driven to seek refuge among strangers.

A peace is made with Portugal (though it hung long) of great concernment to trade; and the people that trade thither, have freedom to enjoy their consciences, without being subjected to the bloody inquisition.

A treaty with France likewise is now depending.

It may be necessary, in the next place, for you to to hear a little of the sea affairs, and to take notice of the great expence of the forces and fleet; and yet 30,000 l. is now abated of the next three months assessment.

These things which I have before-mentioned, are but entrances and doors of hope: you are brought to the edge of Canaan: but if the blessing and presence of God go along with you in the management of your affairs, I make no question but he will enable you to lay the top-stone of this work.

But this is a maxim not to be despised: Though peace be made, yet it is interest that keeps peace, and farther than that, peace is not to be trusted.

The great end of calling this parliament, is, that the work of God may go on, that the ship of this commonwealth may be brought into a safe harbour.

I shall put you in mind, that you have a great work upon you; Ireland to look to, that the beginning of that government may be settled in honour.

That you have before you, the consideration of those foreign states, with whom peace is not made; who, if they see we manage not our affairs with prudence, as becomes men, will retain hopes that we

may

may still, under the disadvantages thereof, break into confusion.

I shall conclude with my persuasion to you, to have a sweet, gracious, and holy understanding one of another; and put you in mind of the counsel you heard this day in order thereunto.

And I desire you to believe, that I speak not to you as one that would be lord over you, but as one that is resolved to be a fellow-servant with you to the interest of this great affair."

§. 4. But this parliament, having chosen Lenthal for their speaker, fell immediately upon the only point which the protector would have kept sacred. They took the instrument of government into consideration, and their first debate was upon this question, "Whether the supreme legislative power of the nation should be in a single person, and a parliament." These debates continued for seven or eight days, till he silenced them by a speech, and a recognition oath imposed on all the members that entered the house. Being restrained therefore from disputing the protector's title, they fell upon the other articles of the instrument. They declared, "That Oliver Cromwell should be protector during life; and limited the number of forces to be kept up in England, Scotland, and Ireland, with provision for the payment of them. They agreed upon the number of ships, that they thought necessary for the guard of the seas; and ordered 200,000 l. a year for the protector's own expence, the salaries of his council, the judges, foreign intelligence, and the reception of ambassadors; and that Whitehall, St. James's, the Mews, Somerset-house, Greenwich, Hampton-court, Windsor, and the manor of York, be kept unsold for the protector's use. They also voted a clause to be inserted, to declare the rights of the people of England, and particularly, that no money should be raised upon the nation but by authority of parliament. And whereas by the instrument of government it was provided, that if the parliament were not fitting at the death of the present protector, the council should chuse a successor; they resolved, that nothing should be determined by the council after his death, but the calling of a parliament, who were then to consider what they would have done. They also approved and confirmed the present lord-deputy of Ireland, the present lords commissioners of the great seal of England, the commissioners of the treasury, and the two chief justices. Among other things, they debated the point of liberty of conscience upon the new government, and agreed to allow it all, who shall not maintain atheism, popery, prelacy, prophaneness, or any damnable heresies, to be enumerated by the parliament."

Many things were said during these debates, which gave great offence to Cromwell and his council. In a word, this parliament was dissolved after a session of five months, by a very tedious and intricate speech *, wherein the protector upbraided them with their late proceedings. And who could wonder at it? Was there ever a man in possession of the supreme authority, who would suffer that authority to be publickly questioned? While they had a liberty of doing all they would for the honour of the nation, could they expect the privilege too of insulting that magistrate, in whose name they were summoned together?

The protector's third parliament, which met on the 17th of September, 1656, was found more complying than either of the former. Some of the members however were excluded, for want of being approved by his highness's council, which occasioned them to petition and remonstrate very strongly against the proceedings of the court. But those who kept their seats, having chosen Sir Thomas Widdrington for their speaker, not only approved of the protector's conduct in the war he had undertaken against Spain, but

---

* This speech was full as long as one of the sermons of those times, and pretty much in the same strain.

Life of Oliver Cromwell.

but paſſed ſeveral acts for ſecuring his perſon and title, for carrying on the preſent war, and for the encouragement of trade; all which received the aſſent of his highneſs, who in a ſhort ſpeech returned them thanks for their care in ſupporting his government.

§. 5. This parliament had not ſat above ſix months, before they drew up a new inſtrument, in order to compliment the protector with the title of king. It met with much oppoſition from the republicans, and the ſoldiers party: but at laſt was carried, and the word King ordered to be inſerted in a blank that was left for that purpoſe; and two other blanks that were left for the parliament, were to be filled up with the words Houſe of commons, and Other houſe. This inſtrument, called "the humble petition and advice of the parliament to his highneſs, was preſented to him by the ſpeaker, who recommended the contents of it in a ſpeech. But the protector, how inclinable ſoever he was to accept of this offer, finding it againſt the humour of the army, and eſpecially that his ſon-in-law Fleetwood and his brother-in-law Deſborough were peculiarly averſe to it, inſtead of giving a ready aſſent, which was expected, deſired "that a committee might be appointed to confer with him, and to offer him better knowledge and ſatisfaction in this great cauſe."

Cromwell, as well as Cæſar, whom he reſembled on many accounts, was not ſo fond of a title which he ſaw would create diſcontent, as to aſſume it at all adventures. Fond enough indeed he would have been of it, if theſe obſtacles had not interfered *: but when
he

---

* Ludlow informs us, that he endeavoured by all poſſible means to perſuade the officers of the army to approve the deſign; for which purpoſe he one time invited himſelf to dine with colonel Deſborough,
and

he found that his beft friends in the army were immoveable, all the arguments of the commons committee, of

and carried lieutenant-general Fleetwood with him. He began to droll with them about monarchy, and fpeaking flightly of it, faid, " It was but a feather in a man's cap, and therefore he wonder'd that men would not pleafe the children, and let them enjoy their rattle." But they being very ferious upon the matter, affured him, " That there was more in it than he perceiv'd: that thofe who put him upon it were no enemies to Charles Stuart; and if he accepted of it, he would draw inevitable ruin on himfelf and friends." Having thus founded them, that he might conclude as he began, he told them, " They were a couple of fcrupulous fellows;" and fo went away. At another time entering more ferioufly into debate with thefe two, he faid, " It was a tempting of God to expofe fo many worthy men to death and poverty, when there was a certain way to fecure them." But they infifting upon the oaths they had taken, he reply'd, that thefe oaths were againft the power and tyranny of kings, but not againft the four letters that made the word KING."

The next day his highnefs fent a meffage to the houfe, requiring their attendance to-morrow morning in the Painted-chamber; intending, as all men thought, there to declare his acceptance of the crown: but in the mean time meeting with his brother Defborough, as he was walking in the park, and acquainting him with his refolution, he received this anfwer from him, " That then he gave the caufe, and his family alfo for loft; and though he refolved never to act againft him, yet he would not act for him after that time." And fo, after fome farther difcourfe, Defborough went home, and there found colonel Pride, whom the protector had knighted; and imparting to him his highnefs's intention to accept the title of king, Pride immediately anfwered, " He fhall not."

of which Whitelock was chairman, tho' they were inculcated for two days together, could not prevail with

not." Desborough asked him, " How he would hinder it ?" Whereupon Pride said, " Get me a petition drawn, and I will prevent it." And so they both went to Dr. Owen, and prevailed on him to draw a petition according to their mind.

The next morning, the house being met, some officers of the army coming to the parliament doors, sent in a message to colonel Desborough, to let him know that they had a petition, and desired him to present it to the house. But he knowing the contents of it, and thinking it not proper for him to take publick notice of it before it was presented, inform'd the house, that certain officers of the army had a petition to present to them; and mov'd that they should be call'd in, and have leave to present it with their own hands; which the house generally agreed to, not thinking the army would oppose their designs. And so the petition being delivered by lieutenant-colonel Mason, was read in the house, and was to this effect; " That they had hazarded their lives against monarchy, and were still ready so to do, in defence of the liberties of the nation: that having observ'd in some men great endeavours to bring the nation again under their old servitude, by pressing their general to take upon him the title and government of king, in order to destroy him, and weaken the hands of those who were faithful to the publick; they therefore humbly desir'd that they would discountenance all such persons and endeavours, and continue stedfast in the old cause, for the preservation of which they for their parts were most ready to lay down their lives." This petition was subscribed by two colonels, seven lieutenant-colonels, and sixteen captains, who, with such officers in the house as were of the same opinion, made up the majority of those relating to that part of the army which was then quartered about the town.

Ludlow

with him to run the rifk of lofing the affections of the foldiers. After long deliberation therefore, and fome clofe conferences with his brother and fon-in-law beforementioned, who ftood firmly to their opinion, he ordered the parliament to attend him in the Painted-chamber, and there in an obfcure fpeech, containing much about confcience, and the pains he had taken to fatisfy himfelf, declared, " that he could not undertake the government with the title of king." Tho' at the fame time he intimated, that he thought the fettlement imperfect without it: and every one might difcover, that the motive of his refufal was rather policy than confcience *.

While Ludlow here obferves, that it was difficult to determine whether the parliament or the protector was moft furpriz'd at this unexpected addrefs. As foon as his highnefs heard of it, he fent for his fon-in-law Fleetwood, and told him, " That he wonder'd he would fuffer fuch a petition to proceed fo far, which he might have hindered, fince he knew it to be his refolution not to accept the crown without the confent of the army; and therefore he defired him to haften to the houfe, and to put them off from doing any thing farther therein." Accordingly the lieutenant-general went immediately thither, and told them, " That the petition ought not to be debated, much lefs to be anfwered, at this time, the contents of it being to defire them not to prefs his highnefs to be king; whereas the prefent bufinefs was to receive his anfwer to what had been formerly offered to him: and thereupon he defired that the debate of it might be put off, till they had received his anfwer." The houfe having agreed to this, and received a meffage from the protector, they met him, and received his refufal of the royal title. Memoirs, p. 586, &c.

* See in the appendix, No. VI. a large account of the arguments offered by the committee of parliament to perfuade him to accept of the title of

While this business was in agitation, the lord Broghill coming one day to Cromwell, and telling him he had been in the city, the protector enquired of him, " what news he had heard there?" Broghill told him, " he had heard he was in treaty with the king, who was to be restored, and to marry his daughter." Cromwell shewing no displeasure at this, his lordship continued, " In the state to which things are reduced, I can see no better expedient: you may bring him in upon what terms you please; and your highness may retain the same authority you now have, with less trouble." To this Cromwell answered, " The king can never forgive his father's blood." Broghill replied, " You are one of the many that were concerned in that, but will be alone in the merit of restoring." Upon which the protector said, " He is so damnably debauch'd, he will undo us all;" and so went off to other discourse, without any emotion; which made his lordship conclude, that he had often thought of the expedient. This story is told by bishop Burnet, who had it from lord Broghill when earl of Orrery *.   §. 6.

of king, and the protector's own reasons for refusing it.

* Mr. Echard tells us of a private application made by king Charles himself to Cromwell, which he says came from the mouth of the dutchess of Lauderdale, who told the same to a person, of whose credit he could make no question. That lady, afterward dutchess of Lauderdale, being a particular friend and acquaintance of Cromwell's, was employed it seems to make a private offer and proposal to him, in substance as follows: " That if he would restore, or permit the king to return to his throne, he would send him a blank paper, for him to write his own terms and limitations, and settle what power and riches he pleased upon himself, family, and friends." This proposal was first communicated to the protector's lady, who liked it very well; believing that, besides other advantages, it would bring absolute indemnity and security to her husband, and
                                                                the

§. 6. Cromwell having refused the title of king, the parliament soon voted, "That he should enjoy the title and authority he had already;" which was in many particulars enlarged beyond what it was by the former instrument, by the new one, called "the humble petition and advice." This instrument consisted of eighteen articles; but I shall only give the substance of the principal ones, as follows. "That his highness, under the title of lord protector, would be pleased to exercise the office of chief magistrate over England, Scotland, and Ireland, and to govern according to all things in this petition and advice: also, that in his life-time he would appoint the person that should succeed in the government after his death. That he would call parliaments consisting of two houses, once in three years at farthest. That those persons who were legally chosen by a free election of the people to serve in parliament, might not be excluded from doing their duties, but by consent of that house whereof they were members. That none but those under the qualifications therein mentioned, should be capable to serve as members in parliament. That the power of the other house be limited as therein prescribed. That the laws and statutes of the land be observed and kept; and no laws altered, suspended, abrogated, or repealed, or new laws made, but by act of parliament. That the yearly sum of a million of pounds sterling be for the maintenance of the navy and army; and 300,000 l. for the support of the government,

the whole family. She therefore took an opportunity, when she was in bed with him, to mention the offer to him, and endeavour'd to persuade him to accept of it, as being of the highest moment to the happiness of himself and relations. But he without minding her arguments and persuasions, presently told her, "She was a fool;" adding this shrewd sentence; "If Charles Stuart can forgive me all that I have done against him and his family, he does not deserve to wear the crown of England."

vernment, besides other temporary supplies, as the commons in parliament should see necessary. That the number of the protector's council should not be above one and twenty; whereof the quorum to be seven, and not under. The chief officers of state, as chancellor, keeper of the great seal, &c. to be approved by parliament. That his highness would encourage a godly ministry in these nations; and that such as do revile or disturb them in the worship of God, may be punished according to law; and where the laws are defective, new ones to be made in that behalf. That the protestant christian religion, as it is contain'd in the old and new testament, be asserted and held forth for the publick profession of these nations, and no other; and that a confession of faith be agreed upon and recommended to the people of these nations; and none be permitted, by words or writings, to revile or reproach the said confession of faith."

This instrument being digested and agreed upon, the house sent to the protector for an audience; which he appointed to be on the 25th of May, in the Banqueting-house. The members waiting upon him accordingly, their speaker Widdrington presented and read the said instrument to him, and desired his assent; which, after a long pause, he with all the gestures of concern and perplexity granted. And thus did his highness accomplish a chief part of what he designed; which was to have his power and authority confirmed by parliament.

§. 7. It was thought proper, after this transaction, that the protector should have a solemn investiture. Notice of this was given to all foreign ambassadors and ministers, and Westminster-hall was prepared and adorned as sumptuously as it could be for a coronation. In short, the ceremony was perform'd on the 26th of June, 1657, with the utmost grandeur and magnificence, amidst the loud acclamations of the people; and there was a fine medal struck on the occasion, which had on one side the protector's bust with his title round it, and on the other an olive-tree flourishing in a field, with the words "non deficient olivæ," by way of allusion to his name.

Things went on amicably between the protector and his parliament, many bills were passed and signed, and the greatest harmony seemed established. But about the beginning of the year 1658, his highness, according to the tenor of the late petition and advice, sent his writs of summons to divers persons, to sit as members of the other, or upper house. The forms of these writs, which were about sixty, was the same used by our monarchs, for the summoning of peers to parliament; and indeed many of the persons summoned were actually peers, and others were made so in the succeeding reign *. These being met in the

house

---

* Their names were, the lord Richard Cromwell, the protector's eldest son; lord Henry Cromwell, his other son, lord deputy of Ireland; Nathaniel Fiennes, and John Lisle, lords commissioners of the great seal; Henry Lawrence, lord president of the council; Charles Fleetwood, lieutenant-general of the army; Bulstrode Whitelock, and William Sydenham, commissioners of the treasury; Robert earl of Warwick, Edmund earl of Mulgrave, Edward earl of Manchester, William viscount Say and Seal, Philip viscount Lisle, Philip lord Wharton, Thomas lord Fauconberg, George lord Eure, John Claypole, esq; Charles Howard, esq; whom the protector made a viscount, John Desborough, and Edward Montague, generals at sea; Sir Charles Wolsley, Sir Gilbert Pickering, Walter Strickland, esq; major-general Skippon, colonel Philip Jones, Sir William Strickland, Francis Rouse, esq; John Fiennes, esq; Sir Francis Russel, Sir Thomas Honeywood, Sir Arthur Haslerigg, Sir John Hobart, Sir Richard Onslow, Sir Gilbert Gerard, Sir William Roberts, lord chief-justice Glynn, lord chief-justice St. John, William Pierpoint,

house of lords, the protector went thither in royal state, and made a speech from the throne, beginning in the old stile, "My lords, and you the knights, citizens, and burgesses of the house of commons."

This step, however, occasioned a division in the lower house, which ended in the dissolution of this his third and last parliament. For several of these new lords being taken from among the commons, his interest was weakened in that house, to which many of the secluded members were also now admitted. Hereupon they fell to examining the authority and jurisdiction of the other house. And his highness finding them obstinate on these points, after having advised them to unity without effect, sent for them by the black rod into the lord's house, where he declared " several urgent and weighty reasons, which made it necessary for him to dissolve this parliament; and accordingly he did dissolve them.

These peremptory summons's and sudden dissolutions, it must be owned, were not agreeable to the English constitution, as it is now settled, and seem to have the appearance of absolute despotism: but many steps that were taken in preceding reigns, by monarchs whose right was in all the forms acknowledged, and who therefore had no excuse for such violent proceedings as Cromwell's situation might some-

point, esq; John Crew, esq; Alexander Popham, esq; Sir Christopher Pack, Sir Robert Tichburn, Edward Whalley, esq; Sir John Barkstead, lieutenant of the tower; Sir George Fleetwood, Sir Thomas Pride, Sir John Hewson, Richard Ingoldsby, esq; James Berry, esq; William Goffe, esq; Thomas Cooper, esq; Edmund Thomas, esq; George Monk, general in Scotland; David earl of Cassils, Sir William Lockhart, Sir Archibald Johnston; William Steel, lord chancellor of Ireland; Roger lord Broghill, Sir Matthew Tomlinson, William Lenthal and Richard Hambden, esqrs. Some of these were knights of the protector's own making.

sometimes require, may serve greatly to alleviate, if not wholly to remove the weight of this accusation; especially if we reflect, that by all the appearances under his administration, it seems evident that Cromwell would never have taken one step contrary to the liberties of parliament, provided they had only been quiet on the article of his authority, which it was not reasonable to think he would suffer to be debated, after he was once in possession.

§. 8. When Cromwell first assumed the government, there were three great parties in the nation all against him, the episcopal party, the presbyterians, and the republicans. It required the greatest skill and dexterity to manage these very opposite factions, and to prevent the ill effects of the plots and conspiracies they were so ready to run into. All this however he was able to accomplish, by the superior force of his genius; and bishop Burnet, who was no friend to the protector's memory, informs us in what manner he proceeded. He had, according to that prelate, only the army to rely upon; and that enthusiastick spirit he had taken so much pains to raise among them, rendered them very intractable: So that he was forced to break and imprison many of his officers; and he flattered the rest as well as he could, going on in his old way of long and dark discourses.

He was apprehensive of assassination, and other plottings, from the cavalier party: as to the former of which, he took a method that proved of great use to him. He would many times openly declare, "'that in a war it was necessary to return upon any side, all the violent things that any of the one side did to the other; and this for the preventing greater mischief, and for bringing men to fair war: and that assassinations were such detestable things, that he would never begin them; but if any of the king's party should endeavour to assassinate him, and fail in it, he would make an assassinating war of it, and destroy

destroy the whole family." And he pretended he had inftruments to do this, whenever he fhould order it. This ftruck fuch a terror, that it proved a better fecurity to him than his guards. And whenever they were plotting againft him, he had his agents and fpies amongft them, to give him notice of their preparations and proceedings; by which means all their fchemes were broken, and their defigns fruftrated, before they could bring them to perfection.

The prefbyterians fo dreaded the fury of the commonwealth party, that they looked upon Cromwell's turning them out to be a happy deliverance for them: and to foften thefe the more, he affured that he would maintain a publick miniftry, with all due encouragement, which the republicans were moftly againft; and he joined them in a commiffion with fome independants to be tryers of all public preachers, who fhould, for the future, be admitted to any benefice. The perfons fo commiffioned did likewife difpofe of all the livings that were in the gift of the crown, of the bifhops, and of the cathedral churches. Neverthelefs, when he perceived that the prefbyterians began to take too much upon them, to be uneafy under the government, or meddle in civil affairs, he found means to mortify them, and let loofe againft them thofe of the other fects, who took pleafure in difputing with their preachers, and interrupting their religious worfhip: and 'tis faid, he was by many heard to glory, " that he had curb'd that infolent fect, that would fuffer none but itfelf." So that they were forced to thank him for permitting them the exercife of their religious worfhip in their own congregations.

The republican party were his greateft enemies, and moft bent on his ruin; looking on him as the perfon who had perfidioufly broken all their meafures, and betrayed their glorious caufe. This party therefore he ftudied by all means to divide among themfelves, and to fet the fifth-monarchy men, and other enthufiafts, againft thofe who proceeded only upon the

principles

principles of civil liberty; such as Algernoon Sidney, Henry Nevill, Martin, Ludlow, Wildman, and Harrington.

As to Vane and his party, who were likewise independants, they indeed, from the time they were turned out of the long parliament, retired quietly into the country, where they endeavoured to prejudice their neighbours against the present government, and yet managed themselves with so much caution, as not to disturb the quiet of the nation, nor give the protector any great advantage against them.

The levellers, many of whom had been the most active agitators in the army, were the most furious and desperate of all the commonwealth party. These, from the time the general assumed the title of protector, which was to them as odious as that of king, professed a mortal hatred to his person; and he knew very well that these men, as well as the last mentioned, had great credit in the army, and with some of the chief officers; so that he more fully dreaded them than all the king's party, and subtily coloured many of the preparations he made against them, as if they had been designed against the other.

The fifth-monarchy men seemed to be in daily expectation of the coming of king Jesus, and the protector found it no easy matter to give them satisfaction; since his assuming the government after this manner, looked like a step to kingship, which they represented as the great anti-christ, which hindred Christ's being set on his throne. To these men he would say with many tears, " that he would rather have taken a shepherd's staff than the protectorship; since nothing was more contrary to his genius, than a shew of greatness: but he saw it was necessary at that time to keep the nation from falling into extreme disorder, and from being open to the common enemy; and therefore he only stept in between the living and the dead, in that interval, till God

God should direct them on what bottom they ought to settle; and then he would surrender the heavy load lying upon him, with a joy equal to the sorrow with which he was affected, while under that shew of dignity." He would also carry himself with great familiarity towards these men, and enter into the terms of their old equality, shutting the door, and making them sit down covered by him, that he might see how little he cared for those distances, which for form's sake he was forced to keep up with others; and their discourse commonly ended in a long prayer.

Thus, with much ado, he pretty well managed the enthusiasts of the commonwealth party. As to the other republicans, many of whom were inclined to deism, he called them 'the heathens,' and acknowledged he could not so easily work upon them. He had some chaplains of all sorts, and became at length more gentle to the episcopal party, who had their meetings in several places about London, without being molested by him. In the end, even the Roman catholicks courted him; and he with wonderful art carried things farther with all parties than was thought possible, considering the great difficulties he had to encounter with. For, that he might the better manage the several factions he stood most in awe of, he made choice of the most active and leading men into his council, by whose influence he had the guiding of all the rest of each party.

§. 9. But notwithstanding this refined management, and the great influence he had over the nation in general, there were several plots and conspiracies formed against him during his protectorship. The first design that was discovered, at the head of which were Mr. Fox, Mr. Gerard, and Mr. Vowel, was to murder him in his way to Hampton-court, to seize the guards, the Tower, and the magazines, and then to proclaim the king. For this Gerard was beheaded on Tower-hill, and Vowel hanged

hanged at Charing-crofs: but Fox, by making an open confeffion, obtained his pardon.

In the fame year, 1654, a defign was formed for a general rifing of the royalifts, in divers parts of the kingdom. But the private intelligence which the protector received of it, on which feveral perfons were apprehended, and many arms feized, prevented the fury of the intended blow. Something however was attempted in the north, but to no effect; the revolters difperfing before any forces arrived againft them, and leaving all their arms. The moft obftinate ftruggle was in the weft, at the time of Salifbury affizes, where the confpirators feized the two judges, and took away their commiffions: but this too was quickly over, without the help of the army. Colonel Penruddock, captain Grove, and a few others, were executed for it at Exeter; and fome of the common people concerned were tranfported to the Weft-Indies. This plot, which was defigned to ruin the protector, ferved but to advance his credit, and confirm his authority. It cleared him of the reproach of inventing plots himfelf, as a pretence to keep up the army; and gave him a good colour of excufe for the order which foon followed, by advice of his council, " that all who had borne arms for the king, and declared themfelves of his party, fhould be decimated, or pay a tenth part of their eftates, to fupport the charge of fuch extraordinary forces, as their feditious practices obliged him to keep up." This was accompany'd with a declaration, " that the charge fhould be laid upon thofe who had occafioned it, and not upon the party who had already been fo much fufferers.

The laft ftruggle of the royal party was about a year before the protector's death. There was not only to be an infurrection in England, but feveral regiments in Flanders commanded by Englifhmen, who were then affifting the Spaniards againft the French and Cromwell, were to have been fuddenly tranfported over. And to promote the rifing at home, a

very

Life of Oliver Cromwell.

very bold paper was induſtriouſly diſperſed, entitled, "Killing no murder;" the deſign of which was to get the protector aſſaſſinated *. It was written by colonel

* The dedication of it runs thus:

To his highneſs Oliver Cromwell.

"May it pleaſe your highneſs,

How I have ſpent ſome hours of the leiſure your highneſs hath been pleaſed to give me, this following paper wil give your highneſs an account. How you will pleaſe to interpret it I cannot tell; but I can with confidence ſay, my intention in it is to procure your highneſs that juſtice nobody yet does you; and to let the people ſee, the longer they defer it, the greater injury they do both themſelves and you. To your highneſs juſtly belongs the honour of dying for the people: and it cannot chuſe but be an unſpeakable conſolation to you in the laſt moments of your life, to conſider, with how much benefit to the world you are like to leave it. 'Tis then only, my lord, the titles you now uſurp will be truly yours: you will then be indeed the deliverer of your country, and free it from a bondage little inferior to that from which Moſes deliver'd his: you will then be the true reformer, which you would now be thought: religion ſhall be then reſtored; liberty aſſerted; and parliaments have their privileges they have fought for: we ſhall then hope, that other laws will have place beſides thoſe of the ſword; and that juſtice ſhall be otherwiſe defined, than the will and pleaſure of the ſtrongeſt: and we ſhall then hope that men will keep oaths again, and not have the neceſſity of being falſe and perfidious to preſerve themſelves, and be like their rulers.

All this we hope, from your highneſs's happy expiration, who are the true father of your country: for while you live, we can call nothing ours; and

colonel Titus, under the borrowed name of William Allen. But so good was the intelligence which his highness kept up, that he seized several of the conspirators before they could get together, and published a pro-

it is from your death, that we hope for our inheritances.

Let this consideration arm and fortify your highness's mind against the fears of death, and the terrors of your evil conscience, that the good you will do by your death will somewhat ballance the evils of your life. And if, in the black catalogue of high malefactors, few can be found, that have liv'd more to the affliction and disturbance of mankind, than your highness hath done; yet your greatest enemies will not deny, but there are likewise as few, that have expired more to the universal benefit of mankind, than your highness is like to do.

To hasten this great good, is the chief end of my writing this paper: and if it have the effect I hope it will, your highness will quickly be out of the reach of men's malice, and your enemies will only be able to wound you in your memory, which strokes you will not feel.

That your highness may be speedily in this security, is the universal wish of your grateful country! This is the desire and prayer of the good and the bad; and, it may be, is the only thing, wherein all sects and factions do agree in their devotions, and is our only common-prayer. But amongst all that put in their requests and supplications for your highness's speedy deliverance from all earthly troubles, none is more assiduous, or more fervent, than he, that, with the rest of the nation, hath the honour to be.

(May it please your highness)

Your highness's present slave and vassal,

W. A.

proclamation for apprehending of others. This was followed by addresses from the city of London to the army, which greatly intimidated all that had engaged for the king; and so upon the execution of Dr. Hewet, Sir Henry Slingsby, and a few of meaner rank, the whole affair blew over.

This attempt, however, was thought the more formidable, because another conspiracy was at the same time on foot, among the fifth-monarchy men. Major-general Harrison was very deep in this affair, and several consultations had been held about it, at a house in Shoreditch. But their proceedings were all known through the means of secretary Thurloe, and the heads of their party seized on the very night appointed for their rendezvous. These were committed to prison, and there kept for a long time; but none of them were executed till after the restoration, for other crimes.

There had, before this, been two bold attempts by some of the republican party. The first was in 1654, when major John Wildman, who had been expell'd the house of commons by the protector, was seized with a paper dictated by him, entitled, "The declaration of the free and well-affected people of England, now in arms against the tyrant Oliver Cromwell, Esq;" But this man, contrary to the expectation of all his friends, was after a short imprisonment set at liberty. The other was in 1656, when Miles Syndercomb, a leveller that had been cashier'd, combined with two of the protector's life-guards, to assassinate him near Brentford. Syndercomb, being betray'd by the other, stoutly denied the fact, but was condemned by lord-chief-justice Glynn. He died before the day appointed for his execution, and was buried on Tower-hill, where a stake was drove through his body.

We have not many instances in history, if any at all, of a person who rose from among the people to the highest authority, that did not stain his administration with more blood, in a judiciary way, than our protector. Let us only compare his executions with those of the second triumvirate at Rome, when all the noblest patriots of that once flourishing commonwealth, were sacrificed to the suspicions of Mark Anthony, and young Octavius. Yet the latter of these, thro' an excess of good fortune, became the delight of his people, the patron and theme of all the learned and ingenious, and the envy of succeeding princes. What less might have been expected of Cromwell, had he lived to get over the remains of prejudice, to put the glorious schemes he had formed in execution, and to shew himself what he really seems to have been, a true friend of liberty, and a lover of mankind in general?

§. 10. In order to make his government secure, at the time when the royalists were plotting his destruction, Cromwell instituted a new order of deputies, under the name of major-generals, who were in the nature of prefects, or governors of provinces. They were to have the inspection of the inferior magistrates in every county, to commit suspected persons into custody, and to put in execution many other directions: there was no appeal from them, but to the protector himself. This office however continued not long: for being invested with great power, the major-generals carried it in a very high and arbitrary manner; which occasioned their suppression by the parliament, at the motion of Mr. Cleypole, the protector's son-in-law.

It was hardly possible, indeed, for any governor, in such a precarious situation, to shew more regard than Cromwell did for the rights and properties of private men. He supplied the benches at Westminster with the ablest of lawyers, whom he had invited to the publick service. Maynard, Twisden, Nudigate, Windham, and other gentlemen of great integrity and learning, were made by him serjeants at law, and Mr. Matthew Hale, afterwards the famous lord chief justice Sir Matthew, was advanced to be a justice juftice of the common pleas. Mr. John Thurloe, who had been fecretary to the chief juftice St. John, was raifed to the office of fecretary of ftate, of which he acquitted himfelf with indefatigable diligence. Milton, the great Milton, was Latin fecretary; a man that would have done honour to the mightieft monarch, to the moft polite and learned court, in the beft of ages. In a word, the fleet and army were well paid; the city of London had the power of its own militia, under their old major-general Skippon; the common people were eafed of fome of their taxes: nor can we better fum up the character of the civil government at this time, than in the following extract, which is chiefly taken from Echard, a moft virulent enemy of the protector and his friends.

" Cromwell, tho' he proceeded in an arbitrary manner againft thofe who contefted his authority, yet in all other cafes, where the life of his jurifdiction was not concerned, he feemed to have a great reverence for the law, and the conftitution, rarely interpofing between party and party; and to do him juftice, there appeared in his government many things that were truly great and praife-worthy. Juftice, as well diftributive as commutative, was by him reftored almoft to its antient grace and fplendor; the judges executed their office without covetoufnefs, according to law and equity, and the laws, except fome few, where himfelf was immediately concerned, being permitted to have their full force upon all, without impediment or delay. Mens manners, outwardly at leaft, became likewife reformed, either by removing the incentives to luxury, or by means of the antient laws now revived, and put in execution. There was a ftrict difcipline kept in his court, where drunkennefs, whoredom, and extortion, were either banifhed, or feverely rebuked. Trade began again to flourifh and profper, and moft things to put on a happy and promifing afpect. The protector alfo fhewed a great regard to the advancement of learning, and was a great encourager of it. The univerfity of Oxford,

Oxford, in particular, acknowledged his highness's respect to them, in continuing their chancellor, and bestowing on the publick library there four-and-twenty Greek manuscripts, and munificently allowing an hundred pounds a year to a divinity-reader. He also ordered a scheme to be drawn for founding and endowing a college at Durham, for the convenience of the northern students.* Towards all who complied with his pleasure, and courted his protection, he manifested great civility, generosity, and bounty. No man affected to seem more tender of the clergy than himself, tho' he would not list himself in any particular sect; saying, " it was his only wish and desire to see the church in peace, and that all would gather into one sheepfold, under one shepherd, Jesus Christ, and mutually love one another." Tho' the publick use of the common-prayer was denied

* In pursuance of this scheme, (which was drawn in consequence of a petition from the city of Durham, the county of Northumberland, and the town of Newcastle) the protector issued a long writ of privy seal, consisting of twenty-three articles, and dated May 15, 1657. It established a provost, two preachers, four professors, four tutors, four schoolmasters or fellows, twenty-four scholars, 12 exhibitioners, and eighteen freeschool scholars; fixed their endowment; gave them the library of the dean and chapter of Durham; with liberty to purchase lands, sue, or be sued; a common seal and statutes, with two visitors, and the privilege of printing bibles; regulated the power of the master and other officers; excused them from watch and ward, &c. Mr. Peck has preserved this piece entire, as also an address from the provost and fellows of the college of Durham to his highness Richard lord protector, &c. dated in December 1658, and full of the praises of his father.

denied to the episcopal party, yet he allow'd the use of their rites in private houses; and milder courses were taken than under the tyranny of others."

CHAP. VIII.

Protector Cromwell's *behaviour towards foreign princes and states, his zeal for the honour of* England, *the protestant religion, and the liberties of mankind.*

§. 1. WE are now to view the protector upon the very pinacle of fortune, where he behaved with all becoming dignity, as he had done in every other situation. It has been remarked of him, that though his great abilities never appeared till they were called into action, yet they were always found superior to the present occasion: so that whatever character he assumed, he filled it to the utmost, or even surpassed our common ideas of grandeur. Having raised himself to the sovereign dignity, he carried it higher, both in peace and war, than any English monarch had done before him. As the titles of dictator and imperator at Rome, which were first invented to ward off the odium attending that of king, were rendered more illustrious by the great men who bore them, than that of king had ever been; so the word protector, which was used originally only for the guardian of a monarch under age, when it was annex'd to the name of Cromwell, though for the same reason that gave rise to dictator and imperator, it signified something more in all the courts of Europe, than either king, emperor, or any other title then in being. In order to make good this affertion, I fhall confider in a few words fome of thofe acts of fovereignty, which he exercifed towards foreign princes and ftates.

As I have hitherto in this effay, fo far as the fubjects would permit, thrown together facts of the fame or a like nature; that I may not here deviate from this method, I fhall firft take a curfory view of the wars in which he was engaged, thofe in particular againft Holland and Spain; then confider him as improving the arts of peace, fo as to make himfelf honoured, courted, and even dreaded by his allies. In both we fhall meet with feveral inftances of his furprifing policy, his true regard for the intereft of his country, and his indefatigable induftry in promoting and executing his defigns.

§. 2. In the year 1652, a war broke out between the two republicks of England and Holland, which produced the moft terrible fea-fights that had ever been known, fome of them lafting for three days fucceffively. The brave admiral Blake, with Pen, Dean, Monk, and Ayfcough, on one fide, were againft the famous De Ruyter, Van Tromp, De Wit, and other gallant Dutch commanders, on the other. The quarrel began upon the Englifh demanding the tenth herring of the Dutch fifhermen on our coaft, in acknowledgment of the fovereignty of the feas. In the feveral engagements of the firft year, the Englifh had fo much the better, that about the beginning of 1653, the ftates fent over letters to the Englifh parliament for putting an end to the war, offering to pay them a large fum, befides acknowledging their fovereignty of the feas. Though Cromwell had not yet affumed the fupreme power, yet he had it fo far in effect, that particular application was made to him in this affair. The negotiation, however, did not fucceed at prefent.

But upon Cromwell's turning out the long parliament, their high mightineffes did not doubt but they fhould make an advantage of the confufion, which

they

Life of OLIVER CROMWELL. 179

they thought muſt ſucceed. They no longer applied therefore for peace, but ſent out a fleet with all imaginable diligence. Cromwell, for his part, was not behindhand with them in his preparations, but gave them ſuch a reception by his admirals, as they did not expect: ſo that after a long and bloody engagement, in which the Engliſh loſt little beſides their admiral Dean, the Dutch were obliged to ſhelter themſelves behind the ſands between Calais and Dunkirk, to prevent the deſtruction of their whole fleet. This made the ſtates ſue again for peace, in the moſt ſubmiſſive manner: to which Cromwell was not averſe, but would allow of no ceſſation till it was actually concluded. Both parties therefore got ready again for an engagement, the Dutch having no leſs than 125 ſail.

They came forth with great confidence of ſucceſs; but ſtill found the Engliſh an over match: for after a fight for two days, in which Van Tromp was killed, and about thirty of their ſhips fired or ſunk, they made all the ſail they could towards the Texel. This victory, tho' it coſt the Engliſh dear, was ſo acceptable to Cromwell and his parliament, that a day of thankſgiving was appointed for it; and gold chains, with fine medals repreſenting a ſea-fight, were given to the admirals for their good ſervices. On the other hand it put the Hollanders into the utmoſt confuſion, and occaſioned ſome dangerous inſurrections of the common people. The ſtates applied themſelves therefore to Cromwell's parliament and council; who would grant them no other terms, than the taking a leaſe, and paying an annual rent for the liberty of fiſhing in the Engliſh ſeas.

But this parliament and council having ſurrendered up their powers to the lord protector, they made a freſh application to him alone; who at laſt, when he ſaw no greater advantages could be expected, granted them a peace upon the following conditions. 1. That they ſhould not permit any of the king's party to reſide within their dominions.

2. That

2 That they should never suffer the prince of Orange to be stadtholder, general, or admiral. 3. That they should restore the island of Polerone in the East-Indies, which they had taken from the English in the reign of king James the first. 4. That they should pay 300,000 l. for the barbarities formerly exercised on the English at Amboyna. 5. That they should never dispute the rights of the English flag. Glorious conditions for the protector! and such as none of our monarchs could procure before him, tho' the terms of the third and fourth articles had been often contested.

§. 3. The greatest difficulty the protector met with, in relation to foreign affairs, was, which side to chuse in the war between France and Spain. Great application was made to him from both sides. Spain, says bishop Burnet, ordered their ambassador de Cardenas, a great and able man, to compliment him, and to engage, that in case he would join with them, they would pay him 100,000 crowns per month, and 200,000 crowns by way of advance, and not make peace till Calais was again recovered to the English, which had now been lost about an hundred years. The prince of Condé likewise, who was then in hostility with France, and supported by Spain, offered to turn protestant, and, upon Cromwell's assisting him, to make a descent in Guienne, where he doubted not but the protestants would join him, and enable him so to distress France, as to obtain for themselves, and for England, what conditions the protector pleased to dictate. But that prince's pretensions, upon farther enquiry, were found to be ill-grounded and vain. Mazarine, on the other hand, endeavoured to outbid Spain, by offering to assist him to take Dunkirk, then in the Spaniards hands, and a place of much more importance than Calais; and at the same time insinuated, that in case he joined with Spain, an army of Huguenots, headed by the king or his brother, should make a descent on England;

land; which, at that time, might be of dangerous consequence to Cromwell, considering how many enemies he had at home.

This, the bishop assures us, was the thing that determined him to join with the French; and in consequence of the treaty, which was concluded soon after, the king and duke were dismissed the kingdom of France with many excuses, some money, and abundance of promises. The prelate mentions another thing, which, he says, had great weight with the protector, while he was yet balancing in his mind about this alliance. One Gage, formerly a priest, coming over from the West-Indies, informed him how weak and how wealthy the Spaniards were there.; which made him conclude, that it would be both a great and an easy conquest to seize their dominions. And this he thought would supply him with such a treasure, as would thoroughly establish his government.

It has been a question much disputed, whether Cromwell, in joining with France against Spain, did really act consistently with the true interest of his country? Most people have maintained the negative; but I think with very little reason. The condition of France, at that time, was far different from what we have seen it in our days. The king was a minor, and the royal family divided among themselves, which had reduced the constitution to a languishing state. Whereas the house of Austria was then united and powerful; and the king of Spain, in particular, was possessed of the Netherlands, just in our neighbourhood, which rendered him formidable, and made it the interest of England to support France against him. Cromwell then, notwithstanding what has been said, might have, and I believe had, more general and national views in this alliance, than have hitherto been ascribed to him.

§. 4. But to put this matter beyond all dispute, and to shew that the Spaniards before Cromwell's time were too much like what we have found them since, which

which made it next to impossible for a man of his spirit not to resent their insults and depredations on his countrymen, we need only read the manifesto penned in Latin by the immortal Milton, and published by the protector while his fleet was in America, to shew " the justice of the cause of this commonwealth against the Spaniards." I shall set down a few passages of it, in order to recommend the perusal of the whole, a translation of which was lately printed *.

After setting forth the state of affairs for many years between the two kingdoms, and shewing how much the two late kings, James and Charles I, had suffered themselves and their subjects to be insulted by the Spaniards, it proceeds: " But as to the disputes that have arisen in the West-Indies, though we, both in the continent itself, and in the islands, have plantations as well as they; and have as good, nay a better right to possess them, than the Spaniards have to possess theirs; and though we have a right to trade in those seas, equally good with theirs; yet, without any reason, or any damage sustained, and that when there was not the least dispute about commerce, they have been continually invading our colonies in a hostile way, killing our men, taking our ships, robbing us of our goods, laying waste our houses and fields, imprisoning and enslaving our people: this they have been doing all along till these present times, wherein we have of late engaged in an expedition against them. For which reason, contrary to what used to be done formerly in the like case, they have detained our ships and merchants, and confiscated their goods almost every where through the Spanish dominions: so that whether we turn our eyes to America or Europe, they alone are undoubtedly to be considered as the authors of the war."

It then sets forth the barbarous treatment of many of our merchants and sailors, giving a long list of particular instances; and goes on thus. " By these, and

* For A. Millar in the Strand.

and many more examples of the same kind, too long to be reckoned up, 'tis abundantly evident, that the king of Spain and his subjects think they are no way bound, by any condition of peace to be performed to us on their part, in these places; since they have habitually exercised all sorts of hostilities against us, nay have even done such things as are more unsuitable, and more grievous than open acts of hostility; and since that cruelty with which they usually treat the English in America, is so contrary to the articles of peace, that it does not so much as seem suitable to the laws of the most bloody war.—

But the king of Spain seems to be convinced, that the sacred bonds of friendship have been first broken on his side: which thing is so clear and manifest, that our adversaries in the controversy are ashamed to deny the fact, and chuse rather to dispute with us concerning the right of possession.—They pretend to have a double title, one founded upon the pope's gift, and another upon their having first discovered those places. As to the first, we know the pope has always been very liberal in his gifts of kingdoms and countries; but in the mean time we cannot but think, that in so doing, he acts in a very different manner from him, whose vicar he professes himself, who would not so much as allow himself to be appointed a judge in the dividing of inheritances.—But we deny his being vested with any such authority, nor do we think there is any nation so void of understanding, as to think that so great power is lodged in him; or that the Spaniards would believe this, or acquiesce in it, if he should require them to yield up as much as he has bestowed.—

Nor is the other title of any greater weight; as if the Spaniards, in consequence of their having first discovered some few parts of America, and given names to some islands, rivers, and promontories, had for this reason lawfully acquired the government and dominion of that new world, But such an imaginary title, founded on such a silly pretence, without being

ing in poffeffion, cannot poffibly create any true and lawful right. The beft right of poffeffion in America, is that which is founded on one's having planted colonies there, and fettled in fuch places as had either no inhabitants, or by the confent of the inhabitants, if there were any; or at leaft in fome of the wild and uncultivated parts of the country, which they were not numerous enough to replenifh and improve.

If this be true, as the Spaniards will be found to hold their poffeffions there very unjuftly, having obtained all of them againft the will of the inhabitants, and, as it were, plucked them out of their very bowels; having laid the foundation of their empire in that place in the blood of the poor natives, and rendered feveral large iflands and countries, that were in a tolerable cafe when they found them, fo many barren defarts, and rooted out all the inhabitants there: fo the Englifh hold their poffeffions there by the beft right imaginable, efpecially thofe iflands where the Spaniards have fallen upon their colonies, and quite demolifhed them; which iflands had no other inhabitants at all, or if they had, they were all flain by the Spaniards, who had likewife deferted thefe places, and left them without any to improve or cultivate them.—Although granting we had beat the Spaniards out of thofe places where we have planted our colonies, out of which they had firft expelled the inhabitants, we fhould have poffefs'd them with better right, as the avengers of the murder of that people, and of the injuries fuftained by them, than the Spaniards, their oppreffors and murderers.—

All thefe things being confidered, we hope the time will come, when all, but efpecially true Englifhmen, will lay afide their private animofities among themfelves, and renounce their own proper advantages, rather than through an exceffive defire of that fmall profit to be made by trading with Spain, which cannot be obtained but upon fuch conditions as are difhonourable, and in fome fort unlawful; and which may likewife be got fome other way; to expofe, as they

now

Life of OLIVER CROMWELL.

now do, the fouls of many young traders, by thofe terms upon which they now live and trade there; and fuffer the lives and fortunes of many chriftian brethren in America, and, in fine, the honour of this whole nation, to be expofed."——

§. 5. Having thus declared the reafons of his proceedings, the protector, in order to make the beft of Gage's information, fitted out a fleet, with a force fufficient, as he thought, to feize Hifpaniola and Cuba. When the time of fetting out this fleet came on, all men wondered whither it fhould be defigned. Some imagined it was to rob the church of Loretto; and this apprehenfion occafioned a fortification to be drawn round it: others talk'd of Rome itfelf; for the protector's preachers often gave out, " that if it were not for the divifions at home, he would go and fack Babylon." Others thought the defign was againft Cadiz, though he had not yet broke with Spain. The French knew nothing of the fecret, and the protector, not having finifhed his alliance with them, was not obliged to impart to them the reafon of his preparations. All he faid about it was this, " that he fent out the fleet, to guard the feas, and to reftore England to its dominion on that element."

This fleet, confifting of about thirty men of war, under the command of vice-admiral Penn, with about four thoufand land foldiers to be commanded by Venables, fet fail the beginning of this year, directly for Barbadoes, where the two commanders were ordered to break open their commiffions. Being fafely arrived there, and new men taken in to increafe the land army, they failed to the ifland of Hifpaniola. Venables landed his men in an ill place, different from the orders he had received from the protector, and marched them through fuch thick woods and uneafy paffages, that the Spaniards, with a very unequal number, beat them back; and they were foon forced to re-embark. To make fome amends for this mifcarriage, they made another defcent on the ifland of Jamaica, and obtained

tained an easy possession of it; which island has ever since remained in the hands of the English: where leaving a good body of foot to secure it, they sailed back to England. The protector was never so much disturbed as at this disaster at Hispaniola; so that Penn and Venables were no sooner come on shore, but he committed them both to the Tower, and could never be prevailed on to trust either of them again *.

§. 6.

* One of our political weekly writers, in a letter upon the fitness of a late design that unfortunately miscarried, has some paragraphs relating to this expedition that are very much to the protector's advantage, and therefore ought not to be here omitted.

"These thoughts on the fitness of the design, says the letter-writer, may, I think, be well supported, by observing the councils and design of Cromwell, in his expedition to the Spanish West-Indies; of which I the rather chuse to speak, because that matter is generally misconceived, and it is misrepresented by our noble historian lord Clarendon.—But Mr. Burchett, in his naval history, hath given us a copy of Cromwell's instructions to Venables, which is superior to all other testimony. Lord Clarendon says, that their orders were very particular, and very positive, that they should land at such a place at Hispaniola, which was described to them. Whereas their orders were at large and general; viz. to pursue such methods as they found proper for the general design of gaining an interest in the Spanish West-Indies; and therefore the instructions say, "We shall not tie you up to a method, by any particular instructions, but only communicate to you what hath been under our consideration."

It appears plainly from these instructions, that his aim was not so piddling as to take St. Domingo, with the island of Hispaniola. Even taking the Havanna, with the island of Cuba, though it was within the compass of his instructions, yet he consider'd it only

as

§. 6. About the time that Penn and Venables set out on this expedition, admiral Blake sailed with another fleet into the Mediterranean, to scour those seas of the Turkish pirates; and not meeting with any of them, he bravely resolved to seek them out in their ports.

as part of the outworks to his greater design; for the treasures are upon the continent, not in the islands. The latter are of use as steps, or securities to the former. He therefore meant a rich settlement on the continent; had his eye particularly on Cartagena, which he intended for the chief seat of the British empire in that part of the world; and which would give a final decision to all disputes, and prevent all further disturbances from Spain.

And immediately upon the news of having taken Jamaica, he lost no time, says lord Clarendon, but sent presently a good squadron of ships, and a recruit of fifteen hundred men, resolving to make continual war on the Spaniards from that place.—

These instructions of Cromwell's were general, as hath been said, to make a conquest as they found themselves able; and the intent was that it should be a holding one. To that end there are two or three methods communicated to the commander in chief, which had been before under the consideration of the council. They are so curious, and so much to our present purpose, that it will not be unacceptable, I believe, to transcribe a part of them.

" The first method is to land on some of the islands, particularly Hispaniola and St. John's [i. e. Porto Rioco] one or both; which being possess'd and brought under obedience, from thence you may send force for the taking of the Havanna, which is the back door to the West-Indies. The taking of the Havanna is so considerable, that we have had thoughts of beginning the first attempt upon that fort and the island of Cuba; and do still judge it worthy of consideration.

Another

ports. He came firſt before Algiers, and ſending to the dey, demanded that all the Engliſh ſhips might be reſtored, and all the Engliſh ſlaves releaſed. The dey hereupon ſent a preſent to Blake, and gave him to underſtand, "that the ſhips and captives already taken belong'd to private men, therefore not ſo much in

Another way is for the preſent to leave the iſlands, and to make the firſt attempt on the main land, in one or more places, between the river Oroonoque and Porto-Bello, aiming therein chiefly at Cartagena, which we would make the ſeat of the intended deſign; wherein if you have ſucceſs, you will probably be maſters of all the Spaniſh treaſure, which comes from Peru, by way of Panama in the South-ſea to Porto-Bello in the North-ſea. You will have houſes ready-built, a country ready planted, and moſt of the people Indians who will ſubmit to you.

There is a third conſideration, relating both to the iſlands and the main, which is to make the firſt attempt upon St. Domingo, or Porto-Rico, one or both, and having ſecured them, to go immediately to Cartagena."

Now it will be obſerved that theſe deſigns were form'd, and the fleet and forces ſent, not a year after the war was proclaimed, but in the year before; he eſteeming that the war was begun by them, when they began to practiſe ſome depredations on the Engliſh, though not to be named with what hath ſince been done. Moreover it will be obſerved that the deſign was ſecret; not ſo ſecret indeed, as to end in nothing, and leave ſuſpicion that no greater matter was ever intended; but ſo as to be concealed from the enemy; not altogether from any ſuſpicion; for that muſt be impoſſible; but from any certain aſſurance; which was ſo far done that the Spaniſh ambaſſador did not believe it, till fraternities were entered into on the Exchange in London, for carrying on plantations at Jamaica. See Craftſman of June 27, 1741.

in his power; but yet they should be restored at a moderate ransom; and if the admiral thought good, they would conclude a peace, and for the future offer no acts of violence to any of the English ships and natives."

A peace being accordingly concluded, Blake sailed from thence to Tunis, where, having made the same demand as at Algiers, instead of the like submission, he received this resolute answer, " that there were their castles of Goletta, and their ships and castles of Porto-Ferino; he might do his worst, for he should not think to fright them with the sight of his fleet." Provoked at this answer, Blake resolved to destroy their ships in Porto-Ferino. Accordingly he ordered his captains to man their long-boats with stout seamen, and sent them into the harbour to fire those ships, whilst the admiral with all his fleet thundered most furiously against their castles. The seamen so bravely performed their parts, that all the Turkish ships of war were soon reduced to ashes, with the loss of only twenty-five men, and forty-eight wounded, on the English side. These were actions of the highest conduct and courage, which made the English name very formidable in those seas.

There was another reason of Blake's sailing into the Mediterranean; which was, to demand satisfaction of all princes and states, that had molested the English in the time of confusion at home. Accordingly, among other places, he sailed to Leghorn, and dispatched his secretary to demand of the great duke of Tuscany 60,000 l. for damages sustained by the English in his dutchy; prince Rupert having taken and sold as many English ships, as amounted to that value, to the great duke's subjects. The duke was willing to pay part of the sum, and desired time to consult the pope about the rest. Blake said, the pope had nothing to do with it, and he would have the whole sum; which was paid him. The duke pretended that the pope ought to pay part of the damage, some of the ships having been sold to his subjects;

accordingly

accordingly the next succeeding pope repaid 20,000 pistoles. Admiral Blake sent home sixteen ships laden with the effects he had received from several states, for satisfaction and damages; and they were ordered to sail up the Thames together, for a pleasant spectacle to the people.

§. 7. The king of Spain, provoked at the late attempt upon the West-Indies, declared war against England; and the protector dispatched orders to admiral Blake, to watch the return of the Spanish plate-fleet, and make what destruction he could upon the coasts of Spain; and thought fit now to finish his alliance with France, sending Lockhart his ambassador thither for that end. His highness undertook to send over an army of six thousand foot; and when the forts of Dunkirk and Mardyke should be taken, they were to be put into his hands.

Admiral Blake, and Montague afterwards earl of Sandwich, having blocked up the port of Cadiz for some weeks, without being able to bring the Spaniards to a fight, were obliged to sail to Wyers-bay in Portugal, to take in supplies. They left behind them captain Stayner, with only seven ships; who, while the commanders were retired, perceived the Spanish plate-fleet making directly to Cadiz. Notwithstanding the small force he had with him; Stayner resolved to fall on the Spaniards; which he did with such success, that in a few hours the whole fleet was spoiled. One ship was sunk; another burnt, in which the viceroy of Mexico, with his lady, perished in the flames: two were forced on ground; one got off, and two remained in the conqueror's hands; which being brought to Portsmouth, the bullion, to the value of two millions, was there landed, and conveyed in carts to London, as a trophy of this great victory *. §. 8.

* See (in the appendix, No. II. of the poems) Mr. Waller's beautiful poem on this victory, entitled, Of a war with Spain, and fight at Sea by general Montague,

§. 8. Blake being returned to Cadiz, and having there rode out the winter of 1657, he received intelligence, that another Spanish plate-fleet, much richer than the former, was coming home; but, for fear of the English fleet, had put into the bay of Santa-Cruz in the Canaries. Upon this Blake weighed anchor April the 13th, and by the 20th stood off of the said bay; where he accordingly found the galleons arriv'd, to the number of sixteen men of war. The bay was secured by a strong castle well furnished with ordnance, besides seven forts more in several parts of it mounted with six, four, and three guns apiece, and united by a line of communication from one fort to another, which was mann'd with musqueteers. Don Diego Diagues, the Spanish admiral, caused all his smaller ships to moor close to the shore, covered by the castles and forts, and posted the six large galleons farther off at anchor, with their formidable broadsides to the sea. A Dutch merchant-man was at this time in the bay, the master whereof perceiving the English were ready to enter, desir'd Don Diego's leave to depart: "For, said he, I am very sure Blake will presently be among us." To which the Don resolutely answered, "Get you gone if you will, and let Blake come if he dares."

Blake having called a council of war, and finding it impracticable to carry off the galleons, resolved to burn them all: to which end he ordered captain Stayner, with a squadron, to stand into the very bay: who by eight the next morning fell furiously on the Spaniards, without the least regard to their forts, and fought them almost an hour. The admiral seconding him, posted some of the larger ships to cannonade the castle and forts; which play'd their parts so well, that the enemy was forced to leave them. Blake for the space of four hours engaged the galleons, which made a brave resistance, but were at last abandon'd by the enemy: as were likewise the smaller vessels, which lay under the forts; which were burnt by Stayner, whilst Blake did the same by the large galleons: so that

that this whole plate-fleet, of ineſtimable value, was utterly deſtroyed, without the loſs of one Engliſh ſhip, and with no more than forty-eight men killed, and an hundred and twenty wounded. The news of this brave and unparallel'd action being brought to England, the parliament ordered a day of thankſgiving for this great ſucceſs; and the protector, at their deſire, ſent the admiral a diamond ring of 500 l. value, and knighted Stayner at his return to England.

§. 9. Blake, after this noble exploit, ſailed back to Spain, whence, after having long kept all their ports in awe, he returned for England. But falling ſick of a fever, he died in the 59th year of his age, juſt as the fleet was entering into Plymouth Sound; where he paſſionately enquired for the land, but found his own element the more proper bed of honour. He had a publick funeral juſtly beſtowed upon him, and the honour of being interred in Henry the ſeventh's chapel. The lord Clarendon ſays, " He was the firſt man that declined the old track, and made it manifeſt, that the naval ſcience might be attained in leſs time than was imagined; and deſpiſed thoſe rules which had been long in practice, to keep his ſhips and his men out of danger, which had been held in former times a point of great ability and circumſpection; as if the principal art requiſite in the captain of a ſhip, had been to be ſure to come home ſafe again. He was the firſt man who brought ſhips to contemn caſtles on ſhore, which had been thought ever very formidable, and were diſcovered by him to make a noiſe only, and to fright thoſe who could rarely be hurt by them. He was the firſt that infuſed that proportion of courage into the ſeamen, by making them ſee by experience, what mighty things they could do, if they were reſolved; and taught them to fight in fire as well as upon water: and tho' he hath been very well imitated and followed, he was the firſt that gave the example of that kind of naval courage, and

bold

Life of OLIVER CROMWELL.

bold and refolute atchievements." A very proper fervant this to fuch a mafter as Cromwell!

Blake had a very great regard to the honour of his country, and the Englifh dominion of the feas. One inftance of his care to preferve this honour, mentioned by bifhop Burnet, I cannot omit. He fays, that Blake happening to be at Malaga with the fleet, before Cromwell made war upon Spain, fome of the feamen going afhore, met the hoft, as it was carrying about, and not only refufed to pay any honour to it, but laugh'd at thofe that did. Whereupon one of the priefts ftirr'd up the people to refent this affront; and fo they fell upon them, and beat them feverely. The feamen returning to their fhip, and complaining of the ufage they had met with, Blake immediately difpatched a trumpeter to the viceroy, to demand the prieft who had been the chief occafion of it; to which the viceroy returned this anfwer, " that he had no authority over the prieft, and fo could not difpofe of him." But Blake fent him word again, " that he would not enquire who had power to fend the prieft to him; but if he were not fent within three hours, he would burn their town. And fo being unable to refift, they fent the prieft to him; who juftifying himfelf upon the rude behaviour of the feamen, Blake anfwered, " that if he had fent a complaint to him of it, he would have punifhed them feverely, fince he would not fuffer his men to affront the eftablifhed religion of any place; but he took it ill, that he fet on the Spaniards to do it; for he would have all the world know, that an Englifhman was only to be punifhed by an Englifhman." And fo he civilly treated the prieft, and difmiffed him, being fatisfied that he had him at his mercy. Cromwell was exceedingly pleafed with this, and read the letters in council with great fatisfaction, telling them, " he hoped he fhould make the name of an Englifhman as great as ever that of a Roman had been."

§. 10. While I am speaking of the protector's great care to assert and maintain the sovereignty of the sea, and the honour of the English nation, a passage occurs from a printed speech made in the house of commons, by Mr. Poultney, in a debate on the complaints of the West-India merchants, two sessions before the present war against Spain was declared. It contains perhaps as remarkable a story as is any where to be met with, and the reflections on it are equally honourable to Cromwell, and worthy of the gentleman that made them, who was neither afraid nor ashamed to introduce the conduct of one we call an usurper, as a pattern to legal kings, and modern ministers.

"We have been negociating and treating with Spain for these twenty years, says this great patriot, about nothing that I know of, unless it was about reparation and security for our merchants; and yet, during that whole time, they have been plundering and abusing our merchants, almost without intermission. If a nation's being subject to daily insults and injuries is not a circumstance, that ought to make it peremptory in its demands, I am sure no circumstance can. This has been our case for many years, and will be our case, till Spain be made to acknowledge, in the most express and particular terms, every one of those rights they now pretend to dispute. Ought not this to make us peremptory in our demands? Ought not it to have made us peremptory long ago? If we had peremptorily insisted upon full satisfaction and reparation, for the very first injury that was offered us, I may venture to affirm, we should never have been exposed to a second. Nay, if we consider that our insults and injuries were inflicted without any ceremony, we ought to have used as little ceremony in the revenging them; and to have taken satisfaction, without being at any great pains to demand it. But, I hope, that is not even yet too late.

This was what Oliver Cromwell did in a like case, that happened during his government, and in a case where a more powerful nation was concerned than
ever

ever Spain could pretend to be. In the histories of his time we are told, that an English merchant-ship was taken in the chops of the channel, carried into St. Maloes, and there confiscated upon some groundless pretence. As soon as the master of the ship, who was an honest quaker, got home, he presented a petition to the protector in council, setting forth his case, and praying for redress. Upon hearing the petition, the protector told his council, he would take that affair upon himself, and ordered the man to attend him next morning. He examined him strictly as to all the circumstances of his case, and finding by his answers that he was a plain honest man, and that he had been concerned in no unlawful trade, he asked him, If he would go to Paris with a letter? The man answered, he could. Well then, says the protector, prepare for your journey, and come to me to-morrow morning. Next morning he gave him a letter to cardinal Mazarine, and told him he must stay but three days for an answer. The answer I mean, says he, is, the full value of what you might have made of your ship and cargo; and tell the cardinal, that if it is not paid you in three days, you have express orders from me to return home. The honest, blunt quaker, we may suppose, followed his instructions to a tittle; but the cardinal, according to the manner of ministers when they are any way pressed, began to shuffle: therefore the quaker returned, as he was bid. As soon as the protector saw him, he asked, "Well, friend, have you got your money?" And upon the man's answering he had not, the protector told him, "Then leave your direction with my secretary, and you shall soon hear from me." Upon this occasion, that great man did not stay to negociate, or to explain, by long tedious memorials, the reasonableness of his demand. No; tho' there was a French minister residing here, he did not so much as acquaint him with the story, but immediately sent a man of war or two to the channel, with orders to seize every French ship they could meet with. Accordingly, they returned in a few days with two or three French prizes, which the protector ordered to be immediately fold, and out of the produce, he paid the quaker what he demanded for the ship and cargo. Then he sent for the French minister, gave him an account of what had happened, and told him there was a balance, which, if he pleased, should be paid in to him, to the end that he might deliver it to those of his countrymen, who were the owners of the French ships, that had been so taken and sold.

This was Oliver Cromwell's manner of negociating; this was the method he took for obtaining reparation. And what was the consequence? it produced no war between the two nations. No; it made the French government terribly afraid of giving him the least offence; and while he lived, they took special care that no injury should be done to any subjects of Great Britain. This shews, that Oliver Cromwell had a genius and a capacity for government; and however unjustly he acquired his power, it is certain that this nation was as much respected abroad, and flourished as much at home, under his government, as it ever did under any government. But when a nation has the misfortune to have a man set at the head of her affairs, who knows nothing of foreign, who knows nothing but the little low detail of offices, and has neither capacity or knowledge beyond what can qualify him for being clerk in the treasury, or some other publick office, it is then no wonder to see that nation despised and insulted abroad, and dissatisfied, mutinous, and seditious at home.

I wish those who have now the direction of our negociations abroad, would assume, if possible, a little of the spirit and courage of Oliver Cromwell. He had as powerful a party to struggle with at home, as ever any minister had; but he never allowed the danger he was in from that party, to deter him from vindicating, upon all occasions, the honour and interest

tereſt of his country abroad. He had too much good ſenſe to manage in ſuch a puſillanimous manner; for he knew that ſuch management would have increaſed the party againſt him, and would have made them more daring, as well as more numerous. If our preſent negociators, or thoſe who have the direction of our negociations, take example by him, I am ſure they will not accept of any general acknowledgments or promiſes."

§. 11. To proceed: As victory crown'd the protector's arms by ſea, ſo his forces by land were not unſuccefsful. The 6000 men which his highneſs was obliged by his treaty with France to provide, being tranſported under the command of Sir John Reynolds, and major-general Morgan, the French had no inclination to begin upon Mardyke or Dunkirk, which when taken, were to be put into Cromwell's hands; but marched to other places, which they were to conquer for their own uſe. But his highneſs's ambaſſador Lockhart made ſuch repeated repreſentations to the cardinal, not witthout ſome menaces, "that his Maſter knew where to find a more punctual friend," that as ſoon as they had taken Montmedy and St. Venant, the army inveſted Mardyke. The French and Engliſh had not lain before this ſtrong place above four days, when it was reduced to a ſurrender upon compoſition, and delivered up wholly in the poſſeſſion of the Engliſh. But preſently after, the French being withdrawn into their winter-quarters, the Spaniards, who were ſenſible of what great importance this place was to the preſerving of Dunkirk, detached a body of horſe and foot to retake it. Among theſe were 2000 Engliſh and Iriſh, commanded by the Duke of York; and they made two very furious ſtorms upon the fort; but were ſtoutly repulſed, and forced to fly, with the loſs of ſeveral brave Commanders. -

Marſhal Turenne commanded the army that took Mardyke; to whom cardinal Mazarine wrote thus, at Lockhart's inftance, before the fiege: " Nothing can be of more fatal confequence to France, than the lofs of Cromwell's friendfhip, and the breach of the union with him; which certainly will be broken, if fome ftrong town is not taken and put into his hands." This conqueft was very grateful to Cromwell, who immediately fent ten men of war to guard the port of Mardyke, and cruize on that coaft. A foreign writer, fpeaking of this matter, fays, " Nothing could flatter the ambition of Cromwell more than this acquifition, knowing that he had thereby won immortal glory: he had, without the lofs of a man, accomplifhed a defign, which the greateft kings of England had often attempted in vain, at the expence of their people's blood and treafure: he had re-eftablifhed the Englifh on the continent, and put them in a condition to make themfelves mafters of both fides of the channel, which had been defpaired of fince the lofs of Calais.

§. 12. Not long after the taking of Mardyke, an attempt was made upon Oftend, but without fuccefs: for fome of the garrifon having contracted with Mazarine to deliver it up, it appeared that this was only a feint, carried on with the privity of the governor, who defended himfelf bravely when the befiegers appeared, killing and taking 1500 French that were landed, and forely galling the Englifh fleet from the forts. But this difappointment had no very ill effect; for prefently after Dunkirk was invefted by the French, affifted by the 6000 valiant Englifhmen, under the infpection of Lockhart, the protector's ambafiador, but more immediately under the command of major general Morgan. Whilft they were carrying on their approaches towards the town, they had intelligence brought them, that the Spanifh general Don John of Auftria, with the prince of Condé, the prince de Ligny, and the dukes of York and Gloucefter, were advancing with 30,000 men to relieve the place. Hereupon the French king and cardinal

dinal were perfuaded to withdraw to Calais, and leave all to be determined by a council of war. In the firft council, which was held without either Lockhart or Morgan, it was refolved to raife the fiege, if the enemy came on. But in the next, when thofe two were prefent, Morgan vehemently oppofed that refolution, alledging, "what a difhonour it would be to the crown of France to have fummoned a place, and broke ground before it, and then raife the fiege and run away;" and defiring the council to confider, that if they raifed the fiege, the alliance with England would be broken the fame hour. Upon which it was refolved, contrary to their former intention, to give battle to the enemy, if they came on, and to maintain the fiege. And the enemy coming on, a defperate fight enfued, in which the Spaniards were in a manner totally routed by the Englifh, before the French came in. At the end of the purfuit, marfhal Turenne, with above 100 officers, came up to the Englifh, and embracing the officers, faid, " They never faw a more glorious action in their lives; and that they were fo tranfported with the fight of it, that they had not power to move, or do any thing.

The Spanifh army being entirely vanquifh'd, the confederates renewed their attempts upon the town of Dunkirk with great vigour and induftry; and the marquifs de Leda, the governor, being mortally wounded, as he was fallying out upon the befiegers, the Spaniards within defired a prefent capitulation: which being granted, this important place was furrendered upon articles on the 25th of June 1658; when it was immediately delivered up into the hands of the Englifh, by the French king and cardinal in perfon, purfuant to the treaty between them and the lord protector.

§. 13. Thus did Cromwell, in a very fhort time, and with little expence either of men or money, render himfelf abfolute mafter of the Britifh channel: but so contrary to his were the measures taken in the succeeding reign of king Charles II. that in the second year of that licentious prince, one of whose chief ends in getting money was to oblige his mistresses, Dunkirk was publickly sold to the French: "which transaction, says bishop Burnet, mightily impaired the king's credit abroad; and the damage we have suffered from it since, has made the bargain often reflected on with severity at home." It was in fact this sale, and the other steps taken in the same reign, that contributed more to the aggrandizing of the French, than any engagement that can be attributed to Cromwell. "It appeared, says another modern writer, when king Charles had sold Dunkirk, which Cromwell kept as a security for England, and the French king had surprised many cities and provinces to a vast increase of empire, that a treaty with Spain was more preferable for the preservation of the balance of power. But was it possible for any such thing as the sale of Dunkirk to enter into such a head as Cromwell's? He would as soon have sold Portsmouth. And had Dunkirk been still kept in English hands, Cromwell's French treaty would never have been complained of."

Sir William Temple assures us farther, that cardinal Mazarine having surmounted his own dangers, and the difficulties incident to a minority, pursued the plan left him by his predecessor, and by the assistance of an immortal body of 6000 English, made such a progress in Flanders, that Cromwell perceived the balance was turned, and grown too heavy on the French side: whereupon he dispatched a gentleman privately to Madrid, to propose there a change of his treaty with France, into one with Spain; by which he would draw his forces over into their service, and make them 10,000, upon condition their first action should be to besiege Calais, and when taken, to put it into his hands. The person sent upon this errand was past the Pyrenees, when he was overtaken by the news of Cromwell's death. This was soon followed by a peace between the two crowns, called the peace of the Pyrenees." Thus we see that with whomsoever the protector sided, his design was to aggrandize and strengthen the English, and to keep the balance of power in his own hands.

§. 14. Though the protector lived but a very short time after the taking of Dunkirk, yet he received greater marks of honour and esteem from the French court, than were shewn to any crowned head in Europe. He sent over the lord Falconbridge, his son-in-law, with a numerous and splendid retinue to Calais, where the king and cardinal then were; who received him as a sovereign prince, the cardinal giving him his right-hand in his apartment, which had never been done to the imperial ambassador, nor even to the pope's nuncio. And when his lordship took his leave, both the king and his minister loaded him with rich presents, some of which were for the protector, and others for himself. The compliment was returned to Cromwell by a very solemn embassy from France, which surpassed most appearances of the same kind. But the protector's death put an end to the further effects of this alliance.

This wonderful man, from the very beginning of his administration, was complimented and courted by most of the powers around him, who acknowledged his sovereignty, and gave him the title of highness. All nations contended, as it were, by their ambassadors, who should render themselves most acceptable to him. Denmark had the favour of being taken into the Dutch treaty, upon the good terms of making the states responsible for 140,000 l. to repair the damage which the English had suffered from the Danes. About the same time, by the negociation of his ambassador Whitelock, he made a firm alliance with the kingdom of Sweden. He forced Portugal to send an ambassador to beg peace, and to submit to make satisfaction for the offence they had committed in receiving prince Rupert, by the payment of a great sum of money.

Even France and Spain, in his earliest days, sued for an alliance with him, and sent over their ministers for that purpose, whom he received with all the state and solemnity of a sovereign prince. He exaggerated nothing therefore in his speech to his second parliament, which he made in favour of his own government.

The truth is, his name became formidable every where. His favourite alliance was with Sweden; for Charles Gustavus and he lived in great conjunction of councils. But the states of Holland so dreaded him, that they took care to give him no manner of umbrage: insomuch that when the king or his brother came at any time to visit their sister, the princess of Orange, a deputation of the states was immediately with them, to let them know they could have no shelter there. All Italy in like manner trembled at his name, and seemed to be under a panick fear, as long as he lived. His fleets scoured the Mediterranean, and the Turks durst not offend him, but delivered up Hyde, the king's ambassador there, who was brought over and executed for assuming that character.

The justice done by him on Don Pantaleon-sa, a very eminent person, and brother to the Portuguese Ambassador, was what mightily raised the reputation of his power. This man had been guilty of a murder, and taken sanctuary in his brother's house, who insisted upon the privilege due to his character. But Cromwell obliged him to deliver up the criminal, who being tried by a jury of half English and half foreigners, was condemned to die; and accordingly was beheaded on Tower-Hill. And it is very remarkable, that on the day of this execution, the Portugal ambassador was obliged to sign the articles of peace between the two nations; whereupon he immediately went out of town. And it is observed of this affair, to the honour of the protector, that whatever reason the house of Austria had to hate his memory, the emperor Leopold, near twenty years after Cromwell's death, brought it as a precedent to justify his carrying off the prince of Furftemburg at the treaty of Cologne, notwithftanding his being a plenipotentiary for the elector of that name. And in the printed manifefto publifhed by the emperor on that occafion, this piece of Cromwell's juftice is related at large.*

Few princes, fays Wellwood, ever bore their character higher upon all occafions, than Oliver Cromwell, efpecially in his treaties with crown'd heads. And it is a thing without example, that is mentioned by one of the beft informed hiftorians of the age, Pufendorf, in his life of the late elector of Brandenburgh; that in Cromwell's league with France and Spain, he would not allow the French king to call himfelf king of France, but of the French; whereas he took to himfelf not only the title of protector of England, but likewife of France. And which is yet more furprifing, and hardly to be believed, but for the authority of the author, the protector's name was put before the French king's, in his inftrument of the treaty.

§. 15. During his adminiftration, there were two fignal inftances given him to fhew his zeal in protecting the proteftants, which advanced his character abroad.

* It was while Don Pantaleon fa lay under fentence of death, that the Latin panegyrick, a tranflation of which is given in the appendix, was prefented to Cromwell, then lord-general only, in order to foften him in favour of that Portuguefe nobleman. This circumftance very much heightens the idea of Cromwell's inflexibility, that it was proof againft one of the moft artful and fine pieces of flattery that perhaps ever was writ; and which was the more dangerous as it came from a foreigner, invefted with a publick character, and at a time when every body was in doubt what fyftem of government the general intended to introduce.

abroad. The duke of Savoy raised a new persecution of the Vaudois, massacring many, and driving the rest from their habitations. Whereupon Cromwell sent to the French court, demanding of them to oblige that duke, whom he knew to be in their power, to put a stop to his unjust fury, or otherwise he must break with them. The cardinal objected to this as unreasonable: he would do good offices, he said, but could not answer for the effect. However, nothing would satisfy the protector, till they oblig'd the duke to restore all that he had taken from his protestant subjects, and to renew their former privileges. Cromwell wrote on this occasion to the duke himself, and by mistake omitted the title of royal highness on his letter; upon which the major part of the council of Savoy were for returning it unopen'd: but one of them representing, that Cromwell would not pass by such an affront, but would certainly lay Villa Franca in ashes, and set the Swiss cantons upon Savoy, the letter was read, and with the cardinal's influence had the desired success. The protector also raised money in England for the poor sufferers, and sent over an agent to settle all their affairs.

At another time there happened a tumult at Nismes, wherein some disorder had been committed by the Huguenots. They being apprehensive of severe proceedings upon it, sent one over, with great expedition and secrecy, to desire Cromwell's intercession and protection. This express found so good a reception, that he the same evening dispatched a letter to the cardinal, with one inclosed to the king; also instructions to his ambassador Lockhart, requiring him either to prevail for a total impunity of that misdemeanor, or immediately to come away. At Lockhart's application, the disorder was overlooked; and, though the French court complained of this way of proceeding, as a little too imperious, yet the necessity of their affairs made them comply. This Lockhart, a wise and gallant man, who was governor of Dunkirk and ambassador at the same time, and in high favour

with

Life of OLIVER CROMWELL.

with the protector, told bishop Burnet, " that when he was sent afterwards ambassador by king Charles, he found he had nothing of that regard that was paid to him in Cromwell's time." *

There

* To these two pieces of history, we may add his letter to the prince of Tarente, as another instance of his regard for the protestant religion. It was written in Latin by Milton, and is thus translated:

" Oliver, protector of the commonwealth of England, Scotland, Ireland, &c. to the most illustrious prince of Tarente, greeting. It was a very great pleasure and satisfaction to me, to perceive by your highness's letter which you sent me, your love of religion, and your extraordinary zeal and concern for the reformed churches, especially considering that you live in a country where such great things are promised to all persons of your rank, if they forsake the orthodox faith, and so many discouragements are laid in the way of those who continue stedfast. Nor was it less pleasing to me, to find that your highness approved of my care and concern for the same religion, than which nothing ought to be more dear and precious to me. And I call God to witness, how desirous I am, according as I have ability and opportunity, to answer the hope and expectation which you say the churches have concerning me, and to manifest it to all. Indeed I should esteem it the best fruit of my labours, and of this dignity, or office, which I hold in this commonwealth, to be put into a capacity of being serviceable either to the enlargement or the safety, or, which is the chief of all, the peace of the reformed church. And I earnestly exhort your highness that you would hold fast to the end the orthodox religion you have receiv'd from your Fathers, with a firmness and constancy of mind equal to the piety and zeal you discover in the profession of it. Nor indeed can there be any thing more worthy of yourself and of your

most

There was yet a farther defign, very advantageous to the proteftant caufe, wherewith Cromwell intended to have begun his kingfhip, had he taken it upon him; and that was, the inftituting a council for the proteftant religion, in oppofition to the congregation de propagandâ fide at Rome. This body was to confift of feven counfellors, and four fecretaries for different provinces. The fecretaries were to have 500 l; falary a-piece, to keep correfpondence every-where. Ten thoufand pounds a year was to be a fund for ordinary emergencies: farther fupplies were to be provided, as occafions required; and Chelfea-College, then an old ruinous building, was to be fitted up for their reception. This was a great defign, and worthy of the man who had formed it.

§. 16, The fecret correfpondence he kept up, from his firft appearance on the theatre of affairs, was what every one wondered at. When he was only deputy of Ireland, he ftopped the lord Broghill in London, as he was going over to the king, to take out a commiffion againft the parliament, and fo wrought on him, that he went over in the parliament's fervice, and continued faithful to Cromwell ever after. And when he was mounted to the fummit of authority, he brought over a company of Jews into England, and gave them toleration to build a fynagogue; becaufe he

moft pious parents; and tho' I could defire all things for your fake, yet I can wifh you nothing better, nothing more excellent in return for the civilities you have fhewn me, than that you fo conduct yourfelf, that the churches, efpecially thofe of your own country, in whofe difcipline you were born with fo happy a difpofition and of fuch a noble family, may find in you a protection anfwerable to the high ftation in which you are placed above others. Farewell. Whitehall, June 26, 1654. Your highnefs's moft affectionate and moft devoted,

OLIVER."

he knew, by reason of their negociation of money in all countries, that they were excellently fitted for the purpose of bringing him intelligence. It was by the information of one of those, who came to him in a poor beggarly habit, that he intercepted a large sum of money, which the Spaniards, who were then at war with him, were sending over in a Dutch ship, to pay their army in Flanders. He also prevailed on Sir Richard Willis, chancellor Hyde's great confident, to let him know all that passed in king Charles's court; pretending, that his aim in discovering the plots of the royalists, for whom he had a great tenderness, was only to disconcert them, that none of them might suffer for their rashness. This practice of Sir Richard's was not discovered till after the protector's death, when he still continued his correspondence with Thurloe, whose under-secretary, Moreland, detected him to the king.

There could not be any considerable person in London, of the royal party, but Cromwell immediately knew of it. He once told lord Broghill, that there was a friend of his in town; and upon his asking Who, said, my lord Ormond; mentioning the day when he arrived, and the place where he now was. Broghill had leave from the protector to go to Ormond, and inform him of all this, that he might make his escape; which was done accordingly.

In matters of greatest moment, the protector trusted none but his secretary Thurloe, and oftentimes not him. An instance of which Thurloe us'd to tell of himself; "that he was once commanded by Cromwell to go at a certain hour to Gray's Inn, and at such a place deliver a bill of 20,000 l. payable to the bearer at Genoa, to a man he should find walking in such a habit and posture as he describ'd him, without speaking one word." Which accordingly Thurloe did: and never knew, to his dying day, either the person or the occasion.

At another time the protector coming late at night to Thurloe's office, and beginning to give him directions

rections about something of great importance and secrecy, he took notice that Mr. Moreland, afterward Sir Samuel Moreland, was in the Room, which he had not obferv'd before; and fearing he might have overheard their difcourfe, tho' he pretended to be afleep upon his defk, he drew a poniard, which he always carried under his coat, and was going to difpatch Moreland upon the fpot; if Thurloe had not with great intreaties prevailed with him to defift, affuring him that Moreland had fat up two nights together, and was now certainly faft afleep.

There was not the fmalleft accident that befel king Charles II. in his exile, but he knew it perfectly well; infomuch that having given leave to an Englifh nobleman to travel, upon condition he fhould not fee Charles Stuart; he afked him, at his return, "If he had punctually obeyed his commands?" Which the other affirming he had; Cromwell reply'd, "It's true you did not fee him; for to keep your word with me, you agreed to meet in the dark, the candles being put out for that end." And withal told him all the particulars that paffed in converfation betwixt the king and him at their meeting.

§. 17. That he had fpies about king Charles, was not ftrange: but his intelligence reached the moft fecret tranfactions of other princes, and when the matter was communicated to but very few: of which we have a notable inftance in the bufinefs of Dunkirk. There was an article, as we have obferved, in the treaty between France and the protector, that if Dunkirk came to be taken, it fhould immediately be delivered up to the Englifh; and his ambaffador Lockhart had orders to take poffeffion of it accordingly. When the French army, being joined by the Englifh auxiliaries, was in its march to inveft the town, Cromwell fent one morning for the French ambaffador to Whitehall, and upbraided him publickly for his mafter's defigned breach of promife, in giving

secret

secret orders to the French general to keep possession of Dunkirk, in case it was taken, contrary to the treaty between them. The ambassador protested he knew nothing of the matter, as indeed he did not, and begg'd leave to assure him, that there was no such thing thought of. Upon which Cromwell pulled a paper out of his pocket, " Here, says he, is a copy of the cardinal's order: and I desire you to dispatch immediately an express, to let him know, that I am not to be imposed upon; and that if he deliver not up the keys of the town of Dunkirk to Lockhart within an hour after it should be taken, tell him I'll come in person, and demand them at the gates of Paris." There were but four persons said to be privy to this order, the queen-mother, the cardinal, the marechal de Turenne, and a secretary, whose name, says Wellwood, it is not fit to mention. The cardinal for a long time blamed the queen, as she might possibly have blabb'd it out to some of her women; whereas it was found, after the secretary's death, that he had kept a secret correspondence with Cromwell for several years; and therefore it was not doubted but he had sent him the copy of the order above-mentioned.

The message had its effect; for Dunkirk was put into possession of the English. And to palliate the matter, the duke and marechal Crequy was dispatch'd into England, ambassador extraordinary, to compliment Cromwell, attended with a numerous and splendid train of persons of quality; among whom was a prince of the blood, and Mancini, Mazarine's nephew, who brought a letter from his uncle, to the protector, full of the highest expressions of respect; and assuring his highness, that " being within view of the English shore, nothing but the king's indisposition (who lay then ill of the small-pox at Calais) could have hinder'd him to come over to England, that he might enjoy the honour of waiting upon one of the greatest men that ever was; and whom, next to his master, his greatest ambition was to serve.

serve. But being deprived of so great an happiness, he had sent the person that was nearest to him in blood, to assure him of the profound veneration he had for his person, and how much he was resolved, to the utmost of his power, to cultivate a perpetual amity and friendship betwixt his master and him." *

To

* Four years before this, viz. on the 29th of March 1654, the French ambassador, M. de Bourdeaux, had an audience of his highness in the banquetting-house, Whitehall, with the same state and ceremony, as is wont to be used towards sovereign princes; when he addressed himself thus to him.

" Your most serene highness has already received some principal assurances of the king my master, of his desire to establish a perfect correspondency betwixt his dominions and England. His majesty, this day, gives to your highness some publick demonstration of the same; and his sending his ambassador to your highness, does plainly shew that the esteem which his majesty makes of your highness, and the interest of his people, have more power in his councils than many considerations, that would be of great concernment to a prince less affected with the one and the other. This proceeding, grounded upon such principles, and so different from what is only guided by ambition, renders the amity of the king my master as considerable for its firmness as it's utility; for which reason it is so eminently esteemed and courted by all the greatest princes and potentates of the earth. But his majesty communicates none to any with so much joy and chearfulness, as to those whose virtuous acts and extraordinary merits render them more conspicuously famous than the largeness of their dominions. His majesty is sensible, that all those advantages do wholly reside in your highness; and that the divine providence, after

so

To conclude; it appears from numberless instances, that as no man practised the arts of government with more policy than Cromwell, so he became more formidable, both at home and abroad, than most princes that had ever sat upon the English throne. It was said, that cardinal Mazarine would change countenance whenever he heard him named; so that it passed into a proverb in France, " that he was not so much afraid of the devil, as of Oliver Cromwell." And this authority Cromwell kept up till the last: for after a long chain of successes, he died in the peaceful possession of the sovereign power, tho' disguised under another name; but left it to a son that little resembled him, one that had neither heart nor abilities to keep it. The protector was buried among our kings, * with a royal pomp, and his death

so many calamities, could not deal more favourably with these three nations, nor cause them to forget their past miseries with greater satisfaction, than by submitting them to so just a government. And since it is not sufficient for the compleating of their happiness, to make them enjoy peace at home, because it depends no less on good correspondency with nations abroad; the king my master does not doubt but to find also the same disposition in your highness, which his majesty here expresses in his letters. After so many dispositions expressed both by his majesty and your highness, towards the accommodation of the two nations, there is reason to believe, that their wishes will be soon accomplished. As for me, I have none greater, than to be able to serve the king my master, with the good pleasure and satisfaction of your highness; and that the happiness I have, to tender to your highness the first assurances of his majesty's esteem, may give me occasion, by my services, to merit the honour of your gracious affection."

* The author of the compleat history of England observes,

death condoled by the greatest princes and states in Christendom, in solemn embassies to his son. It has been observed, that as the ides of March were equally
for-

observes, in his notes, that it remains a question, where his body was really buried. "It was, says he, in appearance in Westminster Abbey. Some report it was carried below bridge, and thrown into the Thames. But it is most probable that it was buried in Naseby Field. This account, continues he, is given, as averr'd, and ready to be deposed, if occasion required, by Mr. Barkstead, son to Barkstead the regicide, who was about fifteen years old at the time of Cromwell's death: "That the said Barkstead his father, being lieutenant of the Tower, and a great donfident of Cromwell's, did, among other such confidents, in the time of his illness, desire to know where he would be buried: To which the protector answer'd, "Where he had obtain'd the greatest victory and glory, and as nigh the spot as could be guess'd where the heat of the action was, viz. in the field at Naseby, Com' Northampton." Which accordingly was thus performed. At midnight, soon after his death, the body (being first imbalm'd and wrapt in a leaden coffin) was in a hearse conveyed to the said field, Mr. Barkstead himself attending, by order of his father, close to the hearse. Being come to the field, they found, about the midst of it, a grave dug about nine feet deep, with the green-sod carefully laid on one side, and the mould on the other; in which the coffin being put, the grave was instantly filled up, and the green-sod laid exactly flat upon it; care being taken that the surplus mould should be clean removed. Soon after the like care was taken that the field should be entirely ploughed up, and it was sown three or four years successively with corn." Several other material circumstances, says the fore-mentioned author, the said Mr. Barkstead, (who now frequents Richard's coffee-
house

fortunate and fatal to Julius Cæfar, fo was the third of September to Cromwell : for on that day he won the two great victories of Dunbar and Worcefter, in 1650 and 1651, and on that day 1658, he died.

houfe within Temple-bar) relates, too long to be here inferted.

As to the ftory of his body being funk in the Thames, it was related by a gentlewoman who attended Oliver in his laft ficknefs, as we are told by the author of the hiftory of England during the reigns of the royal houfe of Stuart. She told him, "that the day after the protector's death, it was confulted how to difpofe of his corpfe; when it was concluded, that, confidering the malice of the cavaliers, it was moft certain they would infult the body of their moft dreadful enemy, if ever it fhould be in their power; to prevent which, it was refolv'd to wrap it up in lead, to put it on board a barge, and fink it in the deepeft part of the Thames; which was undertaken and perform'd by two of his near relations, and fome trufty foldiers, the following night." So that, upon the whole, it remains a doubt whether his body was really carried in that pompous funeral proceffion to Weftminfter-Abbey.

CHAP. IX.

CROMWELL's *character, with a parallel between him and king* CHARLES I.

§. 1. THO' every reader will be able, from what has been faid in the preceding chapters, to form to himfelf an idea of the great man who is the fubject of them; yet, as I apprehend

hend it will be expected from me, that I should sum up the contents of all that as been related, and, with the assistance of what has been written on this head by others, deduce from them a sort of sketch-picture; I shall here attempt that most difficult part of my whole work. And since it has been customary, in order to raise our veneration for the royal sufferer, to oppose the character of king Charles I. to that of Cromwell, I shall take the liberty of comparing them, paragraph by paragraph, in such particulars as will admit of comparison.

Cromwell, as to his person, had a manly stern look, and was of an active healthful constitution, able to endure the greatest toil and fatigue. In school acquirements the king seems to have been his superior; and no wonder, since he was not only born the son of a monarch, but such a monarch as picqued himself more upon his great learning than on his good government. However, if king Charles spoke several languages with a good grace, and had a more than ordinary skill in the liberal sciences: it is also certain that Cromwell had knowledge of the Latin and French tongues, and could both speak and write them; that he was very well read in Greek and Roman history, and not only respected, but patronized men of genius and wit, whom he would even take pains to find out. And the same writer, * who tells us that king Charles writ a tolerable hand for a king, but that his sense was strong, and his stile laconick; assures us likewise, that Cromwell writ a tolerable good hand, † and a stile becoming a gentleman.

§. 2.

---

* Wellwood.

† In Mr. Peck's memoirs of Cromwell's life, may be seen a specimen of his hand writing, engraved from a signature of his name to a writ of summons, dated June 6, 1653. Vide title to the translation of the second panegyrick.

§. 2. Cromwell's natural abilities muſt always have been very great; tho' at firſt he diſcovered none of thoſe extraordinary talents that uſe to gain applauſe, and work upon the affections of the hearers and ſtanders by.* His parts ſeemed to be raiſed as he grew into place and authority, as if he had faculties that lay concealed, till he had occaſion to uſe them. When he was to act the part of a great man, he did it without any indecency, notwithſtanding his want of cuſtom. Tho' his ſpeeches were for the moſt part ambiguous, eſpecially in publick meetings, wherein he rather left others to pick out his meaning than told it himſelf; yet at other times he ſufficiently ſhewed he could command his ſtile as there was occaſion, and would deliver himſelf with ſuch energy and ſtrength of expreſſion, that it was commonly ſaid, every word he ſpoke was a thing. In this part of his character king Charles was no way his ſuperior; for tho' his majeſty ſpoke with a good grace, yet when he grew warm

---

* Sir Philip Warwick, his cotemporary, deſcribes Cromwell's firſt appearance in parliament in the following manner. " A gentleman, ſays he, ſpeaking very ordinarily; apparelled in a plain cloth ſuit, made by an ill country taylor: his linnen mean and not very clean: his band unfaſhionable, with a ſpeck or two of blood upon it: his hat without a hatband: his ſword cloſe to his ſide: his countenance ſwoln and reddiſh: his voice ſharp and untunable; and his elocution full of fervor. Defending ſome libels againſt the queen, he was much hearkened to. But he ſoon improved, and ſhewed himſelf another man; and by the help of good cloaths, converſation and ſucceſs, appeared of a great and majeſtick deportment, and of a lofty and comely preſence; towards which he had ſingular advantages from two great maſters, Mr. Pym and Mr. Hampden, who cunningly made uſe of his bold and enterpriſing ſpirit, at a time when he had nothing to loſe, and very much to expect."

warm in difcourfe, he was apt, fays Dr. Wellwood, to ftammer. And as to his behaviour, it was faid of him, that he beftowed favours with a worfe grace than his fon Charles the Second refufed them, and many times obliterated the fenfe of an obligation by the manner of it.

But what was the ftrongeft indication of Cromwell's great abilities, was the knowledge he fhewed of mankind. No man ever dived into the manners and minds of thofe about him with more penetration, nor fooner difcovered their natural talents and tempers than himfelf. If he chanced to hear of a man fit for his purpofe, tho' never fo obfcure, he fent for him and employed him; fuiting the employment to the perfon, and not the perfon to the employment. Upon this maxim in his government, fays one, depended in a great meafure his fuccefs. And what maxim could be nobler than this, and more worthy of a governor? Had king Charles followed it, and not trufted the management of his weightieft affairs to parafites and priefts, the only creatures who engroffed his favour, his advocates would never have had that popular fubject, his martyrdom, to harangue on, nor the ufurpation of Cromwell to complain of *.

§. 3. The piety and virtue of king Charles, with fome people, are inexhauftible themes of declamation. They

* " How this prince comes to be fo extremely popular amongft many of the clergy, and confequently amongft many of the laity, influenced by them, is obvious enough. He was a very great bigot to the church, to ceremonies, and fhew in religion, and to the power and pomp of churchmen. Thefe he cherifhed, and exalted, and furrendered to them almoft the whole fupremacy; and not only fuffered them to enjoy the ufe of it as a prefent from him, but fuffered them to feize it for themfelves, and even to deny his title to it. [See note at the end of §. 5.] For fuch court

Life of OLIVER CROMWELL.　217

They tell us, he was a proteſtant in the ſtricteſt ſenſe, firm to the church of England, conſtant and regular in devotion: that he was never guilty of any exceſs, never regarded any woman but his queen, and could not bear any diſcourſe that was lewd or profane. All this may be granted, without any prejudice to the character of Cromwell; tho' it is a matter of much doubt, if every particular of what is here ſaid be exactly true. For if, as ſome affirm, he was for a middle way between proteſtants and papiſts; or as others, did even compliment the pope by letter with his uſual title, and was willing to reſtore the revenues of the eccleſiaſtics, which had been divided by Henry VIII, among the nobility; I cannot ſee how he can be eſteemed ſo hearty a proteſtant. But who ever doubted of Cromwell's ſincere zeal for proteſtantiſm, againſt the errors of the church of Rome? Did he not give many ſignal inſtances * of it, both at home and abroad? As to his devotion, we have

as

court and favour to them, for humouring them in their perſecution of the puritans, for his glutting them with power, and becoming their creature rather than ſovereign and head of the church, they promoted and conſecrated all the exceſſes, oppreſſions, and lawleſs meaſures of his reign, becauſe all theſe violences were exerciſed over the laity; and the churchmen were ſo far from feeling them, that they ſhared in his domination, and acted the king too in their place and turn. This is the true ſource of ſo much merit and praiſe; for this he is adored and ſainted; for this he has been often compared to Jeſus Chriſt in his ſufferings; and for this the guilt of murdering him has been repreſented as greater than that of crucifying our Bleſſed Saviour." Vide a Layman's ſermon before the ſociety of Lincoln's-Inn, Jan. 30, 1731.

　＊ See thoſe that we have quoted in the VIIIth chapter.

L

as good a proof of his sincerity therein, as we can have of any such matter; I mean, his whole outward deportment. And it is allowed that he was very temperate, sparing in his diet, and tho' he would sometimes drink freely, yet never to excess: that he was moderate in all other pleasures, and after his first reformation, free from all visible immoralities: that he seemed to be a great enemy to vice, and a lover of virtue; always taking care to suppress the former, and to encourage the latter.

King Charles's high opinion of the royal dignity, and the extraordinary qualities he assumed to himself thereupon, could not but hinder him from being an open and chearful companion. Accordingly we are told, that he was of a grave and melancholic disposition. But Cromwell, at the height of his fortune, was very diverting and familiar in conversation, when among his friends; tho' in publick, for decorum sake, he was more reserved. On these familiar occasions he commonly called for tobacco, pipes, and a candle, and would now and then take a pipe himself. But when business came upon the carpet, he would pass from these relaxations to the most serious discourse, and advise with his friends about his weighty and important affairs. Add to this, that he affected, for the most part, a plainness in his clothes; but in them, as well as in his guards and attendants, he appeared with magnificence upon publick occasions. This shews he had a more true taste of real grandeur and majesty, than many who were born to the enjoyment of them.

§. 4. "It cannot be proved, says Rapin, that king Charles excited the Irish rebellion: however, it may be affirmed, it was not against him that the Irish took arms. The papists, both Irish and English, always looked upon this prince as their protector, and were ever ready to assist him*." If so, and consequently it

---

* Vide note at the end of §. 5.

it should be found that the Irish rebellion was not disagreeable to him, with what face can his advocates call him a merciful prince, and accuse Cromwell of cruelty? Can Cromwell be charged with conniving at any single assassination, much less with permitting the massacre of thousands? He was in his temper good-natured and humane, even to his known enemies. He would sometimes be very merry and jocund with some of the nobility; and would then take occasion to tell them, what company they had lately kept, and when and where they had drank the king and the royal family's health; advising them, when they did so again, to do it more privately: and this without the least sign of passion.

We need not deny personal courage to king Charles, in order to prove that Cromwell was braver than he. It was no great compliment therefore that was passed on him by the French minister, when he called the protector the first captain of the age. His courage and conduct in the field were undoubtedly admirable: he had a dignity of soul, which the greatest dangers and difficulties rather animated than discouraged; and his discipline and government of the army, in all respects, was such as might become the most renowned and accomplished general. Nor was it any diminution of this part of his character, that he was wary in his conduct, and that, after he was declared protector, he always wore a coat of mail under his other clothes. Less caution than he made use of, in the place that he possess'd, and surrounded as he was by secret and open enemies, might have deserved the name of negligence.

§. 5. I come now to that part of the parallel, in which king Charles is thought by many to have had much the advantage, I mean sincerity. Cromwell indeed was a great dissembler*: but was he greater than

---

* I cannot help making a quotation here from a modern historian, who has taken much pains to blacken

than the man who deceived him? Muſt not every one who reads his hiſtory, acknowledge with Rapin, that ſincerity was not the favourite virtue of king Charles? He that made frequent uſe of mental reſervations, concealed in ambiguous terms and general expreſſions, whereof he reſerved the explication for a proper place and ſeaſon; he who gave his aſſent to acts of parliament, the moſt ſolemn promiſe a king of England can make, merely in a belief of their being void in themſelves, and conſequently that he was not bound by the engagement; he who courted the parliament's generals, in whoſe power he was, to reſtore him, with a view all the time to deſtroy them, ruin their maſters, and introduce an arbitrary power by right of conqueſt

blacken Cromwell's character, as there appears to be a good deal of truth in his words, mingled up with ſome malice. He tells us, that the uſurper brought about his ends by the moſt exquiſite hypocriſy, and artful management of the ſeveral tribes of bigots and enthuſiaſts under his command. "Other generals, ſays he, by interpreting omens and uncommon accidents, have accompliſhed mighty things; but none ever knew how to work up the paſſions, and apply the wild whimſies of melancholy men to their particular deſigns, like this ſon of diſſimulation and atheiſm. He had well ſtudied the weakneſs and folly peculiar to every ſect, and could direct their rage and fury to the deſtruction of his enemies; and, when it grew dangerous to himſelf, as artfully play them againſt each other. Princes of old ſent to conſult the oracles of diſtant countries; this prodigy of a man was himſelf the ſoldier's oracle; and, if he ſaid heaven approved his purpoſe, they undertook the moſt hazardous enterprize as chearfully as if an angel had promiſed them ſucceſs." Salmon's hiſtory of England, vol. vii. p. 184. It is not my deſign to prove that Cromwell was not a great diſſembler, but that king Charles actually was ſo too See more concerning the king in the extracts, §. 7.

conqueſt over his own people; could he be the honeſteſt, ſincereſt, beſt man in England, as Cromwell once thought him by miſtake, and others, who cannot now be miſtaken, have ſince repreſented him? Was it ſtrange that the parliament ſhould not confide in his promiſes? or that Cromwell, after diſcovering his intentions, ſhould abandon his intereſt, and even endeavour to countermine him in his own way? I cannot help thinking, that Cromwell had never been that finiſhed diſſembler he afterwards appeared, if the king firſt, and afterwards his own party, had not made it neceſſary to his preſervation; which ſeems to be all he once aimed at: but when he had tried the experiment, and found himſelf an over-match both for the one and the other, he purſued the advantage, till he had joſtled royalty firſt, and afterwards the new-fangled commonwealth monſter, out of all authority, and erected monarchy again in his own perſon upon another baſis, under a name that had not yet become obnoxious.

We are told that Cromwell was an enthuſiaſt. But the good ſenſe that appeared in all his actions, publick and private, is a ſufficient teſtimony that enthuſiaſm had not the aſcendant over him. And indeed, notwithſtanding his pretenſions of grace and regeneration, one would be tempted to think that he could have no real reliſh of the doctrines he profeſſed, but only that he ſuited his diſſimulation to all parties and tempers. Mr. Waller, who was his kinſman, frequently waited on him during his protectorſhip; and, as he often declared, obſerved him to be very well read in antient learning; and that his rude cant and ſpiritual ſimplicity were downright affectation. Waller frequently took notice, that in the midſt of their diſcourſe a ſervant has come in, to tell him ſuch and ſuch perſons attended: upon which Cromwell would riſe, and ſtop them, talking at the door, where he could over-hear him ſay, "The Lord will reveal, the Lord will help," and ſeveral ſuch expreſſions; which, when he returned to Mr. Waller, he excuſed, ſaying,

saying, " Cousin Waller, I must talk to these men after their own way;" and would then go on where they left off. This created in Mr. Waller an opinion, that he secretly despised those whom he seemed to court.

But if Cromwell was no enthusiast, it is certain that king Charles was a very great one. Pomp and ceremony, which were then called decency and good order, with the divine right of episcopacy, as well as royalty, had got so thorough a possession of his understanding, that he could see nothing but through the medium of these. So had he been fashioned by Laud, Neile, Wren, Montague, and the other Sacheverels of those times, that if he may in any sense be called a martyr, it was to the pride and ambition of ecclesiasticks, rather than, as is weakly pretended, to the protestant religion, and the church of England *.

§, 6. I

---

* We have an unexceptionable picture of the principal clergy of this reign, from a speech of the excellent lord Falkland, a nobleman who was afterwards slain in the king's service. " It seemed, says he, their work [the bishops] to try how much of a papist might be brought in without popery, and to destroy as much as they could of the gospel, without bringing themselves into danger of being destroyed by the law. Some of them have so industriously laboured to deduce themselves from Rome, that they have given great suspicion, that in gratitude they desire to return thither, or at least to meet it half way. Some have evidently laboured to bring in an English, though not a Roman, popery : I mean, not only the outside and dress of it, but equally absolute, a blind dependence of the people upon the clergy, and of the clergy upon themselves; and have opposed the papacy beyond the sea, that they might settle one beyond the Water [namely, at Lambeth.] Nay, common fame is more than ordinarily false, if none of them have found a way to reconcile the opinions of Rome to the prefer-

ments

§. 6. I shall continue this parallel only in two instances more, which regard the exercise of their authority;

ments of England, and be so absolutely, directly, and cordially papists, that it is all that fifteen hundred pounds a year can do to keep them from confessing it."—He had said just before, "That they had first depressed preaching to their power, and next laboured to make it such, as the harm had not been much if it had been depressed. The most frequent subjects, even in the most secret auditories, being the divine right of bishops and tithes, the sacredness of the clergy, the sacrilege of impropriations, the demolishing of puritanism and property, the building the prerogative at St. Paul's; the introduction of such doctrines, as, admitting them true, the truth would not recompense the scandal; or of such that were so false, that, as Sir Thomas Moore said of the casuists, they served but to inform them how near they might approach to sin, without sinning.

A late author asserts farther, and it seems upon very good ground, "That archbishop Laud was already affecting the title of holiness, and most holy father. The books of papists were licensed by his chaplains, or approved by himself. New books against popery were by him forbid to be printed; some such already printed were called in. The best protestant books of long standing, and formerly published by authority, were not suffered to be reprinted; not even Fox's famous acts and monuments, a common place book to protestants of their sufferings and burnings under queen Mary, and of the popish cruelty then and before. The very Practice of piety, a protestant book, which had gone through six-and-thirty editions, was not permitted to be reprinted. Bishop Wren put this extraordinary article among those of his visitation: " That the churchwardens in every parish in his diocese should enquire whether any persons presumed to talk of religion at their tables, or in their families." It was made one of

thority; and thefe are, their juftice in the adminiftration of affairs at home, and their zeal for the honour of their country abroad. As to the firft, " King Charles, according to his advocate lord Clarendon, was fo great a lover of juftice, that no temptation could difpofe him to a wrongful action, except

the articles againft bifhop Williams, that he had faid, " He did not allow the priefts to jeer, nor to make invectives againft the people." It was another article againft him, " that he had wickedly jefted on St. Martin's hood." And it was another article againft him, " that he had faid, that the people are God's and the king's, and not the priefts' people; though for this he quoted a national council. Poor Gillebrand, an almanack-maker, was profecuted by the archbifhop in the high-commiffion court, for leaving the names of the old popifh faints out of his calendar, and inferting in their room the names of the proteftant martyrs. Bifhop Cofins of Durham caufed three hundred wax-candles to be lighted up in the church on Candlemas-day, in honour of our lady. He forbad any pfalms to be fung before or after the fermon, but, inftead of pfalms, an anthem in praife of the three kings of Colen. He declared in the pulpit, that when our reformers abolifhed the mafs, they took away all good order. He faid that the king had no more power over the church, than the boy that rubbed his horfes heels. For the clergy had then affumed to themfelves the real fupremacy; and as the crown had taken it from the pope, who had ufurped it, they had ufurped it now from the crown, to the difgrace of the king, the fubverfion of the conftitution, and to their own fhame, and even perjury." Vide examination of the facts and reafonings in the bifhop of Chichefter's fermon before the houfe of lords, Jan. 30, 1731. What muft the king be, who could bear all this, and even fuffer himfelf in defence of thefe ufurpations? See note at the end of §. 2. of this chapter.

cept it was so disguised to him, that he believed it to be just." Upon which Rapin has the following remark. "This, says he, may be true, if applied to particular persons: but besides the justice which a king ought to administer impartially to private persons, there is another sort of justice due from him to all his people in general. With respect to this latter, it may justly be doubted, that lord Clarendon's encomium is inconsistent with the project of altering the constitution, and assuming a power which was certainly illegal."

But more than this: methinks we may even question the whole of lord Clarendon's assertion. Could he be so great a lover of justice, who suffered it to be daily perverted, in the most notorious manner, by the star-chamber and high-commission courts? Were levies upon the people without consent of parliament, and arbitrary imprisonments and fines for non-payment; were those, instances of a tender regard for private property, and the liberty of the subject? But perhaps these were the actions that came disguised to him, so as to appear just. If that was the case, he must either have been more ignorant, or more indolent, than became a king. But the imputation of ignorance he removed himself, when he declared, that " he knew the law as well as any private gentleman in England." What then, did he entirely neglect the examination of affairs? did he leave all to his ministers, the Villiers, the Lauds, and the Straffords? will not even this be allowed? Then let those, who can, acquit him of the many illegal acts of sovereignty, that blacken his reign.

I need not take much pains to prove that Cromwell was herein unlike king Charles; since the worst of his enemies call him a lover of justice, without any such saving clause about the disguising of a wrongful action. Cromwell saw and judged for himself; if an action was disguised, he knew how to unmask it, which he certainly did. Whatever arbitrary proceedings he has been charged with, were only in instances where his authority was controverted; which, as things then were, it was neceſſary to have eſtabliſhed, not for his particular ſecurity alone, but in order that the law, in other caſes, might have due courſe.

And if he claims this preeminence in the adminiſtration at home, what ſhall we ſay of the other point, his maintaining the honour of the Engliſh nation in foreign parts? By this, it has been well obſerved, he gratified the temper which is ſo very natural to Engliſhmen. He would often ſay, "that the dignity of the crown was upon the account of the nation, of which the king was only the repreſentative head; and therefore the nation being ſtill the ſame, he would have the ſame reſpect paid to his miniſters as if he had been a king." Was it not an inſtance without example, that in four or five years he ſhould revenge all the inſults committed on his country during a civil war, retrieve the credit that had been gradually ſinking through two long reigns of near fifty years, extend his dominions in remote parts, acquire the real maſtery of the Britiſh channel, and in fine, render himſelf the arbiter of Europe *? Not a ſingle Briton,

in

---

* "England, ſays M. de Voltaire, (ſpeaking of the ſtate of Europe at the beginning of Lewis XIV's reign) which was much more powerful [than Holland] claimed the ſovereignty of the ſeas, and pretended to balance the ſeveral ſtates of Europe. But Charles I. who aſcended the throne in 1625, ſo far from being able to hold the weight of this balance, found the ſcepter dropping from his hand. His deſign was to raiſe his power to ſuch a height in England, as to make it independent on the laws; and to change the religion eſtabliſhed in Scotland. Too obſtinate to deſiſt from his views, and too weak to put them in execution, this kind huſband and tender father, this good man and ill adviſed monarch, engaged in a civil war, which at laſt brought him to a ſcaffold, where, with his crown, he loſt his life.

This

in his time, but could demand reparation, or at leaft revenge, for injuries fuftained, whether from the corfairs of Barbary, France, or Spain *. Not an oppreffed foreigner claimed his protection, but it was immediately and effectually granted. What fhall we compare to this in the reign of king Charles or his father? Was the honour of the flag then afferted? Were we not duped, defpifed, and infulted? How was the elector Palatine protected, though the fon-inlaw of king James? How was the duke of Rohen affifted, in the proteftant war at Rochelle, notwithftanding the folemn engagement of king Charles, under his own hand? But I have done with comparing of perfons between whom there is fo little fhadow of refemblance; and fhall content myfelf with throwing together a few more fuch particulars with regard to each of them, as I find to be the fentiments of thofe who have written of thefe times.

§. 7. To begin with the king. And here I fhall have recourfe to the words of a modern author †, who

This civil war, begun in the minority of Lewis XIV. prevented England for fome time from concerning itfelf with the interefts of its neighbours, whereby that country loft its efteem and felicity. Its trade was interrupted; fo that all other nations imagined England was buried under its own ruins, when on a fudden, it emerged and grew more formidable than ever under the government of Oliver. This man poffeffed himfelf of the fupreme power, by carrying the gofpel in one hand, a fword in the other, and by wearing the vizor of religion; and, during his adminiftration, he veiled the crimes of an ufurper with the qualities of a great king." Effay on the age of Lewis XIV. p. 26. in Englifh.

* Vide the ftory of the quaker in the preceding chapter.

† Examination of the facts and reafonings in the bifhop of Chichefter's fermon, Jan. 30. 1731.

who has drawn his character I am afraid but too juftly, though perhaps with a little more warmth and freedom of expreffion than were abfolutely neceffary. "The violation, fays he, the repeated and continual violation of his coronation oath; his paffing the bill of rights, and owning all thefe rights to be legal and juft, and thence confeffing that he had broken them all; nay, his violating that very bill in all its parts, almoft as foon as he had paffed it, were but ill marks of a heart very upright and fincere. Of all thefe exceffes he was guilty, at a time when his parliament were well difpofed for the honourable fupport of his government, and free from any defign to diftrefs it, much lefs to alter it; nay, were ready to grant him very noble fupplies, if he would but have fuffered juftice to be done upon public traitors, the infamous inftruments of illegal power, and of mutual diftruft between him and his people.——

He actually committed, or attempted to commit, all the enormities, all the acts of ufurpation, committed by the late king James; levied money againft law; levied forces, and obliged his fubjects to maintain them, againft law; raifed a body of foreign forces to deftroy the law, and enflave his people at once; difpenfed with all the laws; filled the prifons with illuftrious patriots, who defended the law, and themfelves by the law; encouraged and rewarded hireling doctors to maintain that his will was above law, nay itfelf the higheft law, and binding upon the confciences of his fubjects, on pain of eternal damnation; and that fuch as refifted his royal will, refifted God, and were guilty of impiety and rebellion. He robbed cities of their charters, the publick of its money and liberty, and treated his free-born fubjects as flaves born only to obey him.

It is faid, that he was not a papift: perhaps he was not; that is, not a fubject to the pope of Rome: but he was bent upon fetting up an hierarchy in England, refembling that of Rome in all its power and terrors. Nor does it avail, if men are to be perfecuted

cuted and oppreffed for their confcience, whether they fuffer from the tyranny of a Hildebrand, a Luther, or a Laud.—It is certain, that of all the diffenters, none but the papifts had any mercy fhewn them, and thefe were in high favour.———

Had he not laid afide parliaments, [fpeaking of the latter part of his reign] laid them afide for twelve years together ? Had he not made it penal even to talk of parliaments ? Nor does it at all appear, that he ever intended to call another, till the diftreffes brought upon him by his wanton conduct, and by the wife advice of the bifhops, (who involved him in a war with his own people for words and forms, and the violent eftablifhment of prelacy in Scotland) forced him to it. Nay, I think it apparent, that he very early meditated to rule like his brother of France; at leaft, that this bad fpirit was infufed into him by his traiterous counfellors, and particularly animated by the bifhops and clergy.———

His judges were public traitors, enemies to their country, the hirelings of power, wretches who fanctified by the name of law, as many of the clergy did by the name of Chrift, the moft complicated wickedneffes under the fun, that of over-turning all laws human and divine, and of enflaving a whole people. It avails not what fufficiency they had in the knowledge of the law, farther than to condemn them; nor does it avail what has been faid to their advantage, fince facts, the moft notorious, contradict it.—Did king James's judges go greater lengths to legitimate lawlefs power and oppreffion ? Amongft them too were able men; they were therefore the more inexcufable. The truth is, both thefe princes feem to have confidered their judges as the machines and champions of ufurpation, as the abandoned inftruments of cancelling law by chicanery.———

As to his declarations and conceffions, [to his laft parliament] to govern for the future by the known laws of the land, and to maintain the juft rights and privileges of parliaments; I have already taken fome notice how much his actions contradicted his declarations.

tions. He had already contradicted, over and over, all his professions to former parliaments: he had manifested such an affection for lawless power, and such a settled intention to introduce it; such a fondness for the promoters of it, and such dislike of all other men and measures; that it was no wonder his last parliament was loth to trust him, and for guarding themselves with all possible securities against a relapse into their former bondage: and I doubt his readiness in his concessions, was no proof of a purpose to observe them. They still remembered how wantonly he had broke his coronation oath, the bill of rights, and all the ties of law; seized their properties, and imprisoned their persons. And all his compliance seemed only the effects of distress, all his other resources having failed him, nor had he recourse to parliament, till violence, and power, and stratagems, and every scheme of support from any other quarter, had miscarried; and he conformed to old ways, when new would no longer do.

This seemed to be the opinion of the parliament, and this the ground of their distrust. They remembered his professions to former parliaments, and how little his actions had corresponded with these professions; how he had insulted parliaments when he thought he could subsist, however lawlessly, without them; how wantonly he had dissolved them; how barbarously he had used their persons after, such dissolution; a dissolution called by lord Clarendon " unreasonable, unskilful, and precipitate." These jealousies possessed the whole parliament, at least a great majority; and some concurring accidents terribly heightened them, * particularly his supposed tampering with the army in the north, and the Irish massacre. Yet amongst all these alarms, there seems not the least view in that assembly to abolish the monarchy, or to introduce a new government. It was composed of many great and able men, who all con-

* See chap. 1. §. 6. and 7.

curred

curred in putting reftraints upon the king, fuch as he might not be able to break through. What events followed no man forefaw, or could forefee. A war enfued, and on both fides there appeared confiderable men.

Yet the great men who adhered to the king, tho' they thought the parliament too violent, feem to have had no confidence in him, that he meant well to the conftitution : and it was probably owing to fuch their diftruft of his humour and defigns, that after the battle of Edge-hill, where he had the advantage on his fide, they did not proceed to London, where he might have had a chance for being mafter. They who gave him good counfel at Oxford, found but cold countenance, and fome of them were difgraced. ——And, if I remember right, it appears even from my lord Clarendon, that the conceffions which he made, proceeded from no purpofe to obferve them.—

As to what has been further offered, in proof of the king's fincerity and good intentions, namely, his Chriftian fortitude at his death; this reafon will [equally] juftify thofe who doomed him to die. Did not the regicides meet death with great intrepidity, fome of them with raptures? Do not almoft all enthufiafts die fo, even the moft criminal and bloody, even traitors and affaffins? I think the goodnefs of his intention had been more clear, had he fairly owned the many grievous iniquities of his reign, his oppreffion and arbitrary rule. But we fee in this, as in other inftances, the great partiality of men to themfelves and their own actions, and how little their opinions ought to weigh in fuch cafes. Cardinal Richelieu, who had done a thoufand acts of violence and injuftice, faw at his death no guilt in any part of his life, efpecially as a minifter."

There need be nothing added to thefe extracts, which fome perhaps may think abundantly too fevere. But if fuch things are true, why fhould they not be fpoken ? Is the name of king Charles fo very facred, that every name elfe muft be afperfed to preferve serve it spotless? Admit but a very small part of what is here said, and ascribe all the rest to partiality and malice; and I doubt there will still be enough to deprive the royal martyr of much of the veneration that is paid to his memory.

§. 8. I now come to my other character, that of Cromwell. We are told by all parties that he had an absolute command over all his passions and affections, so that he could suit his carriage to all companies and occasions; while himself, founding the opinions of others, artfully concealed his own: that he applied himself so industriously to the business of the commonwealth, and discovered such abilities for the managing of it, that his greatest enemies acknowledged he was not unworthy of the government, if his way to it had been just and innocent. In a word, we have this character of him by lord Clarendon, who professedly hated his memory. "He must have had a wonderful understanding in the natures and humours of men, and as great a dexterity in applying them, who, from a private and obscure birth (though of a good family) without interest or estate, alliance or friendship, could raise himself to such a height, and compound and knead such opposite and contradictory tempers, humours, and interests, into a consistence that contributed to his designs, and to their own destruction; whilst himself grew insensibly powerful enough to cut off those by whom he had climbed, in the instant that they projected to demolish their own building."

Though Cromwell was ambitious to a very high degree, yet at the same time he had a passionate regard for the publick good. It is certain he did more things for the honour and advantage of the nation, notwithstanding his own precarious situation, than had been done for whole ages in the preceding times. Some of them were laboured at long before to no effect, and being dropped upon the restoration, have been since resumed, and carried on with great difficulty.

difficulty. To inftance only in two, the union of the three kingdoms and the reformation of the laws. King James had wifhed, from his firft coming to England, to cement an union between South and North Britain: neither he nor his fon could ever accomplifh it; but Cromwell united not only England and Scotland, but brought in Ireland alfo. How many years was it afterwards, and with what expence and labour, that king James's original plan, which was but half fo extenfive as Cromwell's, was firmly eftablifhed? And then as to the laws, he outvied the beft of our kings that had gone before him, and every one fince him till his prefent moft facred majefty. Edward III. permitted pleading in the Englifh tongue, but he went no farther; whereas Cromwell rendered not only the pleadings, but the practice, and even the laws themfelves into Englifh. And what a noble fcheme this was, is manifefted from the refumption of it in our own days.

If Cromwell united three kingdoms in one, he firft conquered two of thofe kingdoms. Ireland had long been reckoned a demefne of the crown of England, but had never been fo fubdued as to render the natives tractable and docile. They were now at open war with the Englifh parliament, and had got poffeffion of all the garrifons but one or two. But Cromwell foon reduced them to obedience, and put them out of a capacity of being ever fo formidable fince. He did the fame by the hardy Scots; and even took their impregnable caftle of Edinburgh, which, they fay, had never before fubmitted to a conqueror. With all thefe extraordinary qualities, and this wonderful feries of fuccefs, need we think it ftrange that he was the admiration of the age in which he lived, and that thofe who hated him moft, even praifed him in their invectives? That Dryden, Waller, Sprat, and other fine poets, who afterwards infulted his memory, in order to pay their court to the rifing fun, found
themfelves

themselves infpired with his praife *, while his actions were freſh on their minds, and could not help
paying that tribute to his remains, which the mufes
never beftow voluntarily † but on the greateft of men,
the heroes and patrons of mankind ?

§. 9. Having mentioned the poets, I cannot in
juftice but take notice that Mr. Abraham Cowley,
the celebrated wit of that age, was fo far from falling in with this panegyrizing humour of his brethren,
that he has written " a difcourfe by way of vifion,
concerning the government of Oliver Cromwell," with
an exprefs view to render his name and memory odious to all pofterity. But if it be confidered, that Mr.
Cowley had altogether as ftrong perfonal reafons, at
leaft in his own opinion, to prejudice him againft the
protector, as Mr. Waller had to engage him in his
intereft, we fhall have juft grounds to fufpect the im-
partiality of the fatirift, as much as that of the enco-
miaft. Waller had been fined and banifhed in the
heat of the civil war, for a confpiracy againft the
parliament, of which he was a member: he was recalled when Cromwell affumed the fupreme power,
and had his eftate, what was left of it, reftored to
him by the protector ‡. Cowley had all along been
a fharer in the diftreffes of the royal family, and fpent
above twelve years in their fervice abroad; and when

* See the collection of poems inferted in the appendix.
† It muft be confeffed that Waller's relation and
obligations to the protector were fuch, that one can
hardly fay whether the incenfe he offered to him was
altogether voluntary or not: but Dryden, Sprat, and
the others, whofe pieces we have annexed to this
book, had no fuch motive; and therefore the remark
continues juft.
‡ See his life, as printed before many editions of
his works.

it was thought fit, by those on whom he depended, that he should come over into England, and, under pretence of privacy and retirement, take occasion here of giving notice of the posture of affairs; he was seized soon after his arrival, being mistaken for another gentleman, and after examination detained, and put under a severe restraint, from which he was not released without giving a thousand pounds bail, which kept him in England a sort of prisoner at large till after Cromwell's death*; a circumstance that, added to his native loyalty to his master, would hardly fail of souring his temper against the government of those times. Tho' in fact, to an unprejudiced person at this day, if the business he came over upon was really discovered at his examination, it rather proves the lenity than the severity of Cromwell's administration, that a man of Mr. Cowley's dangerous genius and firm attachment to the king, and whom it had been found impossible to bring over to the other party, should have his liberty upon such easy terms. But the light in which Mr. Cowley beheld the protector's authority, made every act of power he exerted, tho' ever so tenderly, look like heavy oppression, and most insupportable tyranny.

Yet when I read this gentleman's above-mention'd discourse, (which is couched in the form of a dialogue between the guardian, or rather governing demon of the deceased protector, and the author,) I cannot but think he has put some arguments into the mouth of his evil spirit, that he seems not able satisfactorily to answer afterwards, and that too in those particulars on which he the most strenuously insists. I will give the reader only two paragraphs, with a few short reflections on them.

"What can be more extraordinary, says our imaginary demon, than that a person of mean birth, no

---

* See the life of Mr. Abraham Cowley, written by Dr. Sprat, and prefixed to Mr. Cowley's works.

fortune,

fortune, no eminent qualities of body, which have sometimes, nor of mind, which have often, raised men to the highest dignities, should have the courage to attempt, and the happiness to succeed in, so improbable a design, as the destruction of one of the most antient, and most solid founded monarchies upon earth? That he should have the power or boldness to put his prince and master to an open and infamous death? To banish that numerous and strongly-allied family? To do all this under the name and wages of a parliament? To trample upon them as he pleased, and spurn them out of doors when he grew weary of them? To raise up a new, and unheard of monster out of their ashes? To stifle that in the very infancy, and set up himself above all things that ever were called sovereign in England? To oppress his enemies by arms, and all his friends afterwards by artifice? To serve all parties patiently for a while, and to command them victoriously at last? To over-run each corner of the three nations, and overcome, with equal facility, both the riches of the south, and the poverty of the north? To be feared and courted by all foreign princes, and adopted a brother to the gods of the earth? To call together parliaments with a word of his pen, and scatter them again with the breath of his mouth? To be humbly and daily petitioned, that he would please to be hired, at the rate of two millions a year, to be the master of those who had hired him before to be their servant? To have the estates and lives of three kingdoms as much at his disposal, as was the little inheritance of his father; and to be as noble and liberal in the spending of them? And lastly (for there is no end of all the particulars of his glory) to bequeath all this with one word to his posterity? To die with peace at home, and triumph abroad? To be buried among kings with more than regal solemnity? And to leave a name behind him, not to be extinguished but with the whole world; which, as it is now too little for his praises, so might it have been too for his conquests, if the

short

short line of his human life could have been stretched out to the extent of his immortal designs?"*

I took notice, at the beginning of this review ‡, of the great absurdity of depriving Cromwell of every great and noble quality, and at the same time ascribing to him such actions as none but a great man was ever known to perform. Mr. Cowley, we see, among the other loyal writers of that age, has fallen into this absurdity, and even put it into the mouth of the protector's apologist, as a thing acknowledged by his own party. But needs there any other answer to the postulatum in the first question, than what is contained in that, and all the questions that follow? It lay upon him to prove, that the man who did all the wonderful things he there enumerates, had no extraordinary qualities either of body or mind: otherwise we are not obliged to admit such an improbability on his mere supposition, against all the evidence of facts, that no man attempts to contradict? The whole dispute therefore concerning his merit, must turn at last, I believe, upon his moral qualifications, and not upon his abilities natural or acquired. And the only question then is (and indeed Mr. Cowley's declamation against him hinges chiefly on that point) whether Cromwell was an honest, not whether he was a great man? and how far what he did will admit of a justification? This is the proposition I have had in view throughout the present essay: every reader must judge, according to his own sentiments of government, and the critical situation of those times, how much I have carried it in his favour. For till the points are settled, in what cases, and how far, resistance to the supreme magistrate be lawful; and at what crisis a man may, to prevent confusion, assume that power to himself which he sees to be falling away from others; I cannot see that we have any certainty to determine these matters by Cromwell's sincerity, which I have almost every

* See Cowley's works 12°. p. 585, in vol. II.
‡ Chap. 1. §. 2.

where given up, especially after his breaking off with the king; but this, I think, is done with no more disadvantage to him, than the king himself is stripped of the same virtue, upon evidence equally valid. And allowing him to be defective in this, and that he was a most finished dissembler (if indeed dissimulation were in him properly a defect) I should be glad to know what other qualification, necessary to the forming a great prince, I will not venture to say a good man, appears to be wanting in him.

But I proceed to my other quotation, in which the author makes his demon discuss the question, Whether the protector were a tyrant in the usurpation of power? The passage runs thus:

"I say, that not only he, but no man ever was so, [a tyrant in the usurpation of power;] and that for these reasons. First, because all power belongs only to God, who is the source and fountain of it, as kings are of all honours in their dominions. Princes are but his viceroys in the little provinces of this world; and to some he gives their places for a few years, to some for their lives, and to others (upon ends and deserts best known to himself, or merely for his indisputable good pleasure) he bestows, as it were, leases upon them, and their posterity, for such a date of time as is prefixed in that patent of their destiny, which is not legible to you men below. Neither is it more unlawful for Oliver to succeed Charles in the kingdom of England, when God so disposes of it, than it had been for him to have succeeded the lord Strafford in the lieutenancy of Ireland, if he had been appointed to it by the king then reigning. Men are in both cases obliged to obey him, whom they see actually invested with the authority, by that sovereign from whom he ought to derive it, without disputing or examining the causes, either of the removal of the one, or the preferment of the other. Secondly, because all power is attended either by the election or consent of the people, and that takes away the objection of forcible intrusion; or else by a conquest of them,

them, and that gives such a legal authority as must be wanting in the usurpation of a tyrant: so that either this title is right, and then there are no usurpers, or else it is a wrong one, and then there are none else but usurpers, if you examine the original pretences of the princes of the world. Thirdly, (which, quitting the dispute in general, is a particular justification of his highness) the government of England was totally broken and dissolved, and extinguished by the confusions of a civil war ; so that his highness could not be accused of possessing himself violently of the antient building of the commonwealth, but to have prudently and peaceably built up a new one out of the ruins and ashes of the former : and he who, after a deplorable shipwreck, can with extraordinary industry gather together the disperfed and broken planks and pieces of it, and with no less wonderful art and facility so rejoin them, as to make a new vessel more tight and beautiful than the old one, deserves, no doubt, to have the command of her (even as his highness had) by the desire of the seamen and passengers themselves. And do but consider lastly, (for I omit a multitude of weighty things that might be spoken upon this noble argument) do but consider seriously and impartially with yourself, what admirable parts of wit and prudence, what indefatigable diligence and invincible courage must of necessity have concurred in the person of that man, who on so contemptible beginnings, and thro' so many thousand difficulties, was able not only to make himself the greatest and most absolute monarch of this nation, but to add to it the entire conquest of Ireland and Scotland (which the whole force of the world, joined with the Roman virtue, could never attain to) and to crown all this with illustrious and heroical undertakings, and successes upon all our foreign enemies ; do but, I say, consider this, and you will confess, that his prodigious merits were a better title to imperial dignity, than the blood of an hundred royal progenitors; and will rather lament

that

that he lived not to overcome more nations, than envy him the conqueſt and dominion of theſe." *

I refer the reader to the author's works for his anſwer at large to the foregoing propoſitions, it being too long to be inſerted here; but muſt inform him beforehand, that if he is not prejudiced by notions of abſolute indefeaſible right, I am apt to think he will imagine Mr. Cowley might, upon the main, as well have let this enquiry alone; and that he has ſtated the points of aſſumption and tranſlation of empire a little too ſtrongly on the protector's ſide, unleſs his own arguments had been better founded, and more concluſive.

To make Cromwell the ſole author of all that confuſion, and diſſolution of government, in which he manifeſtly bore only a part, and that in the capacity of a ſervant; but which he ſingly reſtored again at a critical time to his own advantage; and yet to deny him every great endowment, moral and intellectual; nay the very honour of having once ſaid a wiſe and witty thing; 'this is more of the ſame abſurdity that was before exploded, and what might well enough make his antagoniſt "fall a laughing, as the author himſelf expreſſes it, at the ſimplicity of his diſcourſe."†

As to the reſt, there may be much truth in what he advances upon moral and chriſtian principles, and ſomewhat immoral and unchriſtian in a few of the Machiavellian maxims above recited: yet the admitting of all this does not derogate from Cromwell's abilities, nor leſſen the merit of his making a good uſe of power, when he might, without controul, have abuſed it to the vileſt purpoſes.

* Vol. II. p. 594, &c.
† Page 617.

APPENDIX.

APPENDIX.

No. I.

A LETTER of the marquis of Montrofs to king Charles I. delivered during the treaty of Uxbridge, and which was the occafion of breaking off the conferences.

May it pleafe your majefty,

THE laft difpatch I fent your majefty was by my worthy friend, and your majefty's brave fervant, Sir William Rollock, from Kintore, near Aberdeen, dated the 14th of September laft; wherein I acquainted your majefty with the good fuccefs of your arms in this kingdom, and of the battles the juftice of your caufe has won over your obdured rebel fubjects. Since Sir William Rollock went, I have traverfed all the north of Scotland, up to Argyle's country, who durft not ftay my coming, or I fhould have given your majefty a good account of him ere now. But at laft I have met with him yefterday to his coft; of which your gracious majefty be pleafed to receive the following particulars.

After I had laid wafte the whole county of Argyle, and brought off provifions for my army of what could be found, I received information, that Argyle was got together with a confiderable army made up chiefly of his own clan, and vaffals, and tenants, with others of the rebels that joined him; and that he was at Inverlochy, where he expected the earl of Seaforth, and the Sept (family) of the Fraziers, to come up to him with all the forces they could get together. Upon this intelligence I departed out of Argyleshire, and marched thro' Lorn, Glencow, and Aber, till I came to Lockness; my design being to fall upon Argyle, before Seaforth, and the Fraziers could join him. My march was thro' inaccessible mountains, where I could have no guides but cowherds, and they scarce acquainted with a place but six miles from their own habitations. If I had been attacked but with one hundred men in some of these passes, I must have certainly returned back; for it would have been impossible to force my way, most of the passes being so strait, that three men could not march a-breast. I was willing to let the world see, that Argyle was not the man his highland men believed him to be, and that it was not impossible to beat him in his own highlands. The difficultest march of all, was over the Lochaber mountains, which we at last surmounted, and came upon the back of the enemy when they least suspected us, having cut off some scouts we met four miles from Inverlochy. Our van came within view of them about five o'clock in the afternoon, and we made a halt till our rear was got up, which could not be done till eight at night. The rebels took the alarm and stood to their arms, as well as we, all night, which was moon-light, and very clear. There were some few skirmishes between the rebels and us all the night, and with no loss on our side, but one man. By break of day I ordered my men to be ready to fall on upon the first signal; and I understood since by the prisoners, the rebels did the same. A little after the sun was up both armies met, and the rebels fought for some time with great bravery; the prime of the Campbels giving the first onset as men that deserved to fight in a better cause. Our men, having a nobler cause, did wonders, and came immediately to push of pike, and dint of sword, after their first firing. The rebels could not stand it,

but,

but, after some resistance at first, began to run, whom we pursued for nine miles together, making a great slaughter; which I would have hindered, if possible, that I might save your majesty's rebel subjects; for well I know your majesty does not delight in their blood, but in their returning to their duty. There were at least fifteen hundred killed in the battle, and the pursuit; among whom were a great many of the most considerable gentlemen of the name of Campbell, and some of them nearly related to the earl. I have saved and taken prisoners several of them, that have acknowledged to me their fault, and lay all the blame on their chief. Some gentlemen of the low lands, that had behaved themselves bravely in the battle, when they saw all lost, fled into their old castle; and upon their surrender I have treated them honourably, and taken their parole, never to bear arms against your majesty. We have of your majesty's army about two hundred wounded, but I hope few of them dangerously. I can hear but of four killed, and one of them whom I cannot name to your majesty but with grief of mind, Sir Thomas Ogilvy, of whom I wrote to you in my last. He is not yet dead, but they say he cannot possibly live, and we give him over for dead. Your majesty had never a truer servant, nor there never was a braver honester gentleman. For the rest of the particulars of this action, I refer myself to the bearer, Mr. Hay, whom your majesty knows already, and therefore I need not recommend him.

Now, sacred Sir, let me humbly intreat your majesty's pardon, if I presume to write you my poor thoughts and opinion about what I heard by a letter I received from my friends in the south last week, as if your majesty was entering into a treaty with your rebel parliament in England. The success of your arms in Scotland does not more rejoice my heart, than that news from England is like to break it. And whatever comes of me, I will speak my mind freely to your majesty; for it is not mine, but your majesty's interest I seek. When I had the honour of waiting upon your

APPENDIX.

majesty the last, I told you at full length what I fully understood, of the designs of your rebel subjects in both kingdoms; which I had occasion to know, as much as any one whatsoever, being at that time, as they thought, entirely in their interest. Your majesty may remember how much you said you were convinced I was in the right in my opinion of them. I am sure there is nothing fallen out since, to make your majesty change your judgmemt in all those things I laid before your majesty at that time. The more your majesty grants, the more will be asked; and I have too much reason to know, that they will not rest satisfied with less than making your majesty a king of straw. I hope the news I have received about a treaty may be a mistake; and the rather, that the letter wherewith the queen was pleased to honour me, dated the 30th of December, mentions no such thing. Yet I know not what to make of the intelligence I received, since it comes from Sir Robert Spotswood, who writes it with great regret; and it's no wonder, considering that no man living is a more true subject, than he. Forgive me, sacred sovereign, to tell your majesty, that in my poor opinion, it is unworthy of a king to treat with rebel subjects, while they have the sword in their hands. And tho' God forbid I should stint your majesty's mercy, yet I must declare the horror that I am in, when I think of a treaty, while your majesty and they are in a field with two armies; unless they disband, and submit themselves entirely to your majesty's goodness and pardon. As to the state of affairs in this kingdom, the bearer will fully inform your majesty in every particular. And give me leave, with all humility, to assure your majesty, that thro' God's blessing, I am in the fairest way to reduce this kingdom to your majesty's obedience. And if the measures I have concerted with your other loyal subjects fail me not, which they hardly can, I doubt not but before the end of this summer I shall be able to come to your majesty's assistance with a brave army; which, backed with the justice of your majesty's cause, will make the rebels in England,

APPENDIX. 245

England, as well as in Scotland, feel the juft rewards of rebellion. Only give me leave, after I have reduced this country to your majefty's obedience, and conquered from Dan to Beerfheba, to fay to your majefty then, as David's general did to his mafter, "Come thou thyfelf, left this country be called by my name;" for, in all my actions, I am only at your majefty's honour and intereft, as becomes one that is to his laft breath,

May it pleafe your majefty,

Your majefty's moft humble,

moft faithful, and

moft obedient fervant and fubject,

Innerlochy
in Lochaber,
Feb. 3. 1645.   -   MONTROSS.

No. II.

The fubftance of Cromwell's firft conference with the members and officers concerning fettling the nation. Whitelock's memoirs, p. 516, a.

LENTHALL the fpeaker began thus: My lord, this company were very ready to attend your excellency; and the bufinefs you are pleafed to propound to us, is very neceffary to be confidered. God hath given marvellous fuccefs to our forces under your command, and if we do not improve thefe mercies to fome fettlement, fuch as may be to God's honour, and the good of this comonwealth, we fhall be very much blame-worthy.

Harrifon.

Harrison. I think that which my lord general hath propounded, is to advise us to a settlement both of our civil and spiritual liberties, and so that the mercies which the Lord hath given in to us, may not be cast away; how this may be done is the great question.

Whitelock. It is a great question indeed, and not suddenly to be resolved; yet it were pity that a meeting of so many able worthy persons as I see here, should be fruitless. I should humbly offer in the first place, whether it be not requisite to be understood, in what way this settlement is desired, whether of an absolute republick, or with any mixture of monarchy.

General Cromwell. My lord commissioner Whitelock hath put us upon the right point; and indeed it is my meaning, that we should consider, whether a republick, or a mix'd monarchical government will be best to be settled; and if any thing monarchical, then in whom that power shall be placed.

Sir Tho. Widdrington. I think a mix'd monarchical government will be most suitable to the laws and people of this nation; and if any monarchical, I suppose we shall hold it most just to place that power in one of the sons of the late king.

Fleetwood. I think that the question, Whether an absolute republick, or a mix'd monarchy, be best to be settled in this nation, will not be very easy to be determined.

Lord-chief-justice St. John. It will be found that the government of this nation, without something of monarchical power, will be very difficult to be so settled, as not to shake the foundation of our laws, and the liberties of the people.

Lenthall. It will breed a strange confusion to settle a government of this nation, without something of monarchy.

Desborough. I beseech you, my lord, why may not this, as well as other nations, be govern'd in the way of a republick.

Whitelock. The laws of England are so interwoven with the power and practice of monarchy,

that

that to settle a government without something of monarchy in it, would make so great an alteration in the proceedings of our law, that you have scarce time to rectify, nor can we well foresee the inconveniencies which will arise thereby.

Whalley. I do not well understand matters of law; but it seems to me the best way, not to have any thing of monarchical power in the settlement of our government. And if we should resolve upon any, whom have we to pitch upon? The king's eldest son hath been in arms against us, and his second son likewise is our enemy.

Sir Thomas Widdrington. But the late king's third son, the duke of Gloucester, is still among us, and too young to have been in arms against us, or infected with the principles of our enemies.

Whitelock. There may be a day given for the king's eldest son, or for the duke of York his brother, to come in to the parliament; and upon such terms as shall be thought fit, and agreeable both to our civil and spiritual liberties, a settlement may be made with them.

General Cromwell. That will be a business of more than ordinary difficulty: but really, I think, if it may be done with safety, and preservation of our rights, both as Englishmen and as christians, that a settlement with something of monarchical power in it would be very effectual.

※※※※※※※※※※＊※※※※※※※※※

No. III.

A remarkable conference between general Cromwell and Whitelock on the same subject. Whitelock, p. 548. b. & seq.

THE lord-general Cromwell meeting with commissioner Whitelock one evening in the park, saluted him with more than ordinary courtesy, and desired

desired to have some private discourse with him. Whitelock waited on him accordingly, and after some previous discourse, the lord-general proceeded thus: "Your lordship hath observed most truly the inclinations of the officers of the army to particular factions, and to murmurings, that they are not rewarded according to their deserts; and others, who have ventured least, have gained most, and they have neither profit nor preferment, nor place in government, which others hold, who have undergone no hardships nor hazards for the commonwealth; and herein they have too much of truth; yet their insolence is very great, and their influence on the private soldiers works them to the like discontents and murmurings.

Then as for the members of parliament, the army begins to have a strange distaste against them, and I wish their pride, and ambition, and self seeking, ingrossing all places of honour and profit to themselves and their friends, and their daily breaking forth into new and violent parties and factions; their delays of business, and designs to perpetuate themselves, and to continue the power in their own hands; their meddling in private matters between party and party, contrary to the institution of parliaments, and their injustice and partiality in those matters, and the scandalous lives of some of the chief of them; these things, my lord, do give too much ground for people to open their mouths against them, and to dislike them. Nor can they be kept within the bounds of justice, and law or reason, they themselves being the supreme power of the nation, liable to no account to any, nor to be controuled or regulated by any other power, there being none superior, or co-ordinate with them. So that unless there be some authority and power so full and so high, as to restrain and keep things in better order, and that may be a check to these exorbitancies, it will be impossible in human reason to prevent our ruin."

Whitelock answered: "I confess the danger we are in, by these extravagancies and inordinate powers, is more than I doubt is generally apprehended; yet as to that part of it which concerns the foldiery, your excellency's power and commiſſion is ſufficient already to reſtrain and keep them in their due obedience: and bleſſed be God, you have done it hitherto, and I doubt not but by your wiſdom you will be able ſtill to do it. As to the members of parliament, I confeſs the greateſt difficulty lies there, your commiſſion being from them, and they being acknowledged the ſupreme power of the nation, ſubject to no controuls, nor allowing any appeal from them. Yet, I am ſure, your excellency will not look upon them as generally deprav'd: too many of them are much to blame in thoſe things you have mentioned, and many unfit things have paſſed among them; but I hope well of the major part of them, when great matters come to a deciſion."

The lord-general reply'd, "There is little hopes of a good ſettlement to be made by them, really there is not; but a great deal of fear, that they will deſtroy again what the Lord hath done gracioully for them and us. We all forget God, and God will forget us, and give us up to confuſion; and theſe men will help it on, if they be ſuffered to proceed in their ways; ſome courſe muſt be thought on to curb and reſtrain them, or we ſhall be ruined by them."

Upon this Whitelock ſaid, "We ourſelves have acknowledged them the ſupreme power, and taken our commiſſions and authority in the higheſt concernments from them; and how to reſtrain and curb them after this, it will be hard to find out a way for it."

The general then put this ſhort queſtion to Whitelock, "What if a man ſhould take upon him to be king?" Whitelock ſaid, "He thought that the remedy would be worſe than the diſeaſe:" And the general aſking him, "Why he thought ſo," he proceeded; "As to your own perſon, the title of king would be of no advantage, becauſe you have the full kingly power in you already, concerning the militia, as you are general: as to the nomination of civil officers, thofe whom you think fitteft are feldom refufed; and altho' you have no negative vote in the paffing of laws, yet what you diflike will not eafily be carried; and the taxes are already fettled, and in your power to difpofe the money raifed. And as to foreign affairs, tho' the ceremonial application be made to the parliament, yet the expectation of good or bad fuccefs in it, is from your excellency; and particular follicitations of foreign minifters are made to you only. So that I apprehend indeed lefs envy, and danger, and pomp, but not lefs power and real opportunities of doing good in your being general, than would be if you had aflumed the title of king."

Cromwell replied, " I have heard fome of your profeffion obferve, that whoever is actually king by election, the acts done by him are as lawful and juftifiable, as if done by a king, who had the crown by inheritance; and that by an act of parliament in king Henry the feventh's reign, it was fafer for the people to act under a king, let his title be what it will, than under any other power.

Whitelock agreed to the legality, but much doubted the expediency of it; and being afked, " What danger he apprehended in taking this title," he anfwered, " The danger I think would be this: one of the main points of controverfy betwixt us and our adverfaries, is, Whether the government of this nation fhall be eftablifhed in monarchy, or in a free ftate or commonwealth? And moft of our friends have engaged with us, upon the hopes of having the government fettled in a free ftate, and to effect that, have undergone all their hazards and difficulties; they being perfuaded (though I think much miftaken) that under the government of a commonwealth, they fhall enjoy more liberty and right, both as to their fpiritual and civil concernments, than they fhall under monarchy, the preffures and diflike whereof are fo frefh in their memories and fufferings. Now if your excellency fhall take upon you the title of king, this ftate of your caufe will be thereby wholly determined

mined, and monarchy established in your person; and the question will be no more, whether our government shall be by a monarch or by a free state, but, whether Cromwell or Stuart shall be our king and monarch. And that question, wherein before so great parties of the nation were engaged, and which was universal, will by this means become in effect a private controversy only; before it was national, what kind of government we should have; now it will become particular, who shall be our governor, whether of the family of the Stuarts, or of the family of the Cromwells. Thus the state of our controversy being totally changed, all those who were for a commonwealth (and they are a very great and considerable party) having their hopes therein frustrated, will desert you; your hands will be weakened, your interest streightened, and your cause in apparent danger to be ruined."

The general here acknowledged that Whitelock spoke reason, and ask'd him, " What other thing he could propound, that might obviate the present dangers and difficulties, wherein they were all involv'd." Whitelock confess'd, it would be the greatest difficulty to find out such an expedient; but said, he had some things in his private thoughts upon this matter, which he fear'd were not fit or safe for him to communicate. But upon the general's pressing him to dissolve them, and promising there should be no prejudice come to him by any private discourse betwixt them, and assuring him, he should never betray his friend, and that he should take kindly whatever he should offer; Whitelock began thus: " Give me leave then first to consider your excellency's condition. You are invironed with secret enemies. Upon your subduing the publick enemy, the officers of your army account themselves all victors, and to have had an equal share in the conquest with you. The success which God hath given us, hath not a little elated their minds, and many of them are busy, and of turbulent spirits, and are not without their designs how

they

they may difmount your excellency, and fome of themfelves get up into the faddle; how they may bring you down, and fet up themfelves. They want not counfel and encouragement herein, it may be, from fome members of the parliament, who may be jealous of your power and greatnefs, left you fhould grow too high for them, and in time over-mafter them; and they will plot to bring you down firft, or to clip your wings."

The general upon this thanked Whitelock for fo fully confidering his condition: " It is, faid he, a teftimony of your love to me and care of me, and you have rightly confider'd it; and I may fay, without vanity, that in my condition yours is involv'd and all our friends, and thofe that plot my ruin will hardly bear your continuance in any condition worthy of you. Befides this, the caufe itfelf may poffibly receive fome difadvantage, by the ftrugglings and contentions among ourfelves. But what, Sir, are your thoughts for prevention of thofe mifchiefs that hang over our heads?"

Whitelock then proceeded: " Pardon me, Sir, in the next place a little to confider the condition of the king of Scots. This prince being now by your valour, and the fuccefs which God hath given to the parliament, and to the army under your command, reduc'd to a very low condition, both he, and all about him, cannot but be very inclinable to hearken to any terms, whereby their loft hopes may be reviv-ed of his being reftored to the crown, and they to their fortunes and native country. By a private treaty with him you may fecure yourfelf, and your friends, and their fortunes; you may make yourfelf and your pofterity as great and permanent, to all human probability, as ever any fubject was, and provide for your friends: you may put fuch limits to monarchical power, as will fecure our fpiritual and civil liberties, and you may fecure the caufe in which we are all engaged; and this may be effectually done, by having the power of the militia continue in yourfelf, and
whom

APPENDIX. 25

whom you shall agree upon after you. I propound therefore for your excellency to send to the king of Scots, and have a private treaty with him for that purpose."

The general hereupon told him, he thought he had much reason for what he propounded: But, said he, it is a matter of so high importance and difficulty, that it deserves more time of consideration and debate, than is at present allowed us: we shall therefore take a farther time to discourse of it.

Whitelock says, " With this the general broke off, and went to other company, and so into Whitehall, seeming by his countenance and carriage displeased with what I had said. Yet he never objected it against me in any publick meeting afterwards: only his carriage towards me from that time was altered, and his advising with me not so frequent and intimate as before.

No. IV.

IN the instrument of government, subscribed the sixteenth of December 1653, by Cromwell when he was lord protector, it was declared that the members for the future be thus elected, to the end that the kingdom might be more equally represented.

Bedford, county 5, town 1.
Berks, county 5, Abingdon 1, Reading 1.
Bucks, county 5, Buckingham 1, Ailesbury 1, Wic‑ comb 1.
Cambridge, county 4, Isle of Ely 2, Cambridge, town 1, University 1.
Chester, county 4, city 1.
Cornwall, county 8, Launceston 1, Truro 1, Pen‑ ryn 1, Eastlow and Westlow 1.
Cumberland county 2, Carlisle 1.

Derby,

APPENDIX.

Derby, county 4, town 1.
Devon, county 11, Exeter 2, Plymouth 2, Dartmouth, Clifton and Hardernefs 1, Totnefs 1, Tiverton 1, Honiton 1.
Dorfet, county 6, Dorchefter 1, Weymouth and Melcomb-Regis 1, Lyme-Regis 1, Pool 1.
Durham, county 2, city 1.
Effex, county 13, Malden 1, Colchefter 2.
Gloucefter, county 5, city 2, Tewkfbury 1, Cirencefter 1.
Hereford, county 4, city 1, Lempfter 1.
Hertford, county 5, town 1, St. Albans 1.
Huntingdon, county 3, town 1.
Kent, county 11, Canterbury 2, Rochefter 1, Maidftone 1, Dover 1, Sandwich 1, Queenborough 1.
Lancafter, county 4, town 1, Prefton 1, Liverpool 1, Manchefter 1.
Leicefter, county 4, town 2.
Lincoln, county 10, city 2, Bofton 1, Grantham 1, Stamford 1, Great Grimfby 1.
Middlefex, county 4, London 6, Weftminfter 2,
Monmouth, county 3.
Norfolk, county 10, Norwich 2, Lynn 2, Yarmouth 2.
Northampton, county 6, town 1, Peterborough 1.
Nottingham, county 4, town 2.
Northumberland, county 3, Newcaftle 1, Berwick 1.
Oxon, county 5, city 1, univerfity 1, Woodftock 1.
Rutland, county 2.
Salop, county 4, Shrewfbury 2, Bridgenorth 1, Ludlow 1.
Stafford, county 3, town 1, Litchfield 1, Newcaftle 1.
Somerfet, county 11, Briftol 2, Taunton 2, Bath 1, Wells 1, Bridgewater 1.
Southampton, county 8, town 1, Winchefter 1, Portfmouth 1, Wight Ifle 2, Andover 1.
Suffolk, county 10, Ipfwich 2, Bury St. Edmonds 2, Dunwich 1, Sudbury 1.
Surry, county 6, Southwark 2, Guildford 1, Rygate 1.
Suffex, county 9, Chichefter 1, Lewes 1, Eaft-Grimftead 1, Arundel 1, Rye 1.

APPENDIX. 255

Westmoreland, county 2.
Warwick, county 4, town 1, Coventry 2.
Worcester, county 5, city 2.
Wells, county 10, New Sarum 2, Marlborough 1, Devizes 1.
York, West-riding 6, East-riding 4, North-riding 4, city 2, Hull 1, Beverley 1, Scarborough 1, Richmond 1. Leeds 1, Hallifax 1.
Anglesea, county 2.
Brecon, county 2.
Cardigan, county 2.
Caermarthen, county 2.
Denbigh, county 2.
Flint, county 2.
Glamorgan, county 2, Cardiffe 1.
Merioneth, county 1.
Montgomery, county 2.
Pembroke, county 3, Haverford West 1.
Radnor, county 2.

No. II.

A Debate between the committee of the house of commons in 1657, and O. Cromwell, upon the humble petition and advice of the parliament, by which he was desired to assume the title of KING.

ON April the 11th, [according to Whitelock, on the 4th] the protector was attended by the committee, appointed by the parliament, to receive and answer his doubts and scruples relating to their request and advice, that he would assume the title of king; but the protector being unwilling to disclose his own sentiments, till he was informed of the reasons by which the parliament had been determined, the following arguments were offered by the committee, which

which confisted of 100 members; thofe who were deputed to treat on this fubject, being,

 Oliver St. John, lord chief juftice.
 Lord chief juftice Glynne.
 Mr. Whitelock, one of the commiffioners of the treafury.
 Mr. Lifle, } Commiffioners of the great feal.
 Mr. Fines,
 Lord Broghill.
 Sir Charles Wolfeley.
 Sir Richard Onflow.
 Colonel Jones.

N. B. We have taken their arguments in one feries or difcourfe, as they are given by a modern compiler; the whole debate, as it was printed in 1660, being fo tedious and intricate, that it would rather 're than entertain the reader, unlefs he were more-than ordinarily curious to know what was faid on fo unprecedented a fubject.

May it pleafe your highnefs,

IT is with great fatisfaction, that we fee ourfelves deputed by the parliament to confer with your highnefs, upon the fettlement of the publick tranquility, and the eftablifhment of fuch a form of government as may beft promote the great ends for which government was inftituted, for which we have been fo long labouring, and for which we have hazarded our fortunes and our lives. We doubt not of finding your highnefs ready to concur in any lawful meafures, that can contribute to the happinefs of the publick, to the pacification of thofe differences that have fo divided them, and to the perpetuity of that freedom which has been fo dearly purchafed, and fo fuccefsfully defended. And we cannot forbear to inform you that, in our opinion, in the opinion of the parliament, and

of

of the people who are reprefented by it, thefe purpofes cannot be effectually profecuted by your highnefs without affuming not the office only, but the title likewife of king.

Your highnefs may demand why, having already made you protector, invefted you with the office of chief magiftrate, and intrufted you with the care of our liberties, our commerce, and our honour, we are now grown weary of our inftitution, and defire to reftore a title, which a long feries of wicked adminiftraion has made it proper to abrogate? to this we can eafily anfwer, that our requeft is the requeft of the people, the people whofe intereft is chiefly to be confidered, and to whom it is your higheft honour to be a faithful fervant. That they have a right to judge for themfelves, to promote their own happinefs by their own meafures, and to diftinguifh their fervants by what name or titles they fhall judge moft proper, cannot be denied. Monarchy has always been thought by this nation, the moft eligible form of government, and the title of KING has been always confidered by them as effential to it. The office has never been complained of, nor the title changed, even by thofe parliaments that have made the ftricteft enquiries into the defects of our conftitution, and have had power to reform whatever they difliked. The office in general was always regarded as ufeful and neceffary, and the title was reverenced, when the conduct of him that held it was condemned. It is never prudent to make needlefs alterations, becaufe we are already acquainted with all the confequences of known eftablifhments and antient forms; but new methods of adminiftration may produce evils which the moft prudent cannot forefee, nor the moft diligent rectify. But leaft of all are fuch changes to be made as draw after them the neceffity of endlefs alterations, and extend their effects through the whole frame of government.

That the change of the title KING to that of PROTECTOR, or any other, would affect the remoteft links

links of subordination, and alter the whole constitution, is evident, at the most superficial and transient view of the laws and customs of the nation. Every officer of justice acts in the king's name, and by the king's authority, an authority that gives life and efficacy to law, and makes every sentence valid and binding. In all criminal cases the law knows not any prosecutor but the king, nor can inflict any punishment but in his name.

If it be urged, that the judges have already taken their commissions in the name of the lord protector, and supposed his authority and that of the king to be the same, let it be remembred that the judges themselves were far from concurring in their opinions; they whose province is to justify the proceedings of the government to the people, were not satisfied themselves, and even those that complied with least reluctance pleaded rather the resistless force of necessity, than the authority of law or the evidence of reason; and let us not reduce our judges to say, when either the captious or conscientious enquirer shall demand the reasons of their conduct, that they act not as they ought but as they must.

In desiring you to assume this title, the parliament has regard not only to conscience but prudence, not only to the people's happiness but to your safety. The office of protector is new and unheard of till now, and by consequence unknown to the law, nor understood with regard to its relation to other parts of the constitution; so that neither the duties of the protector are known by the people, nor those of the people by the protector: such ignorance and uncertainty can produce nothing but disputes, murmurs, and confusions.

The knowledge of our duty is necessarily previous to the practice of it, and how can any man know his duty to a magistrate to whose authority he is a stranger? The limits of obedience to a protector are settled by no law, nor is there any statute in being that condemns any attempt to shake off his authority. For this reason it is not without long hesitation and
im-

importunate perfuafion, that juries are prevailed upon to affign the name, and fix the guilt of treafon to any confpiracies againft your life or government. The king's authority is fupported by the law, and his perfon is exempt from violation; but the protector's office has no fuch fanction, and his power may therefore be, if not juftly, yet legally refifted; nor is his perfon fecured any otherwife than that of the meaneft fubject.

The protector is indeed, in a ftate of greater difficulty and embarraffment than any other member of the community: he is obliged to obey the laws, but with regard to his office is not protected by them; he is reftrained by the law from any exorbitant exertions of power, but not fupported by it in the due exercife of his authority: thofe who act by the protector's commiffion, can receive from him no other power than fuch as he is invefted with, a power which the laws of the nation, thofe laws which on all occafions every man muft appeal, difavow, and reject. So that no man can be obliged by law to admit the determinations of the courts as obligatory and conclufive; and how great the number is of thofe who deny any moral or confcientious reafon for obedience to the prefent government, your highnefs needs not to be informed. Thefe men, however at prefent fubjected, are at leaft formidable by their multitudes, and it is always more eligible to procure a chearful and willing, than conftrain an involuntary and reluctant obedience. All thefe men allow the authority of regal government, and profefs their willingnefs to fubmit to it; fo that all opinions unite in this point, and all parties concur to make a compliance with this requeft neceffary to your highnefs.

Nor is it only for your own fake that this defire is warmly prefs'd, but for the fecurity of thofe whofe endeavours have contributed to the eftablifhment of the prefent government, or fhall hereafter act by your authority. All thofe who receive commiffions from the king, by whatever means exalted to the throne, are

APPENDIX.

are secured from prosecution and punishment in any change of affairs, by the statute of the eleventh year of Henry the seventh; but the name of protector can confer no such security, and therefore the cautious and vigilant will always decline your service, or prosecute your affairs with diffidence and timidity, even the honest and scrupulous will be fearful of engaging where they have nothing but their own opinion to set in ballance against the law; and the artful and the avaricious, the discontented and the turbulent, will never cease to contrive a revolution by which they may revenge the wrongs that they imagine themselves to have received, and riot in the spoils of their enemies.

The present alienation of the crown of these realms from him who pretends to claim them by his birth, may be compared to a divorce, which may, by the mutual consent of both parties, be set aside. It is therefore necessary, to prevent any future reunion, that the crown be consigned to another.

Were the reasons for your assumption of this title less weighty than they appear, the desire of parliament ought to add to their efficacy. It is not to be conceived that we are able to assign all the arguments that might be formed by the united and concurrent wisdom of so numerous and discerning an assembly, an assembly deputed by the whole people to judge and act for them. The desires of a parliament are never to be considered as sudden starts of imagination, or to be rejected as trivial, or unworthy of consideration: the desire of the parliament, is the voice of the people: nor can it, indeed, be now disregarded, without breaking all the rules of policy, and neglecting the first opportunity of reinstating the nation in tranquillity. The parliament, the only authority which the nation reverences, has now first attempted to establish a legal and settled government, by conferring on your highness the title of KING, which you therefore cannot refuse without encouraging the enemies of our government, by showing not only, that the chief magistrate of the nation bears a title unknown to the law,

law, but even such as is disproved by the parliament, that parliament which himself called.

But the parliament is far from desiring that their authority alone should enforce their desire, for which they have so many and so strong reasons to alledge; nor are their own reasons alone to be considered, but the authority of all former parliaments, who have ever been to the last degree cautious of admitting the least change in any thing that related to the constituent part of our government.

When king James, after his accession to the crown of England, was desirous of changing his title to that of king of Great Britain, the parliament refused to admit any alteration in the regal stile; not that they discovered any apparent ill consequences arising from it, but because they did not know how far it might affect the constitution, nor to what farther alterations it might make way.

In the late parliament, when it was proposed that the name of parliament should be changed to that of representative of the people, the proposal was for the same reason disapproved. " Nolumus leges Angliæ mutari" was a fixed principle of the antient barons, and certainly nothing can shew greater weakness than to change without prospect of advantage. Long prescription is a sufficient argument in favour of a practice against which nothing can be alledged; nor is it sufficient to affirm that the change may be made without inconvenience, for change itself is an evil, and ought to be balanced by some equivalent advantage, and bad consequences may arise, though we do not foresee them.

But the consequences of the change now proposed are neither remote nor doubtful; by substituting the name and office of protector in the place of those of king, we shall immediately alarm the people, we shall awaken the jealousy of the wife, and the fears of the timorous; there will be indeed some reasons for apprehension and suspicion, which designing men will not fail to exaggerate for their own purposes. The first

first question that will naturally arise will be, what is this new office of protector, upon what law is it founded, and what are the limits of his authority? To these enquiries what answer can be returned? Shall it be said that his authority is independent, despotick, and unlimited? Where then is the liberty for which the wisest and best men of this nation has been so long contending? What is the advantage of all our battles and all our victories? If we say that the authority of the protector is bounded by the laws, how shall we prove the assertion? What law shall we be able to cite, by which the duties of the protector to the people, or those of the people to the protector, are marked out.

This then is the great reason upon which the parliament have made their request. The people are to be governed according to the law, and the law acknowledges no supreme magistrate but the KING. It is necessary to the good administration of the state, that the duty both of governors and subjects should be known, limited, and stated, that neither the governors may oppress the people, nor the people rebel against the governors: the parliament therefore desires that the office and title of KING may be restored as they are understood in their whole extent, and in all their relations. Every man is well informed when the king acts in conformity to the law, and when he transgresses the limits of his authority. But of the power of the protector they know nothing, and therefore will suspect every thing: nor indeed can their suspicions be reasonably censured; for till they are informed what are the claims of this new magistrate, how can they know their own rights?

If your highness should injure, or oppress any man, to what law can he appeal? He may, indeed, discover that the king could not have attacked his property, but will never be able to prove that the protector is subject to the same restraint; so that neither your highness is protected by the law when you do right, nor the subject redressed if you should do wrong.

The

The end for which monarchy has been for some time suspended, is the happiness of the people, and this end can only be attained by reviving it. The question may indeed be brought to a short issue, for either the office of protector is the same with that of KING, or something different from it; if it be the same, let us not be so weak as to impose upon ourselves, or so dishonest as to endeavour to deceive others, by rejecting the name while we retain the thing; let not an aversion to an idle sound, to a name reverenced by the people, and approved by the parliament, incite you to reject the petition of the whole nation, to raise difficulties in the distribution of justice, and awaken themselves in the minds of all those who attend more to names than things, who will always be the greatest number, and whose satisfaction ought therefore to be endeavoured by all lawful compliances.

It is a certain truth, that old institutions are, merely because they are old, preferable to new plans, in their nature equally good; because a very small part of mankind judges from any other principles than custom, and it will be long before new titles attract their regard, esteem, and veneration.

But if the office of protector be not only in its denomination, but in nature also, absolutely new, we are then yet in a state of uncertainty, confusion, and misery: we have the bounds of his authority to settle, the rights of parliament to state, all our laws to new-model, and our whole system of government to constitute afresh. An endless and insuperable task, from which we intreat your highness to exempt us, by assuming, according to the advice of parliament, the office and title of KING.

The

The protector having defired fome time to confider the arguments that had been offered, returned on April the 13th (the 7th, as may be collected from White-lock) his anfwer to this effect.

My lord,

THOUGH I am far from imagining myfelf qualified to controvert a queftion of fo great importance, with the learned members of this committee, efpecially as the arguments have been founded chiefly upon the laws and antient conftitution of this nation, with which I have had no opportunity to be well acquainted; yet, fince it may be reafonably required of me either to yield to your reafons, or to affign the difficulties and objections that hinder me from yielding, I fhall attempt to confider and difcufs them diligently and diftinctly.

It has been urged, with great appearance of ftrength, that the title of KING is the only title by which the laws acknowledge the chief magiftrate of this nation; that the title cannot be changed without fuppofing a change in the office; and that a change in the office would be a dangerous innovation, productive of debate, jealoufy, and fufpicion; that the limits of this new-erected authority would be unknown to the people, as being unfettled by the law; that the people are beft pleafed with inftitutions which they have long known; and that therefore it would neither contibute to the publick happinefs, nor to our own fecurity, to obtrude upon the nation titles and offices either new in reality or in appearance.

The apprehenfion that the parliaments have always expreffed of changes and innovations, has been made appear by two remarkable inftances; and to fhew the neceffity of reftoring the title of KING it has been alledged, that not only the dangers and difcontents that novelty produces will be efcaped by it; but that both the chief magiftrate, and thofe that act by his authority,

APPENDIX.

rity, will be more effectually protected by the laws of the nation.

These are the chief arguments that have dwelt upon my memory. Arguments doubtless of force, and such as do not admit of an easy confutation, but which, however, in my opinion, prove rather the expediency than necessity of reviving monarchy under its antient title, and as such I shall consider them; for where absolute inevitable necessity is contended for, the controversy will be very short; absolute necessity will soon appear by the impossibility of shewing any method of avoiding it; and where any expedient may be proposed that may probably produce the same effects, necessity vanishes at once. Very few actions are really necessary; most of them are only expedient, or comparatively preferable to other measures that may be taken. Where there is room for comparisons, there is room for diversity of opinions.

That the title of king is not necessary, how long soever it may have been in use, or what regard soever may have been paid it, is plain from the very nature of language; words have not their import from the natural power of particular combinations of characters, or from the real efficacy of certain sounds, but from the consent of those that use them, and arbitrarily annex certain ideas to them, which might have been signified with equal propriety by any other. Whoever originally distinguished the chief magistrate by the appellation of king, might have assigned him any other denomination, and the power of the people can never be lost or impaired. If that might once have been done, it may be done now; for surely words are of no other value than their significations; and the name of king can have no other use than any other word of the same import.

That the law may be as regularly executed, and as chearfully obey'd, though the name of king be entirely rejected, is, in my opinion, plain, from the experience both of the time in which I have administred the government, and of that when the execution of the laws was intrusted to the (custodes libertatis Angliæ) keepers of the liberty of England, in which justice has been as regularly, as equally, and as expeditiously distributed, as in the happiest days of the most celebrated kings. The judges did, indeed, hesitate for some time about the legality of their commissions, but a short deliberation freed them from their doubts; and certainly their authority ought to be of weight, as they have been excelled by none of their predecessors in learning or abilities.

That I have never interrupted the course of justice, all the judges can attest, and I believe, affirm with equal confidence, that it has not been more obstructed by any other impediment than in former times; so that the title of KING appears by no means necessary to the efficacy of the law.

Such obedience has been paid to the supreme magistracy under two different denominations, neither of which were established by a parliamentary sanction; and why should we imagine any other title would obtain less regard, when confirmed by the power to which the title that you now contend for owes its validity?

There was once a time when every office, and the title annexed to that office, was newly invented and introduced; from what did it derive its legality, and its importance, at its first introduction, but from general consent? The great, the binding, the inviolable law, is the consent of the people: without this nothing is right, and supported by this nothing can be wrong. Antiquity adds nothing to this great sanction, nor can novelty take away its authority. What is now determined by the people, or by their proper representatives, is of equal validity with the earliest institutions; and whether they will be governed by a supreme magistrate under the title of KING, or any other, the government is equally lawful.

As therefore neither reason nor experience can prove, that this title is absolutely essential to the due administration of justice, it is proper to enquire how far it

may

may be convenient, what proportions of advantage or detriment will arise from it. In this inquiry I hope that the honesty of my intentions, and the purity of my heart, will not be mistaken. I hope that neither hypocrisy nor artifice will be imputed to my open declarations, and sincere professions; declarations and professions which I make not hastily and negligently, but with care, reflection, and deliberate caution, in the presence of the Almighty power, by whose providence I have been guided, and in whose presence I stand. I hope it will not be imagined, that I reject the title of KING from fondness for that of protector, a name and an office to which I was far from aspiring, and which I only did not refuse when it was offered me: nor did I then accept it as imagining myself qualified to govern others, who find it sufficiently difficult to regulate my own conduct, nor even from a confidence, that I should be able much to benefit the nation; the only motive by which I was induced to engage in so arduous and invidious an employment, was the desire of obviating those evils which I saw impending over the nation, and to prevent the revival of those disputes in which so much blood had been already shed, and which must inevitably involve us in endless confusion.

Having these prospects before me, I thought it not lawful to reject an opportunity of preventing calamities, even when there was no hope of promoting happiness; I therefore could not but accept, what at the same time I could not ardently desire. For nothing can deserve to be pursued with eagerness and assiduity but the power of doing good, of conferring real and solid benefits upon mankind. And surely, while the only end for which greatness and authority are desired, is publick good, those desires are at least lawful, and perhaps worthy of applause; they are certainly lawful, if he that entertains them has, by a long and diligent examination of his own heart, an examination serious and sincere, without any of those fallacious arts by which the conscience is too frequently deceived, satisfied himself that his ultimate views are not his own honour or interest, but the welfare of mankind, and the promotion of virtue, and that his advancement will contribute to them.

Having informed you by what means I was raised to the protectorship, and for what reasons I accepted it, I may properly proceed to deliver my own sentiments of the office in which I have engaged, that it may appear, from my own notions of my present situation, how little it can be preferred by me, on account of any personal views, to that which the parliament now offers; and that whatever arguments I shall make use of in this question are not dictated by private interest, but by a sincere and unfeigned regard for the happiness of the nation.

I have often considered, with a degree of attention suitable to the importance of the inquiry, what is the nature of my present office, and what is the purpose which I am principally to have in view; and could never attain to any farther determination than that I was the chief constable of the nation, and was intrusted with the care of the publick peace. This trust I have endeavoured faithfully to discharge, and have been so far successful, that peace has never been long interrupted; and whatever miseries have been feared or felt, we have enjoy'd the blessing of quiet; a blessing, in my opinion, too valuable to be hazarded by any unnecessary or inconsiderate innovations, and for the sake of which I think it therefore necessary to decline the title which is now offered me.

This argument will not, perhaps, be immediately understood; nor is it easy for me to make it intelligible without giving an account of some past transactions, too long to be excused but by the importance of the subject.

At the beginning of the late war between the king and parliament, I observed that in all encounters the royalists prevailed, and our men, though superior in number, or other advantages, were shamefully routed, dispersed, and slaughtered; and discoursing upon this
subject

subject with my worthy friend Mr. John Hampden, a name remembered by most of you with reverence, I told him, that this calamity, formidable as it was, admitted, in my opinion, of a remedy, and that by a proper choice of soldiers the state of the war might soon be changed. You are, says I, in comparing our forces with those of the enemy, to regard, in the first place, the difference between their education and habitual sentiments. Our followers are, for the most part, the gleanings of the lowest rank of the people, serving-men discarded, and mechanics without employments, men used to insults and servility from their cradles, without any principles of honour, or incitements to overbalance the sense of immediate danger. Their army is crouded with men whose profession is courage, who have been by their education fortified against cowardice, and have been esteemed throughout their lives in proportion to their bravery. All their officers are men of quality, and their soldiers the sons of gentlemen, men animated by a sense of reputation, who had rather die than support the ignominy of having turned their backs. Can it be supposed, that education has no force, and that principles exert no influence upon actions? Can men that fight only for pay, without any sense of honour from conquest, or disgrace from being overcome, withstand the charge of gentlemen, of men that act upon principles of honour, and confirm themselves and each other in their resolutions by reason and reflection? To motives such as these, what can be opposed by our men that may exalt them to the same degree of gallantry, and animate them with the same contempt of danger and of death? Zeal for religion is the only motive more active and powerful than these, and that is in our power to inculcate. Let us chuse men warm with regard for their religion, men who shall think it an high degree of impiety to fly before the wicked and profane, to forsake the cause of heaven, and prefer safety to truth; and our enemies will quickly be subdued.

This advice was not otherways disapproved than as

difficult

difficult to be put in execution. This difficulty I imagined myself in some degree able to surmount, and applied all my industry to levy such men as were animated with the zeal of religion, and to inflame their fervour: nor did the effect deceive my expectation; for when these men were led to the field, no veterans cou'd stand before them, no obstructions could retard, or danger affright them; and to these men are to be attributed the victories that we have gained, and the peace that we enjoy.

Of this account there may be many uses: it may contribute to confirm us in our perseverance in this cause, that it has hitherto succeeded by the endeavours of good men; it may tend to the confirmation of religious men in their purposes of an holy life, that those principles are more efficacious and powerful than any other: but with regard to the present dispute, I mean only to observe how highly these men are to be valued, how much of our regard they may justly claim, and how weak it would be to alienate them from us by reviving a title which they have been taught to abhor.

It may be urged, that to refuse obedience to lawful authority, under whatsoever name, is not consistent with the character of piety; and that to abhor the title and office of KING, the title lawfully conferred, and the office justly administred, is not so much religion as prejudice, and rather folly than conscience. Nor can I deny either of these assertions; I am far from thinking it lawful to with-hold obedience from lawful government, and freely confess, that to reverence or detest a mere name is equally weak. And I am confident, that those good men of whom I have been speaking, will obey the legislative power, by what title soever exercised; and with regard to their scruples, however unreasonable, it is my opinion, that they who have done and suffered so much, deserve that some indulgence should be shewed, even to their weakness, and that they should not be grieved with imaginary hardships, or perplexed with tormenting scruples without necessity: their readiness to comply with authority is a plea for tenderness and regard,

APPENDIX.

regard, which will contribute to unite their endeavours with ours, for the suppression of those who seem to look upon it as their duty to oppose all government, and whose opinions lead them to imagine all human authority impious and detestable.

The reason for which these men will be offended at the revival of the title and office of KING, a reason which, I confess, has some weight with me, and may, perhaps, more strongly affect weaker minds, if any such there are, is this: We are, indeed, principally to consult the scriptures as the rule of our consciences, but we are likewise to have regard to the visible hand of God, and the dispensations of providence, by which the scripture may be often very clearly and usefully explained: in these explications, indeed, we may easily be deceived; and therefore ought not to depend upon them with a presumptuous degree of confidence, but to use them with caution, modesty, and a careful attention to every circumstance that may rectify our mistakes; but we certainly ought not to pass great events over without reflection, observation, or regard.

When, in conformity to this rule, I consider the late revolution that has happened in this nation, and see that not only the royal family is subdued and exiled, but the name and title eradicated by the providence of God, it appears in me no less than presumption to attempt to restore it. How just these proceedings were with regard to those that transacted them, I am not now to dispute; nor need I say how I would act, were the same circumstances to recur: I only desire you to remember, that neither by me, nor by those who invested me with this authority, was the title abolished, but by the long parliament. It is sufficient for my purpose to remark, that the title was not laid aside by caprice, or accidental disgust, but after ten years war, by long and sober deliberation; and what is this less than the hand of God? When I see that by these instruments of vengeance he has not only expelled the family, but blasted the title; would not an attempt to restore it be like an endeavour to build up Jericho, to defeat the designs of providence, and oppose the great Ruler of the universe?

These are the reasons for which I think the office and title of KING neither necessary nor expedient: whether they ought to convince you I am not able to determine, nor wish they should have any force which their own weight does not give them. In the desire of a firm and settled form of government, the great end for which this proposal is made, I concur with the parliament, and hope that no reasons or resolutions of mine will in the least tend to obstruct it; for a firm and legal establishment, as it is the only method by which happiness and liberty can be secured, is equally the concern of every wise and honest man; and whoever opposes it, deserves nothing less than to be mark'd out as an enemy to his country. I would not wish, that this great design should be frustrated by a compliance with my inclinations; for settlement and order are surely necessary, whether royalty be necessary or not: whatever may contribute to this, I intreat you steadily to pursue: nor should I advise even to deny that gratification to the particular prejudices or passions of private men, that may secure their affections to good for the advancement of it. For my part, could I multiply my person, or dilate my power, I should dedicate myself wholly to this great end, in the prosecution of which I shall implore the blessing of God upon your counsels and endeavours.

On the 13th of April (according to Whitelock), the committee attended the protector, and offered the following reply.

AS the request of the parliament is of too great importance to be either granted or refused without long deliberation, we have thought it necessary to attend your highness a second time, that this great question, after having been on both sides attentively consider'd, may at last be diligently discuss'd, and determin'd with that caution which is always to be used,

where

where the happiness and tranquillity of the public is evidently concern'd.

That the title of KING is not absolutely and physically necessary to government, will be readily admitted; for, if government can subsist an hour, or a day, without it, no man can affirm that it is absolutely necessary. Necessity in this sense has no place in political transactions. Laws themselves are not absolutely necessary; the will of the prince may supply them, and the wisdom and vigilance of a good prince make a people happy without them. Natural necessity allows no room for disputation, being always evident beyond controversy, and powerful beyond resistance. Therefore in all debates of this kind, by necessity, moral necessity is to be understood, which is nothing more than a high degree of expedience, or incontestable reasons of preference.

That the title of KING is in this sense necessary to the government of these nations, may perhaps be proved; but an attempt to prove it seems in the present state of the question superfluous, because the request of the parliament is in itself a reason sufficient to overbalance all that has been urged in opposition to it. And it may therefore rather be requir'd of your highness to prove the necessity of rejecting that title which the whole people of England intreat you to accept.

For nothing less than necessity ought to be put in balance with the desires of the whole people legally represented. But how can such necessity be evinced? Or whence can it arise? That either monarchy, or any other form of government, is contrary to the revealed will of God, cannot be pretended. No kind of government is unlawful in its own nature, nor is any one dignified with a higher degree of the Divine approbation than another: political institutions are like other contracts, in which such stipulations are to be made as the contracting parties shall judge conducive to their happiness, and they must therefore vary according to the various opinions of those that make them: but when made they are all obligatory and inviolable: There is therefore no necessity from the divine commands either of accepting this title, or refusing it; there is nothing in the name of a king either sacred, as some have had the weakness to assert, or profane, as others have imagined with no better reason. The necessity on either side must therefore be accidental, and arise from circumstances and relations. And surely the prescription of many hundred years, the authority of the law, and the approbation of the people, are circumstances that will constitute the highest degree of political necessity.

That monarchy under the title of KING has all the sanction that antiquity can give, is too evident for controversy; but it may perhaps be questioned how far the sanction of antiquity deserves to be regarded. The long continuance of any practice, which might have been altered or disused at pleasure, is at least a proof that no inconveniences have been found to arise from it; and a custom not in itself detrimental becomes every day better established, because the other part of life will be regulated with relation to it, till what was merely arbitrary at first, appears in time essential and indispensable. The nation might doubtless, when government was first instituted here, have chosen any other constitution no less lawfully than that of monarchy; but monarchy, either by deliberation or chance, was established, and the laws have all been made in consequence of that establishment, and so strongly connected with it, that they must stand or fall together. The king is obliged to act in conformity to the laws, and the law can only act by commission from the king. The prerogative of our monarchs, and the authority of our laws, it has been already the task of several ages to regulate and ascertain; a task which must be again begun, if the supreme magistrate has another title.

If it be urged, that this labour may be spared by one general act, declaring the power of the protector the same with that of our former kings, what then have we been

been contending for? A mere name & an empty found! yet a found of such importance as to be preferred to the voice of the whole people. But this certainly will not be propofed, becaufe if fuch an act be public, all muft be immediately convinced, that they are governed as before by a king; and therefore all objections to our antient conftitution remain in their full ftrength.

But indeed the long continuance of monarchy is an irrefragable proof, that in the opinion of the people there have hitherto arifen no lafting or heavy calamities from it, and that therefore nothing can reafonably be feared from reviving it, at leaft nothing equivalent to the difcontent that will be produced by a total alteration of our conftitution, and the apprehenfions which a new power, or new title, muft certainly create; a title of which the import is unknown, and a power of which the limits are unfettled.

Antiquity, which to the wife and inquifitive is often only a proof of general approbation, becomes to the vulgar a foundation for reverence. Inftitutions and cuftoms are long continued becaufe they are good, and are reverenced becaufe they have been long continued. Thus the danger of changing them grows every day greater, as the real ufefulnefs is always the fame, and the accidental efteem of them is always increafing. To fhew how much this regard to antiquity contributes to the good order of the world, and how inevitably it arifes from the prefent ftate of things, is not at prefent requifite; fince experience may convince us of its influence, and the experience of our own times above any other, in which we have almoft every day been changing the form of government, without having been able to fatisfy either ourfelves or the people. Whether any of the fchemes that have been tried, were in themfelves preferable to that of monarchy, it is difficult to determine; but this at leaft is obvious, if they were not preferable, monarchy ought to be reftored; and if they were, there needs no farther proof of the affection of the people to the antient conftitution, fince they would be content with no other, tho' of greater excellence ;

cellence; but, after years spent in fruitlefs experiments, have returned back to monarchy with greater eagernefs.

Nor was the difapprobation of thefe new forms merely popular, but the refult of long deliberation, and careful inquiry, in thofe whofe opinions ought moft to be regarded in queftions of this kind. Some of the judges themfelves, even of thofe whofe learning and integrity are above diftruft, refufed to act by any other commiffion than that of the king; and, as it was obferved in our laft conference, thofe that complied, pleaded no other reafon for their conduct, than neceffity, a reafon which can laft no longer, fince that neceffity is now at an end.

Nor can it be wondered, that thofe whofe lives have been laid out upon the ftudy of the laws, have conceived the ftrongeft ideas of the neceffity of this title; a title fuppofed by the law fo effential to our conftitution, that the ceffation of its influence, even for a few days, might fubvert or endanger it, as the deftruction of one of the elements would throw the natural world into confufion. For this reafon it is a fix'd principle, "That the king never dies," that the regal authority is never extinct, and that there has in effect been no more than one king fince the firft eftablifhment of monarchy. For, during the time that the regal authority fhould be fufpended, the law muft ceafe from its operations; no crime could be punifhed, nor any queftion of property be decided; all power to punifh, and all authority to decide, being derived immediately from the king, whofe office therefore cannot be abrogated: for no authority can be taken away but by a fuperior power, and this nation has never known or acknowledged any power independent on that of the king. The authority of parliament, and the rights of the people, can boaft no deeper foundation, or ftronger eftablifhment. The power of parliament has no efficacy, but as it co-operates with that of the king, nor can one deftroy the other without a general diffolution of our government: thefe two concurrent powers are

the

APPENDIX.

the essential parts of our constitution, which, when either of them shall cease, is equally destroyed.

These considerations are surely sufficient to vindicate the judges, whom it would be to the last degree unreasonable to blame, for their steady adherence to the laws, which it is the business of their office to maintain; but it is not to be imagined, that the same motives influenced the bulk of the people to this general desire, which was so apparently prevalent throughout the nation. General effects must have general causes, and nothing can influence the whole nation to demand the restoration of monarchy, but universal experience of the evils produced by rejecting it; evils too evident to be concealed, and too heavy to be borne. One of these, and perhaps not the least, is the interruption of justice, which has not been administred but by the assistance of the army, the last expedient that ought to be made use of.

That the laws did not lose more of their authority, and justice was not more evaded, is indeed not to be ascribed to the forms of government which these years of distraction have produced, but to the care, integrity, and reputation of those men in whose hands the great offices were placed: who were reverenced by the people on account of their own characters, rather than from any regard to the powers by whom they were commissioned; powers which yesterday produced, and which were expected to perish to-morrow. For every title, except that of KING, which antiquity had made venerable, is considered only as the issue of momentary caprice, and subject to be changed by the inconstancy that erected it, as soon as any inconvenience shall be discovered to arise from it; because what is raised by one act of parliament, may, by another, be destroyed, and such alterations it is reasonable to expect: for as no form of government is without its defects, while it remains part of every man's right to propose a new scheme, which he will always think more beneficial than any other, every man that has any real or fansied amendments to offer, will be impatient till

they

they have been try'd, and will endeavour to facilitate the reception of them, by exaggerating the difadvantages of the prefent plan, and heightening the difcontents that arife from them. Thus fhall we go on from change to change, from expedient to expedient. Thus fhall we attempt to remove one evil by introducing another, and gain nothing by all our fatigues, perplexities, and fufferings, but new conviction of the neceffity of complying with the laws and the people.

It is indeed no great proof of regard to the nation, to deny any legal requeft: perhaps more may be faid, without the leaft deviation from truth and juftice. The people, for whofe fake only government is conftituted, have a right to fettle the forms of it, and this petition is only an exertion of that natural privilege which cannot be forfeited. All government muft derive its legality either from the choice of the people by whom it was eftablifhed, or from their confent after its inftitution: the prefent government was erected without their concurrence; and it is to be inquired, whether it be not now diffolved by their petition to diffolve it.

But whether this petition may be lawfully refufed or not, prudence at leaft requires that it be complied with; for it is abfolutely neceffary to the happinefs of any adminiftration, that the people love and efteem their governors. The fupreme magiftrate muft therefore affume the title of KING, for no title that has not the fanction of the parliament, and is therefore fubject to an immediate change, can be equally reverenced with that which has been eftablifhed by the approbation of many generations, the authority of many parliaments, and which the experience of the whole nation has proved to be without thofe dangers that may be juftly fufpected in any new inftitution, which can never be confider'd in its whole extent, or purfued to all its confequences.

Nor can the nation in this demand be charged with inconftancy in their refolutions, or inconfiftency in their conduct: for that the war was begun not againft

the

the office of king, but againſt the perſon of him who was then inveſted with it, and diſcharged it in a manner contrary to the intention for which he was intruſted with it, is apparent from four declarations of parliament; nor is it leſs known that the firſt breach of unanimity amongſt the friends of liberty was produced by the abolition of this title, and may therefore be probably repaired by the revival of it.

If it be urged, that the queſtion, which relates only to a name, be trifling and unimportant; it may be replied, that the leſs is demanded, the greater contempt is ſhewn by a refuſal. That titles are more than empty ſounds, may be proved not only from the preſent diſpute, but from the antient conſtitutions, and the determination of former parliaments, by which the title of KING was declared eſſential to the conſtitution, in the reigns of Edward IV. and Henry VII. and yet a ſtronger proof of regard to titles, was given by the parliament of Henry VIII. in which it was enacted, that the title of lord of Ireland ſhould be changed to that of king, that the difficulties ariſing from the ambiguity of the title might be removed. Even the late convention, called together without the election or concurrence of the people, found the prejudice ariſing from mere titles of ſo great force, that they were obliged to aſſume the name of a parliament, that their determinations might eſcape contempt.

Thus the requeſt of the parliament, appears not only reaſonable, but neceſſary; not only conſiſtent with the preſent diſpoſition of the people, but conformable to the ſentiments of all former acts: and certainly nothing ſhould produce a refuſal of ſuch a requeſt, except the impoſſibility of granting it.

But the objections raiſed by your highneſs ſeem very far from implying any neceſſity of declining the title ſo unanimouſly offer'd you, and ſo earneſtly preſſed upon you, being founded upon ſuppoſitions merely conjectural. For your firſt aſſertion, that the office does not neceſſarily require the ſame title, has been already conſidered; and it has been ſhewn, that there can be no reason in altering the title, if the power be the same; and that the supreme magistrate cannot be invested with new powers without endless confusion, and incredible jealousies. It is therefore of no great force to object, that many good men will be dissatisfied with the revival of the title: for tho' it must be granted, that those who have assisted us in shaking off oppression, have a claim to our gratitude; and that piety, tho' erroneous, deserves indulgence; yet both gratitude and indulgence ought to be limited by reason. In things indifferent, considerations of tenderness and respect may turn the balance; but we have not a right to consult the satisfaction of a few, however great their merits may have been, at the expence of the public tranquility, and the happiness of succeeding generations. The satisfaction of particulars may be endeavoured by particular provision; but if, in questions of universal importance, we have regard to any thing but universal good, and the great laws of reason and justice, we shall be tossed in endless uncertainty. " He that observeth the wind shall never sow, and he that regardeth the clouds shall never reap." He that attends to mutable circumstances, and waits till nothing shall oppose his intention, shall design for ever without execution. When are we to hope for settlement, if general unanimity must introduce it? Whatever shall be determined, multitudes will still remain dissatisfied, because mens opinions will always be various. It was not with universal approbation that the title of protector was assumed, or that any change has hitherto been made; but since some discontent will always be found, whatever measures shall be taken, let not the satisfaction of private men be preferr'd to that of the parliament, to the determination of which all good men will readily submit.

Still less weight has the objection drawn by your highness from the visible dispensation of providence, of which we know too little to direct our actions by them, in opposition to evident reason, to certain facts, and revealed precepts; lights which we always are commanded

manded to ufe, and of which the two firſt can feldom, and the laſt never deceive us. If we confider this poſition, that becaufe providence has once blaſted the title of KING, or fuffer'd it to be blaſted, it is therefore never to be revived, it will foon appear, that we cannot admit it in its whole extent, and purfue it through all its confequences, without involving ourfelves in endlefs difficulties, and condemning our own conduct.

If providence hath blaſted the office of KING, how can it be proved, that the fupreme power, in any fingle head, under whatfoever title, even the power which you now poffefs, is not equally interdicted? The acts of parliament extend equally to all titles, and declare againſt monarchy under every name.

But the confequences of this propofition do not terminate in this inconfiſtency of conduct, but extend equally to every determination; for if what has been once deſtroyed by providence be for ever after interdicted, what will remain of which the ufe is lawful? what is there of which we have not at fome time been deprived by providence, or which providence has not at fome time made the inſtrument of our punifhment? May not the diffolution of the long parliament be interpreted as a blaſt from heaven with equal juſtice, and the people be reprefented no more? But in reality, the proceedings of providence are not intended as the rules of action; we are left to govern our own lives by virtue and by prudence. When a form of government is deſtroyed, for juſt reafons it is blaſted by providence, and lofes its efficacy; when with equal reafons it is reſtored, then providence again fmiles upon it, and the fanction of heaven renews its validity. If royalty was deſtroyed by Providence, who can deny, that the fame Providence directs it to be revived? Is not the refolution of the parliament equally a proof on either fide? or have we any arguments to prove, that the people co-operate with Providence lefs when they require than when they reject a KING? Let us wave fuch inconclufive arguments, and dubious conjectures; and guide ourfelves by the ſteady light of religion,

reafon,

reason, and experience. That a juſt demand is not to be refuſed, religion will inform us: reaſon will teach us, that the magiſtrate is to conform to the laws, and not the laws yield to the magiſtrate; and the experience of many ages may inſtruct us, that the king has nothing to fear from compliance with the parliament. At leaſt if any danger ſhould ariſe from the meaſures now propoſed, it will ariſe from the performance, not neglect of our duty; and we may therefore encounter it with that reſolution which a conſciouſneſs of the approbation of God ought to inſpire.

The PROTECTOR's final Anſwer.

N. B. This diſcourſe is in many parts remarkably obſcure, as well from the negligence and ignorance of the copiers and printers, as from frequent alluſions to occurrences known to the perſons with whom Cromwell was conferring, but not mentioned in any hiſtory which it is now in our power to conſult: we have therefore collected ſuch of the arguments as we can apprehend the full meaning of, and have omitted ſome unintelligible paſſages, and others which related to other articles in the petition.

On the 26th of April (and in another conference May 11.), the protector made the following reply:

My Lords,

HAVING ſeriouſly reflected on the demand of the parliament, and the learned arguments produced by the committee to ſupport it, I think it unreaſonable any longer to delay ſuch a reply as it is in my power to make, becauſe it is both due to the great body by whom you are deputed, and neceſſary to the diſpatch of public affairs, which ſeem to be entirely ſuſpended.

APPENDIX. 283

suspended, and to wait for the decision of this question; a question which I cannot yet think of so much importance as it is represented and conceived.

The arguments produced in the last conference I shall not waste time in repeating, because they were little different from those formerly produced; only graced with new decorations, and enforced with some new instances. With respect to the chief reason, the known nature of the title of KING, the fix'd and stated bound of the authority imply'd by it, its propriety with regard to the laws, and the veneration paid to it by the people, I have nothing to add, nor think any thing necessary beyond what I have already offered. I am convinced, that your authority is sufficient to give validity to any administration, and to add dignity to any title, without the concurrence of antient forms, or the sanction of hereditary prejudices.

All government intends the good of the people, and that government is therefore best by which their good may be most effectually promoted: we are therefore, in establishing the chief magistracy of these kingdoms, chiefly to inquire, what form or what title will be most willingly admitted; and this discovery being once made, it will easily be established by a single act of parliament, concurring with the general desire of the people.

It may indeed be urged, that in rejecting the title of KING I deny the request of the parliament, and treat the representatives of the people with a degree of disregard which no king of England ever discover'd. But let it be consider'd how much my state differs from that of a legal king, claiming the crown by inheritance, or exalted to supreme authority by the parliament, and governing by fix'd laws in a settled establishment. I hold the supreme power by no other title than that of necessity. I assumed the authority with which I stand·invested, at a time when immediate ruin was falling down upon us, which no other man durst attempt to prevent; when opposite factions were rushing into war, because no man durst interpose, and command

mand peace. What were the dangers that threaten'd us, and upon what principles the factious and disobedient attempted to interrupt the public tranquillity, it may not be at this time improper to explain.

The parliament, which had so vigoroufly withstood the encroachments of the regal power, became themselves too desirous of absolute authority; and not only engrofs'd the legiflative, but ufurp'd the executive power. All caufes civil and criminal, all queftions of property and right, were determin'd by commitees; who, being themfelves the legiflature, were accountable to no law; and for that reafon their decrees were arbitrary, and their proceedings violent; oppreffion was without redrefs, and unjuft fentence without appeal. All the bufinefs of all the courts of Weftminfter was tranfacted in this manner; and the hardfhips were ftill more lamented, becaufe there was no profpect of either end or intermiffion. For the parliament was fo far from intending to refign this unlimited authority, that they had formed a refolution of perpetuating their tyranny; and, apprehending no poffibility of a diffolution by any other power, determin'd never to diffolve themfelves.

Such and fo oppreffive was the government plann'd out to us, and for our pofterity; and under thefe calamities muft we ftill have languifh'd, had not the fame army which reprefs'd the infolence of monarchy, relieved us with the fame fpirit from the tyranny of a perpetual parliament, a tyranny which was equally illegal and oppreffive.

When, after their dangers and labours, their battles and their wounds, they had leifure to obferve the government which they had eftablifhed at fo much expence, they foon perceived, that unlefs they made one regulation more, and crufh'd this many-headed tyranny, they had hitherto ventured their lives to little purpofe, and had, inftead of afferting their own and the people's liberty, only changed one kind of flavery for another.

They therefore diffolved the parliament, which would

would never have diſſolv'd itſelf; and that the nation might not fall into its former ſtate of confuſion, intreated me to aſſume the ſupreme authority, under the title of PROTECTOR; a title which implies not any legal power of governing in my own right, but a truſt conſign'd to me for the advantage of another: this truſt I have faithfully diſcharged, and, whenever the means of ſettling the public ſhall be found, am ready to give an account of it, and reſign it.

The neceſſity which compelled me to accept it, was, indeed, not wholly produced by the illegal reſolutions of the parliament, but was much heighten'd by the ungovernable fury of wild fanatics, and tumultuous factions, who, to eſtabliſh their new ſchemes, would have ſpread ſlaughter and deſolation thro' the kingdom, and ſpared nothing, however cruel or unjuſt, that might have propagated their own opinions.

Of theſe, ſome were for abrogating all our ſtatutes, and aboliſhing all our cuſtoms, and introducing the judicial law of Moſes as the only rule of judgment, and ſtandard of equity. Of this law every man was to be his own interpreter, and conſequently was allowed to judge according to his paſſions, prejudices, or ignorance, without appeal. Every man was then to commence legiſlator: for to make laws, and to interpret them for his own uſe, is nearly the ſame.

Another ſet of men there was, who were yet more profeſſedly for inveſting every man with the power of determining his own claims, and judging of his own actions; for, it was among them a principle fix'd and uncontrovertible, that all magiſtracy was forbidden by God, and therefore unlawful and deteſtable.

It is unneceſſary to ſay what muſt have been the ſtate of a nation, in which either of theſe parties had exalted themſelves to power, and how uſefully that man was employed, who, ſtepping on a ſudden into the ſtate of dominion, had ſpirit to controul, and power to ſuppreſs them.

The reproaches thrown upon my conduct by the ignorant or ill-affected, I ſometimes hear, but with the neglect

neglect and scorn which they deserve; I am acquitted by my own conscience, and I hope by the best and wisest men. I am convinc'd, that I was called by Providence to the power which I possess, and know that I desire it no longer than is necessary for the preservation of peace, and the security of liberty, that liberty which I have never violated, and that peace, which amidst murmurs and discontents, threats and complaints, I have yet never suffer'd to be broken. That I aspire to unlimited authority, and therefore assume a title unknown to the nation, is a reproach easily cast, and as easily contemned: my power has been the offspring of necessity, and its extent has been bounded only by the occasions of exerting it. If a settlement is now proposed, and previously to it, a legal establishment of my authority, it may be limited by you. Under whatever title it shall be conferred upon me, that title will then be valid, and those limitations cannot be transgress'd.

May 11.] With regard to the particular TITLE which you have so warmly recommended to me, I cannot yet prevail upon myself to accept it. When I consider your arguments, I cannot find them inevitably conclusive: and when I examine my own conscience in solitude, I find it yet unsatisfied. The desire of parliament is indeed a powerful motive, but the desire of parliament cannot alter the nature of things: it may determine me, in things indifferent, to chuse one rather than another; but it cannot make those actions lawful which God has forbidden, nor oblige me to do what, though perhaps lawful in itself, is not lawful in my private judgment.

Upon the calmest reflection, I am convinced, that I cannot without a crime comply with their demand; and therefore, as I am far from believing, that those who sit for no other end than to preserve the liberty of the nation, can design any infraction of mine, I declare that I cannot undertake the administration of the government under the title of KING.

APPENDIX.

No. VI.

POEMS on OLIVER CROMWELL, by Mr. Waller, Mr. Dryden, Mr. Sprat, Mr. Locke, &c.

I. A PANEGYRIC to OLIVER CROMWELL, lord protector. Of the present greatness, and joint-interest of his highness, and this nation.

By Edmund Waller, Esq; in the year 1654.

WHILE with a strong, and yet a gentle hand,
  You bridle faction, and our hearts command;
Protect us from ourselves, and from the foe;
Make us unite, and make us conquer too;
Let partial spirits still aloud complain;
Think themselves injur'd, that they cannot reign;
And own no liberty, but where they may,
Without controul, upon their fellows prey.
 Above the waves as Neptune shew'd his face,
To chide the winds, and save the Trojan race;
So has your highness (rais'd above the rest)
Storms of ambition tossing us represt.
Your drooping country, torn by civil hate,
Restor'd by you, is made a glorious state;
The seat of empire, where the Irish come,
And the unwilling Scot, to fetch his doom.
The sea's our own, and now all nations greet,
With bending sails, each vessel of our fleet.
Your pow'r resounds, as far as winds can blow,
Or swelling sails upon the globe may go.
 Heav'n, that has plac'd this island to give law,
To balance Europe, and her states to awe,
In this conjunction does on Britain smile,
The greatest leader to the greatest isle.

          Whether

APPENDIX.

Whether this portion of the world were rent
By the wide ocean from the continent,
Or thus created; it was sure design'd
To be the sacred refuge of mankind.
Hither th' oppressed shall henceforth resort,
Justice to crave, and succour, of your court;
And shew your highness, not for ours alone,
But for the world's protector shall be known.
    Fame swifter than your winged navy flies
Thro' ev'ry land that near the ocean lies,
Sounding your name, and telling dreadful news
To all that piracy and rapine use.
With such a chief the meanest nation blest,
Might hope to lift her head above the rest:
What may be thought impossible to do
For us embraced by the sea and you?
    Lords of the world's great waste, the ocean, we
Whole forests send to reign upon the sea;
And ev'ry coast may trouble and relieve,
But none can visit us without your leave.
Angels and we have this prerogative,
That none can at our happy seat arrive;
While we descend at pleasure, to invade
The bad with vengeance, or the good to aid.
    Our little world, the image of the great,
Like that, amidst the boundless ocean set,
Of her own growth has all that nature craves,
And all that's rare, as tribute from the waves.
As Egypt does not on the clouds rely,
But to the Nile owes more than to the sky:
So what our heav'n, or what our earth denies,
Our ever constant friend the sea supplies.
The taste of hot Arabia's spice we know,
Free from the scorching sun that makes it grow:
Without the worm in Persian silks we shine,
And without planting, drink of ev'ry vine.
To dig for wealth we weary not our limbs;
Gold, tho' the heaviest metal, hither swims.
Ours is the harvest where the Indians mow;
We plough the deep, and reap what others sow.

Things

APPENDIX.

Things of the nobleſt kind our own ſoil breeds;
Stout are our men, and warlike are our ſteeds:
Rome, tho' her eagle thro' the world had flown,
Could never make this iſland all her own.
Here the third Edward, and the Black Prince too,
France-conqu'ring Henry flouriſh'd, and now You;
For whom we ſtay'd, as did the Grecian ſtate,
'Till Alexander came to urge their fate.

When for more worlds that Macedonian cry'd,
He wiſt not Thetis in her lap did hide
Another yet, a world reſerv'd for you,
To make more great than that he did ſubdue.
He ſafely might old troops to battle lead
Againſt th' unwarlike Perſian, or the Mede,
Whoſe haſty flight did from a bloodleſs field
More ſpoil than honour to the victor yield.
A race unconquer'd, by their clime made bold,
The Caledonians, arm'd with want and cold,
Have, by a fate indulgent to your fame,
Been from all ages kept for you to tame.
Whom the old Roman wall ſo ill confin'd,
With a new chain of garriſons you bind:
Here foreign gold no more ſhall make them come,
Our Engliſh iron holds them faſt at home.

They that henceforth muſt be content to know
No warmer regions than their hills of ſnow,
May blame the ſun, but muſt extol your grace,
Which in our ſenate hath allow'd them place.
Preferr'd by conqueſt, happily o'erthrown,
Falling they riſe, to be with us made one:
So kind dictators made, when they came home,
Their vanquiſh'd foes free citizens of Rome.

Like favour find the Iriſh with like fate
Advanc'd to be a portion of our ſtate;
While by your valour, and your bounteous mind,
Nations, divided by the ſea, are join'd.

Holland, to gain your friendſhip, is content
To be our out-guard on the continent:
She from her fellow-provinces would go,
Rather than hazard to have you her foe,

O In

In our late fight, when cannons did diffuse,
Preventing posts, the terror of the news,
Our neighbour princes trembled at their roar;
But our conjunction makes them tremble more.
    Your never-failing sword made war to cease,
And now you heal us with the arts of peace;
Our minds with bounty and with awe engage,
Unite affections, and restrain our rage.
Less pleasure take brave minds in battle won,
Than in restoring such as are undone:
Tygers have courage, and the rugged bear;
But man alone can whom he conquers spare.
To pardon willing, and to punish loth,
You strike with one hand, but you heal with both:
Lifting up all that prostrate lie, you grieve
You cannot make the dead again to live.
    When fate or error had our age misled,
And o'er these nations such confusion spread,
The only cure which could from heav'n come down,
Was so much pow'r and clemency in one:
One, whose extraction from an antient line,
Gives hope again, that well-born men may shine:
The meanest, in your nature mild and good,
The noble rest secured in your blood.
    Oft have we wonder'd, how you hid in peace
A mind proportion'd to such things as these:
How such a ruling spirit could restrain,
And practise first over yourself to reign.
Your private life did a just pattern give,
How fathers, husbands, pious sons should live:
Born to command, your princely virtues slept
Like humble David's, whilst the flock he kept.
But when your troubled country call'd you forth,
Your flaming courage, and your matchless worth,
Dazling the eyes of all that did pretend,
To fierce contention gave a prosp'rous end.
Still as you rise, the state, exalted too,
Finds no distemper while it's chang'd by you;
Chang'd like the world's great scene, when without noise
The rising sun night's vulgar lights destroys.

                                      Had

APPENDIX.

Had you some ages past this race of glory
Run, with amazement we should read your story:
But living virtue, all atchievements past,
Meets envy still to grapple with at last.
This Cæsar found; and that ungrateful age,
With losing him, fell back to blood and rage,
Mistaken Brutus thought to break their yoke,
But cut the bond of union at that stroke.
That sun once set, a thousand meaner stars
Give a dim light to violence and wars;
To such a tempest as now threatens all,
Did not your mighty arm prevent the fall.

If Rome's great senate could not wield the sword,
Which of the conquer'd world has made them lord;
What hope had ours, while yet their pow'r was new,
To rule victorious armies, but by you?
You, who had taught them to subdue their foes,
Could order teach, and all their heats compose;
To ev'ry duty could their minds engage,
Provoke their courage, and command their rage.
So when a lion shakes his dreadful mane,
And angry grows, if he that first took pain
To tame his youth, approach the haughty beast,
He bends to him, but frights away the rest.

As the vext world, to find repose at last,
Itself into Augustus' arms did cast:
So England now does, with like toil oppress'd,
Her weary head upon your bosom rest.
Then let the muses, with such notes as these,
Instruct us what belongs unto our peace:
Your battles they hereafter shall indite,
And draw the image of our Mars in fight;
Tell of towns storm'd, of armies over-run,
And mighty kingdoms by your conduct won;
How, while you thunder'd, clouds of dust did choke
Contending troops, and seas lay hid in smoke.
Illustrious arts high raptures do infuse,
And ev'ry conqueror creates a muse:
Here in low strains your milder deeds we sing;
But there, my lord, we'll bays and olives bring

To crown your head; while you in triumph ride
O'er vanquish'd nations, and the sea beside;
While all your neighbour-princes unto you,
Like Joseph's sheaves, pay reverence, and bow.

II. Of a war with Spain, and fight at sea, by general Montague. In the year 1656. By Mr. Waller.

NOW for some ages had the pride of Spain
Made the sun shine on half the world in vain;
While she bid war to all that durst supply
The place of those her cruelty made die:
Of nature's bounty men forbore to taste,
And the best portion of the earth lay waste.
   From the new world her silver and her gold
Come, like a tempest, to confound the old;
Feeding, with these, the brib'd electors hopes,
Alone she gave us emperors and popes;
With these accomplishing her vast designs,
Europe was shaken with her Indian mines.
   When Britain, looking with a just disdain,
Upon this gilded majesty of Spain,
And knowing well that empire must decline,
Whose chief support and sinews are of coin,
Our nation's solid virtues did oppose
To the rich troublers of the world's repose.
   And now some months, encamping on the main,
Our naval army had besieged Spain:
They that the whole world's monarchy design'd,
Are to their ports by our bold fleet confin'd;
From whence our red-cross they triumphant see,
Riding without a rival on the sea.
Others may use the ocean as their road;
Only the English make it their abode,
Whose ready sails with ev'ry wind can fly,
And make a cov'nant with th' inconstant sky:
Our oaks secure, as if they there took root,
We tread on billows with a steady foot.

Mean while the Spaniards in America,
Near to the line, the fun approaching faw,
And hop'd their European coaft to find
Clear'd from our ships by the autumnal wind;
Their huge capacious galleons, ftuft with plate,
The lab'ring winds drive flowly tow'rds their fate.
 Before St. Lucar they their guns difcharge,
To tell their joy, or to invite a barge:
This heard fome fhips of ours (tho' out of view),
And fwift as eagles to the quarry flew:
So heedlefs lambs, which for their mother bleat,
Wake hungry lions, and become their meat.
 Arriv'd, they foon begin the tragic play,
And with their fmoky cannons banifh day;
Night, horror, flaughter, with confufion meet,
And with their fable arms embrace the fleet;
Thro' yielding planks the angry bullets fly,
And of one wound hundreds together die:
Born under diff'rent ftars, one fate they have,
The fhip their coffin, and the fea their grave.
 Bold were the men which on the ocean firft
Spread their new fails, when fhipwreck was the worft:
More danger now from man alone we find,
Than from the rocks, the billows, or the wind.
They that had fail'd from near th' Antarctic pole,
Their treafure fafe, and all their veffels whole,
In fight of their dear country ruin'd be,
Without the guilt of either rock or fea:
What they would fpare, our fiercer art deftroys,
Surpaffing ftorms in terror and in noife.
 Once Jove from Ida did both hofts furvey,
And, when he pleas'd to thunder, part the fray:
Here heav'n in vain that kind retreat fhould found;
The louder cannon had the thunder drown'd.
Some we made prize, while others, burnt and rent,
With their rich lading, to the bottom went:
Down finks at once (fo fortune with us fports)
The pay of armies, and the pride of courts.
Vain man! whofe rage buries as low that ftore,
As avarice had digg'd for it before;

What earth in her dark bowels could not keep
From greedy hands, lies fafer in the deep,
Where Thetis kindly does from mortals hide
Thofe feeds of luxury, debate, and pride.
   And now into her lap the richeft prize
Fell, with the nobleft of our enemies:
The marquis, glad to fee the fire deftroy
Wealth, that prevailing foes were to enjoy,
Out from his flaming fhip his children fent,
To perifh in a milder element;
Then laid him by his burning lady's fide,
And, fince he could not fave her, with her dy'd.
Spices and gums about them melting fry,
And, phœnix-like, in that rich neft they die.
Alive, in equal flames of love they burn'd,
And now together are to afhes turn'd;
Afhes more worth than all their fun'ral coft,
Than the huge treafure which was with them loft.
   Thefe dying lovers, and their floating fons,
Sufpend the fight, and filence all our guns:
Beauty and youth, about to perifh, finds
Such noble pity in brave Englifh minds,
That the rich fpoil forgot, their valour's prize,
All labour now to fave their enemies.
How frail our paffions! how foon changed are
Our wrath and fury to a friendly care!
They that but now, for honour and for plate,
Made the fea blufh with blood, refign their hate;
And, their young foes endeav'ring to retrieve,
With greater hazard than they fought they dive.
   With thefe returns victorious Montague,
With laurels in his hand, and half Peru.
Let the brave generals divide that bough;
Our great protector hath fuch wreaths enough.
His conqu'ring head has no more room for bays:
Then let it be as the glad nation prays;
Let the rich ore be forthwith melted down,
And the ftate fix'd, by making him a crown.

III.

APPENDIX.

III. To Oliver Cromwell: by Mr. John Locke.

A Peaceful fway the great Auguftus bore,
O'er what great Julius gain'd by arms before.
Julius was all with martial trophies crown'd;
Auguftus for his peaceful arts renown'd.
Rome calls them great, and makes them deities;
That for his valour; this, his policies.
You, mighty prince, than both are greater far,
Who rule, in peace, that world you gain'd by war:
You fure from heav'n a finifh'd hero fell,
Who thus alone two pagan gods excel.

IV. Heroic ftanzas on the late protector Oliver Cromwell. Written after his funeral, by Mr. Dryden.

AND now 'tis time; for their officious hafte,
Who would before have borne him to the fky,
Like eager Romans, ere all rites were paft,
Did let too foon the facred eagle fly.

Though our beft notes are treafon to his fame,
Join'd with the loud applaufe of public voice;
Since heav'n, what praife we offer to his name,
Hath render'd too authentic by its choice:

Though in his praife no arts can lib'ral be,
Since they whofe mufes have the higheft flown,
Add not to his immortal memory,
But do an act of friendfhip to their own:

Yet 'tis our duty, and our int'reft too,
Such monuments as we can build, to raife,
Left all the world prevent what we fhou'd do,
And claim a title in him by their praife.

How fhall I then begin, or where conclude,
To draw a fame fo truly circular?
For in a round what order can be fhew'd,
Where all the parts fo equal perfect are?

His grandeur he deriv'd from heav'n alone;
For he was great ere fortune made him so;
And wars, like mists that rise against the sun,
Made him but greater seem, not greater grow.

No borrow'd bays his temples did adorn,
But to our crown he did fresh jewels bring:
Nor was his virtue poison'd, soon as born,
With the too early thoughts of being king.

Fortune (that easy mistress to the young,
But to her antient servants coy and hard)
Him, at that age, her fav'rites rank'd among,
When she her best-lov'd Pompey did discard.

He, private, mark'd the faults of others sway,
And set as sea-marks for himself to shun;
Not like rash monarchs, who their youth betray,
By acts their age too late would wish undone.

And yet dominion was not his design;
We owe that blessing not to him, but heav'n,
Which to fair acts unsought rewards did join:
Rewards that less to him than us were giv'n.

Our former chiefs, like sticklers of the war,
First fought t'inflame the parties, then to poise;
The quarrel lov'd, but did the cause abhor,
And did not strike to hurt, but make a noise.

War, our consumption, was their gainful trade:
He inward bled, whilst they prolong'd our pain;
He fought to hinder fighting, and essay'd
To stanch the blood by breathing of the vein.

Swift and resistless thro' the land he past,
Like that bold Greek who did the east subdue,
And made to battles such heroic haste,
As if on wings of victory he flew.

He fought secure of fortune as of fame:
Still by new maps the island might be shown,
Of conquests which he strew'd where-e'er he came,
Thick as the Galaxy with stars is sown.

His

His palms, tho' under weights they did not stand,
Still thriv'd; no winter could his laurels fade;
Heav'n in his portrait shew'd a workman's hand,
And drew it perfect, tho' without a shade.

Peace was the prize of all his toil and care,
Which war had banish'd, and did now restore:
Bolognia's walls thus mounted in the air,
To seat themselves more surely than before.

Her safety rescu'd Ireland to him owes,
And treach'rous Scotland, to no int'rest true;
Yet bless'd that fate which did his arms dispose
Her land to civilize, as to subdue.

Nor was he like those stars, which only shine
When to pale mariners they storms portend;
He had his calmer influence, and his mien
Did love and majesty together blend.

'Tis true, his count'nance did imprint an awe,
And nat'rally all souls to his did bow;
As wands of divination downward draw,
And point to beds where sov'reign gold doth grow.

When, past all off'rings to Feretrian Jove,
He Mars depos'd, and arms to gowns made yield;
Succesful councils did him soon approve
As fit for close intrigues, as open field.

To suppliant Holland he vouchsaf'd a peace,
Our once bold rival in the British main.
Now tamely glad her unjust claim to cease,
And buy our friendship with her idol, gain.

Fame of th' asserted sea, through Europe blown,
Made France and Spain ambitious of his love;
Each knew that side must conquer he would own;
And for him fiercely, as for empire, strove.

No sooner was the Frenchman's cause embrac'd,
Than the light monsieur the grave don outweigh'd:
His fortune turn'd the scale where it was cast,
Though Indian mines were in the other laid.

When abfent, yet we conquer'd in his right;
For tho' that fome mean artift's fkill were fhown
In mingling colours, or in placing light;
Yet ftill the fair defignment was his own:

For from all tempers he could fervice draw;
The worth of each with its allay he knew;
And, as the confident of nature, faw,
How fhe complexions did divide and brew.

Or he their fingle virtues did furvey,
By intuition in his own large breaft,
Where all the rich ideas of them lay,
That were the rule and meafure to the reft.

When fuch heroic virtue heav'n fets out,
The ftars, like commons, fullenly obey;
Becaufe it drains them when it comes about;
And therefore is a tafk they feldom pay.

From this high fpring our foreign conquefts flow,
Which yet more glorious triumph do portend,
Since their commencement to his arms they owe,
If fprings as high as fountains may afcend.

He made us freemen of the continent,
Whom nature did like captives treat before;
To nobler preys the Englifh lion fent,
And taught him firft in Belgian walks to roar.

That old unqueftion'd pirate of the land,
Proud Rome, with dread the fate of Dunkirk heard;
And trembling wifh'd behind more Alps to ftand,
Although an Alexander were her guard.

By his command, we boldly crofs'd the line,
And bravely fought where fouthern ftars arife;
We trac'd the far-fetch'd gold unto the mine,
And that which brib'd our fathers made our prize.

Such was our prince; yet own'd a foul above
The higheft acts it could produce or fhew;
Thus poor mechanic arts in public move,
Whilft the deep fecrets beyond practice go.

Nor died he when his ebbing fame went less,
But when fresh laurels courted him to live;
He seem'd but to prevent some new success,
As if above what triumphs earth can give.

His latest victories still thickest came,
As near the centre motion doth increase;
Till he, press'd down by his own weighty name,
Did, like the vestal, under spoils decease.

But first the ocean, as a tribute, sent
That giant prince of all her wat'ry herd;
And th' isle, when her protecting genius went,
Upon his obsequies loud sighs conferr'd.

No civil broils have since his death arose;
But faction now by habit does obey;
And wars have that respect for his repose,
As winds for Halcyons, when they breed at sea.

His ashes in a peaceful urn shall rest,
His name a great example stands, to show
How strangely high endeavours may be blest,
Where piety and valour jointly go.

V. To the happy memory of the late protector, Oliver Cromwell. By Mr. Sprat of Oxon, afterwards bishop of Rochester.

A Pindaric ODE.

I.

'TIS true, great name, thou art secure
    From the forgetfulness and rage
Of death, or envy, or devouring age;
Thou canst the force and teeth of time endure:
    Thy fame, like men, the elder it doth grow,
    Will of itself turn whiter too,
    Without what needless art can do;
Will live beyond thy breath, beyond thy herse,
Tho' it were never heard or sung in verse.

  Without our help thy memory is safe;
  They only want an epitaph,
  That do remain alone
  Alive in an inscription,
Remembred only on the brass, or marble stone.
'Tis all in vain what we can do:
  All our roses and perfumes
  Will but officious folly shew,
  And pious nothings, to such mighty tombs.
  All our incense, gums, and balm,
  Are but unnecessary duties here;
  The poets may their spices spare,
Their costly numbers, and their tuneful feet:
That need not be embalm'd, which of itself is sweet.

II.

We know to praise thee is a dangerous proof
  Of our obedience and our love:
  For when the sun and fire meet,
  The one's extinguish'd quite;
And yet the other never is more bright:
  So they that write of thee, and join
  Their feeble names with thine,
Their weaker sparks with thy illustrious light,
  Will lose themselves in that ambitious thought;
  And yet no fame to thee from hence be brought.
  We know, bles'd spirit, thy mighty name
  Wants no additions of another's beam;
  It's for our pens too high, and full of theme;
The muses are made great by thee, not thou by them.
  Thy fame's eternal lamp will live,
  And in thy sacred urn survive,
Without the food of oil, which we can give.
'Tis true; but yet our duty calls our songs,
  Duty commands our tongues:
  Tho' thou want not our praises, we
  Are not excus'd for what we owe to thee:
For so men from religion are not freed;
  But from the altars clouds must rise,
  Tho' heav'n itself doth nothing need,
And tho' the Gods don't want an earthly sacrifice.

              III.

APPENDIX.

III.

Great life of wonders, whofe each year
  Full of new miracles did appear!
  Whofe ev'ry month might be
  Alone a chronicle, or hiftory!
  Others great actions are
  But thinly fcatter'd here and there;
  At beft, but all one fingle ftar;
  But thine, the milky way,
All one continued light of undiftinguifh'd day:
They throng'd fo clofe, that nought elfe could be feen,
  Scarce any common fky did come between.
  What fhall I fay, or where begin?
Thou may'ft in double fhapes be fhown,
Or in thy arms, or in thy gown;
Like Jove fometimes with warlike thunder, and
Sometimes with peaceful fceptre in his hand;
  Or in the field, or on the throne;
In what thy head, or what thy arm hath done.
  All that thou didft was fo refin'd,
  So full of fubftance, and fo ftrongly join'd,
  So pure, fo weighty gold,
  That the leaft grain of it,
  If fully fpread and beat,
Would many leaves, and mighty volumes hold.

IV.

Before thy name was publifh'd, and whilft yet
  Thou only to thyfelf wert great;
  Whilft yet thy happy bud
  Was not quite feen, or underftood;
It then fure figns of future greatnefs fhew'd;
  Then thy domeftic worth
  Did tell the world what it would be,
  When it fhould fit occafion fee,
When a full fpring fhould call it forth:
  As bodies in the dark and night
Have the fame colours, the fame red and white,
  As in the open day and light;
    The fun doth only fhow
That they are bright, not make them fo:

So whilſt but private walls did know
What we to ſuch a mighty mind ſhould owe,
   Then the ſame virtues did appear,
Though in a leſs and more contracted ſphere,
As full, though not as large as ſince they were:
   And like great rivers fountains, though
     At firſt ſo deep thou didſt not go;
   Tho' then thine was not ſo enlarg'd a flood;
Yet when 'twas little, 'twas as clear, as good.

V.

'Tis true, thou waſt not born unto a crown;
   Thy ſceptre's not thy father's, but thy own:
   Thy purple was not made at once in haſte,
   But, after many other colours paſt,
   It took the deepeſt princely dye at laſt.
   Thou didſt begin with leſſer cares,
And private thoughts took up thy private years:
   Thoſe hands, which were ordain'd by fates
   To change the world, and alter ſtates,
   Practis'd at firſt that vaſt deſign
   On meaner things with equal mein.
That ſoul, which ſhould ſo many ſceptres ſway,
   To whom ſo many kingdoms ſhould obey,
Learn'd firſt to rule in a domeſtic way:
So government itſelf began
   From family, and ſingle man;
Was by the ſmall relation, firſt,
   Of huſband, and of father, nurs'd;
And from thoſe leſs beginnings paſt,
To ſpread itſelf o'er all the world at laſt.

VI.

But when thy country (then almoſt inthrall'd)
   Thy virtue, and thy courage call'd;
When England did thy arms intreat,
And 't had been ſin in thee not to be great;
   When ev'ry ſtream, and ev'ry flood,
Was a true vein of earth, and ran with blood;
   When unus'd arms, and unknown war,
   Fill'd ev'ry place, and ev'ry ear;

When

APPENDIX.

When the great ſtorms, and diſmal night,
    Did all the land affright;
'Twas time for thee to bring forth all our light.
  Thou left'ſt thy more delightful peace,
  Thy private life, and better eaſe;
  Then down thy ſteel and armour took,
  Wiſhing that it ſtill hung upon the hook:
  When death had got a large commiſſion out,
    Throwing her arrows and her ſting about;
  Then thou (as once the healing ſerpent roſe)
  Waſt lifted up, not for thyſelf, but us.

VII.

Thy country wounded was, and ſick, before
  Thy wars and arms did her reſtore:
  Thou knew'ſt where the diſeaſe did lie,
  And, like the cure of ſympathy,
    Thy ſtrong and certain remedy
    Unto the weapon didſt apply:
Thou didſt not draw the ſword, and ſo
    Away the ſcabbard throw;
      As if thy country ſhou'd
  Be the inheritance of Mars and blood:
But that when the great work was ſpun,
  War in itſelf ſhould be undone;
That peace might land again upon the ſhore,
    Richer and better than before;
  The huſbandmen no ſteel ſhould know,
  None but the uſeful iron of the plough;
  That bays might creep on ev'ry ſpear:
And tho' our ſky was overſpread
    With a deſtructive red,
'Twas but till thou our ſun didſt in full light appear.

VIII.

When Ajax dy'd, the purple blood,
  That from his gaping wound had flow'd,
    Turn'd into letters; ev'ry leaf
    Had on it wrote his epitaph:
So from that crimſon flood,
Which thou, by fate of times, wert led
    Unwillingly to ſhed,
  Letters and learning roſe, and were renew'd.

Thou fought'st not out of envy, hope, or hate,
   But to refine the church and state;
And like the Romans, whate'er thou
   In the field of Mars didst mow,
Was, that a holy island hence might grow.
   Thy wars, as rivers raised by a show'r,
     Which welcome clouds do pour,
     Though they at first may seem
To carry all away with an enraged stream:
Yet did not happen, that they might destroy,
   Or the better parts annoy;
But all the filth and mud to scour,
   And leave behind another slime,
To give a birth to a more happy pow'r.

IX.

In fields unconquer'd, and so well
   Thou didst in battles and in arms excel,
   That steelly arms themselves might be
   Worn out in war as soon as thee.
Success so close upon thy troops did wait,
   As if thou first hadst conquer'd fate;
     As if uncertain victory
     Had been first overcome by thee;
As if her wings were clipp'd, and could not flee;
     Whilst thou didst only serve,
Before thou hadst what first thou didst deserve.
   Others by thee did great things do,
Triumph'dst thyself, and mad'st them triumph too;
   Tho' they above thee did appear,
   As yet in a more large and higher sphere,
Thou, the great sun, gav'st light to ev'ry star.
     Thyself an army wert alone,
     And mighty troops contain'dst in one:
   Thy only sword did guard the land,
   Like that which, flaming in the angel's hand,
     From men God's garden did defend:
   But yet thy sword did more than his,
Not only guarded, but did make this land a paradise.

APPENDIX.

X.
Thou fought'ſt not to be high or great,
  Not for a ſceptre or a crown,
  Or ermin, purple, or the throne;
    But, as the veſtal heat,
Thy fire was kindled from above alone.
  Religion, putting on the ſhield,
  Brought thee victorious to the field.
Thy arms, like thoſe, which antient heroes wore,
    Were given by the God thou didſt adore;
    And all the ſwords thy armies had,
    Were on an heav'nly anvil made;
    Not intereſt, or any weak deſire
  Of rule, or empire, did thy mind inſpire;
    Thy valour, like the holy fire
  Which did before the Perſian armies go,
  Liv'd in the camp, and yet was ſacred too;
    Thy mighty ſword anticipates
  What was reſerv'd for heav'n and thoſe bleſs'd feats,
And makes the church triumphant here below.

XI.
Tho' fortune did hang on thy ſword,
  And did obey thy mighty word;
  Tho' fortune for thy ſide and thee,
  Forgot her lov'd unconſtancy;
  Amidſt thy arms and trophies thou
  Wert valiant and gentle too,
Woundeſt thyſelf, when thou didſt kill thy foe.
  Like ſteel, when it much work has paſt,
  That which was rough does ſhine at laſt;
Thy arms by being oft'ner us'd did ſmoother grow:
  Nor did thy battles make thee proud or high;
    Thy conqueſt rais'd the ſtate, not thee:
  Thou overcam'ſt thyſelf in ev'ry victory.
    As when the ſun, in a directer line,
    Upon a poliſh'd golden ſhield doth ſhine,
  The ſhield reflects unto the ſun again his light:
So when the heavens ſmil'd on thee in fight,
    When thy propitious God had lent

  Succefs and vict'ry to thy tent,
 To heav'n again the victory was fent.
XII.
England, till thou didft come,
Confin'd her valour home :
'Then our own rocks did ftand
Bounds to our fame as well as land,
  And were to us, as well
  As to our enemies, unpaffable.
 We were afham'd at what we read,
  And blufh'd at what our fathers did,
Becaufe we came fo far behind the dead.
The Britifh lion hung his mane, and droop'd,
  To flavery and burden ftoop'd;
  With a degen'rate fleep and fear
  Lay in his den, and languifh'd there;
   At whofe leaft voice before,
A trembling echo ran through ev'ry fhore,
  And fhook the world at ev'ry roar:
Thou his fubdu'd courage didft reftore,
 Sharpen his claws, and in his eyes
 Mad'ft the fame dreadful lightning rife;
Mad'ft him again affright the neighb'ring floods;
His mighty thunder founds through all the woods:
  Thou haft our military fame redeem'd,
  Which was loft, or clouded feem'd:
  Nay, more; heav'n did by thee beftow
On us, at once, an iron age, and happy too.
XIII.
Till thou command'ft, that azure chain of waves,
  Which nature round about us fent,
  Made us to ev'ry pirate flaves,
 Was rather burden than an ornament;
 Thofe fields of fea, that wafh'd our fhores,
Were plow'd and reap'd by other hands than ours:
  To us, the liquid mafs,
  Which doth about us run,
  As it is to the fun,
  Only a bed to fleep on was;
          And

And not, as now, a pow'rful throne,
To shake and sway the world thereon.
Our princes in their hand a globe did shew,
   But not a perfect one,
   Compos'd of earth, and water too.
But thy commands the floods obey'd,
Thou all the wilderness of water sway'd;
Thou didst but only wed the sea,
Not make her equal, but a slave to thee.
Neptune himself did bear thy yoke,
   Stoop'd and trembled at thy stroke:
   He that ruled all the main,
   Acknowledg'd thee his sovereign:
   And now the conquer'd sea doth pay
More tribute to thy Thames, than that unto the sea.

XIV.

Till now our valour did ourselves more hurt;
   Our wounds to other nations were a sport;
   And as the earth, our land produc'd
Iron and steel, which should to tear ourselves be us'd.
Our strength within itself did break,
   Like thund'ring cannons crack,
   And kill'd those that were near,
While th' enemies secur'd and untouch'd were.
   But now our trumpets thou hast made to sound
   Against our enemies walls in foreign ground;
And yet no echo back to us returning found.
   England is now the happy peaceful isle,
   And all the world the while
Is exercising arms and wars,
With foreign, or intestine jars.
The torch extinguish'd here, we lend to others oil.
   We give to all, yet know ourselves no fear;
   We reach the flame of ruin and of death,
   Where-e'er we please our swords t' unsheath,
Whilst we in calm and temp'rate regions breath
   Like to the sun, whose heat is hurl'd
   Thro' ev'ry corner of the world;
   Whose flame thro' all the air doth go,
And yet the sun himself the while no fire doth know.

XV.

XV.

Befides the glories of thy peace
  Are not in number, nor in value, lefs.
    Thy hand did cure, and clofe the fcars
      Of our bloody civil wars;
  Not only lanc'd, but heal'd the wound,
    Made us again as healthy, and as found:
    When now the fhip was well-nigh loft,
    After the ftorm upon the coaft,
    By 'ts mariners endanger'd moft;
    When they their ropes and helms had left,
    When the planks afunder cleft,
  And floods came roaring in with mighty found,
Thou a fafe land, and harbour, for us found,
And favedft thofe that would themfelves have drown'd:
A work which none but heav'n and thou could do,
    Thou mad'ft us happy whe'er we would or no:
    Thy judgment, mercy, temperance fo great,
    As if thofe virtues in thy mind had feat:
    Thy piety, not only in the field, but peace,
    When heav'n feem'd to be wanted leaft:
    Thy temples not, like Janus, open were
      Only in time of war,
      When thou hadft greater caufe of fear;
      Religion and the awe of heav'n poffeft
  All places, and all times alike, thy breaft.

XVI.

Nor didft thou only for thy age provide,
    But for the years to come befide:
  Our after-times, and late pofterity,
    Shall pay unto thy fame as much as we;
    They too are made by thee.
  When fate did call thee to a higher throne,
    And when thy mortal work was done;
  When heav'n did fay it, and thou muft be gone;
    Thou him to bear thy burden chofe,
Who might (if any could) make us forget thy lofs:
    Nor hadft thou him defign'd,
      Had he not been
  Not only to thy blood, but virtue, kin;
  Not only heir unto thy throne, but mind.

'Tis he shall perfect all thy cares,
And with as fine a thread weave out thy loom :
So one did bring thy chosen people from
    Their slavery and fears;
Led them through their pathless road,
    Guided himself by God ;
He brought them to the borders ; but a second hand
Did settle, and secure them in the promis'd land.

VI. Upon the late storm, and the death of the protector O. Cromwell, ensuing the same. By Mr. Waller.

WE must resign ! heav'n his great soul does claim,
    In storms as loud as his immortal fame !
His dying groans, his last breath shakes our isle,
And trees uncut fall for his fun'ral pile !
About this palace their broad roots are tost
Into the air : so Romulus was lost.
New Rome in such a tempest miss'd their king,
And from obeying fell to worshipping.
On Oeta's top thus Hercules lay dead,
With ruin'd oaks and pines about him spread :
The poplar too, whose bough he wont to wear
On his victorious head, lay prostrate there.
Those his last fury from the mountain rent :
Our dying hero, from the continent,
Ravish'd whole towns ; and forts, from Spaniards reft,
As his last legacy to Britain left.
The ocean, which so long our hopes confin'd,
    Could give no limits to his vaster mind ;
Our bounds enlargement was his latest toil,
Nor hath he left us pris'ners to our isle :
Under the tropic is our language spoke,
And part of Flanders hath receiv'd our yoke.
From civil broils he did us disengage ;
Found nobler objects for our martial rage ;

                              And,

APPENDIX.

And, with wife conduct, to his country shew'd
Their antient way of conquering abroad.
Ungrateful then, if we no more allow
To him, that gave us peace and empire too.
Princes that fear'd him, griev'd, concern'd to see
No pitch of glory from the grave is free.
Nature herself took notice of his death,
And, sighing, swell'd the sea with such a breath,
That to remotest shores her billows roll'd,
Th' approaching fate of her great ruler told.

From the Cambridge verses, written upon the lord protector's death.

VII. In obitum serenissimi domini, Olivarii Cromwelli, hujus reipublicæ protectoris.

FLORES non Paphios, rosas
    Huc ferte, aut violas; munera non rogant
Hæc manes Olivarii:
    Sed tela & clypeos, Martia præmia,
Ferte, & laurigeras date
    Laudes exequiis egregii ducis;
Quo fama Angliacæ nitet
    Gentis, præteritæ reddita gloriæ.
Hic est qui patriæ diu
    Amissas penitus restituit suæ
Leges; qui furias pius
    Bellonæ indigenæ composuit truces;
Et cujus Scotus horruit
    Tot funesta tepens sanguine prælia.
Nostri non semel impetum
    Victricemque manum sensit Hibernia
Herois. Gladiis feri
    Hujus subsidium consocialibus
Ambirunt proceres prece
    Gallorum: potuit non sine prælio

APPENDIX. 311

Quem dirus Batavus sibi
  Immanis valido jungere fœdere;
Classis cum laceras rates
  Fudisset proprio Marte Britannica.
Sic hostes animo suos,
  Dum vivus, domuit; sed, Libitina, te
Lassam nomine deprimens,
  Invictus pariter vixit & interit.

B. S. Coll. S. Petri Soc. M. A.

No. VII.

The substance of a panegyric of the lord general Oliver Cromwell, as presented to him by the Portuguese embassador don Juan Roderiguez de Saa Meneses, Conde de Penaguaia. Written in Latin, as pretended, by a learned Jesuit, his excellency's chaplain; but, as more probably supposed, by the celebrated Mr. John Milton, Latin secretary to Cromwell.

WHEN I had often and long revolved in mind those illustrious examples, which, from an assiduous reading of the antients of heroic time, I had treasured up in my memory, there occurred to me a certain species of humanity superlatively excellent, formed out of the virtues of them all, which I proposed to myself as an idea, to which I might compare the protraits of whatever eminent men I could meet with in the present age. And indeed it has so happened, by the will of fortune, that I have travelled over the greatest and most noble part of Europe; in which peregrination I both accidentally lit of, and industriously found, many who shone forth in every kind of praise, whom, as they respectively excelled, I compared with the species that resided in my mind, and observed how

nearly

nearly each came up to, or fell short of it; and from that similitude assigned to every one his own proper rank. Some there were, who, upon a comparison of their virtues, made up that resemblance in part; others, who almost represented it; but not one, I must ingenuously own, who expressed it fully. That, indeed, seemed a thing rather to be wished than hoped for. For who was there who could, in every respect, bring together all the ornaments of the gown and the sword, so as to equal the idea I had formed from them?

But my voyage into Britain forbad me to despair. Britain, which, by being divided from the rest of the globe, made, in the opinion of the antients, a world of itself, has presented me with that which the other could not afford. There was an expectation already raised from the extraordinary fame of the person, but such an expectation as rather inflamed a desire, than produced a hope of finding in him what I had feigned in my wish. I was even afraid, lest, as fame is wont to magnify things beyond their due, that the present virtue of the man, eminent as it was, would not sustain the expectation it had raised. You, general Cromwell, the honour of your country, the safeguard of the commonwealth, the ornament of England, you are the man I mean. No sooner did I light on you, and thoroughly inspect your accomplishments, and critically compare them with those I had collected in my own idea, but I persuaded myself, that you either equalled, or at least came nearer to than any other, this image of a perfect hero.—I was overjoyed, that now I had found you: I remained possessed of so vast a desire: for I had seen, in you I had seen, the picture of all policy, and of all public virtue, most compleatly delineated.

But, not to dwell in generals, let us consider those virtues and endowments which made up that form that I had feigned in my mind, and compare them, as we proceed, with your actions and accomplishments; that we may, by the comparison, determine if the latter come up to the former.

First,

APPENDIX.

First then, I had conceived, as a very desirable thing, a nobility that was pure, splendid, honourable; and at the same time, free from delicacy, free from vanity. I divided from it all meanness, luxury, haughtiness, vaunting of itself. That which is solid, subject to no shame, promotive of no pride; far above every thing mean, near approaching to magnificence; from which nobody might detract, and which might detract from nobody; clear indeed and conspicuous, but not so as to obscure the lustre of others; which would not be satisfied with itself alone, or abstain from action from an opinion that it had honour enough in its own blood; but would spur on to fame, and wish still to increase in virtue; not tending to make the possessor careless, but brave, not indolent, but industrious; this was the nobility that pleased me.

Such a nobility as this, most illustrious Cromwell, have we found yours to be; pure, solid, true: full, not of paint, but of juice: made up, not so much of flowers, as of seeds: not wrapt up in smoke, and vanishing in air; but open and clear; aspiring, by firm gradations, to the highest things. You may boast yourself in this, but not grow proud. This nobility may neglect no man, and will be neglected of none: it need not desire light from you, but splendor only; it is not void of praise, but breathing out a plenitude of glory.

To nobility (which, because it is derived from others, is more frequently called theirs, than our own) I added a study of letters, by which nature should be cultivated, the mind polished and subdued, and reason sharpened. Yet this, in a person instructed for the commonwealth, and trained up for political affairs, I wished might be moderate. For, as the art of governing a commonwealth, for the most part, is active and practical; it should rather consist of counsel and prudence, than of speculative and theoretical knowledge and wisdom. It is necessary therefore for him, who is brought up to the art of ruling and commanding, to be tinged indeed with a study of letters, which may reasonably inform him, and banish ignorance and unskilfulness

skilfulness from his mind; yet not to be so deeply tutored, as to comprehend them absolutely and exactly in every point. For, I know not by what means, this thorough knowledge of the sciences, at the same time that it sharpens the intellect, dulls the soul, and interrupts its close attention to the administration of public affairs: perhaps because it wastes the spirits necessary for action, and, by gradually consuming them, causes the mind, in proportion as it is deprived of them, to grow languid. Those applications of the wit and mind are tender things; they do not fancy the sun and the croud, but delight in shade and retirement. Noise and business disturb them: they shrink up at the horror of arms, and are even affrighted at the bawling of the forum. Like noble and delicate maidens, they must rather be kept safe at home, than brought forth into engagements and perils. Wherefore the most celebrated generals of antiquity have so addicted themselves to the instructions of their preceptors, as rather to adorn, than to profess, those studies: they have applied themselves just so much to them, as might serve to nourish, not to overwhelm, their minds. It was this course that the hero Achilles held under Chiron and Phœnix; Alexander, under Aristotle; Epaminondas, under Lysias; Scipio, under Panætius. And tho' Pericles, among the Greeks, and Julius Cæsar, among the Romans, may have passed for scholars; yet certainly their praise (whereof both obtained a very great share) is comprised chiefly in their eloquence; which consists more in force and nature, than in art and precept. For this reason it is delivered down to us, that the one thundered when he spoke, and that the other pronounced every thing with the same spirit he fought with.

You, O most excellent Cromwell, have applied your mind to the study of letters in this manner, copying exactly what I had observed in these, and other famous captains of antiquity. You have gathered up the literary dust at Cambridge, without deepening the tracks of learning. You have garnished your understanding

APPENDIX.

standing with those arts, which become a liberal nature; you have rubbed off the rust of your mind; you have sharpened the edge of your wit; you have gained such a character, as not to be reckoned an ill scholar, and fitted yourself, by the rudiments of the sciences, to manage the highest offices of the commonwealth. You have given us, in fact, such a specimen of your capacity, that you may make it appear, if you was disposed to go on in the pursuit of learning, how very able you are to equal the greatest masters; just as Julius Cæsar did, whose steps you so nearly tread in, according to the testimony of Cicero himself, that prince in every kind of learning. And in conducting the commonwealth you have chose to imitate that Cæsar rather than Cicero, by preferring the harsh, incessant, and laborious employment of a general, to the delicate and sedentary office of a senator. It did not become that hand to wax soft in literary ease, which was to be inured to the use of arms, and harden'd with asperity; that right hand to be wrapt up in down among the nocturnal birds of Athens, by which thunderbolts were soon after to be hurled among the eagles which emulate the sun.

For what belongs to their method of life, the best generals were always honest and frugal citizens; and, when their country did not want their assistance, applied themselves busily to domestic affairs, and to private difficulties, if they any way occurred. They professed ethics and œconomics as the groundwork and help of politics, both in their own personal practice of virtue, and in the good order and example they kept up in their families. For neither will he, who cannot govern himself, ever keep his family in due bounds; nor will the commonwealth ever be ruled by him, who cannot tell how to order his own houshold aright. Nor is the glory indeed less of being the best of citizens, than of being the best of generals; since the former must be the effect of a man's own industry and virtue, the latter may happen thro' the aid of the many, and is often the work of fortune. That man, in a word, who will not deport himself as an orderly citizen, must be a dangerous man to his country. For this reason the best of men have endeavoured to approve their fidelity and affection to their country by their own manners. Thus, even in the latest times of Roman liberty, did the two Marci, Marcus Cato and Marcus Brutus, excel. Of these, O Cromwell, you have so imitated the manners, that you have expressed them to the very life.

Betaking yourself to your own paternal house, which you had received and made noble and large, and having married a most excellent wife, you lived, while a private person, in such a manner as that you might pass for a master of probity; not void of all vices only, which is some little praise, but full of all virtues. You delighted in a noble and generous issue, to whom nothing but worthy things could be acceptable. There was in them a judgment, steady, true, mature; which manifested their integrity: a spirit, free from lust and avarice, which despised every thing that was mean. To these was added a prudence, persuading things agreeable to reason. It was easy therefore for them to embrace virtue, and to produce it for an example to the world. As a family, formed by such living lessons, imbibes a knowledge of the most perfect manners, and conforms itself to its preceptor; there did not seem, to the most rigid Stoic, any duty wanting in it, that was founded in justice and equity. Cincinnatus lived not more innocently; Serranus, not more incorruptly; Cato, he that was censor, not more justly.

One might have imagined, even at this time, that he could divine what was to happen, and thus prepared himself beforehand for the admiration of the commonwealth. Severe, within the bounds of humanity; humane, within the bounds of severity; easy, yet grave; moderate, yet majestic; sparing, without sordidness; liberal within measure, yet often offended at parsimony; so prone to bounty, that he seemed to repine, on some occasions, that the excess of it was a fault. That he might indulge more to others, he denied many things to himself; yet his indulgence never extended to licentiousness: he bridled his own anger, to correct that passion in others; and by his example restrained riot, and kept all to their duty. He cultivated friendships with eagerness, and would never rashly conceive enmities; yet was very tenacious of them when once conceived. He always allowed more to love, and less to hatred; would bear with some things, be angry at a few, and seemingly disregard a great many; and in this dissimulation he ever discovered a shrewd and penetrating wit.

With these endowments, both implanted by nature, and acquired by industry, you appeared to be born and made for the commonwealth. You prevented your dignities with your merits; and, before you obtained them, plainly shewed yourself worthy to wear them. Nor did you thrust yourself into honours, except only when the fortune of the commonwealth required your assistance. It was a religious and constant practice of the antient heroes, to wait for, and not make, occasions of helping the commonwealth; lest, being led by a study of ambition, they should seem to obtrude themselves into offices, and to set more by their own private advantages than the common concerns. And indeed an honest and good citizen ought not, uncalled, to turn statesman. But he may look upon himself as called, either when asked in the name of the people, or when the miserable state of public affairs implore his assistance. We read that Camillus acted thus, when the Senones, a people of Gaul, invading Rome, he gathered up what soldiers he could find at Ardea, whither he was banished, and with them defeated and put to flight the enemy. Cincinnatus, who was sent for from the plough to drive their enemies the Æqui from the Roman people, is not to be preferred to that generous exile.

The public necessity is of great weight; and greater is the force of compassion for him who silently suffers an injury, than for him who implores our aid to be delivered from such a misfortune; since there is reason to think that the mouth of the former is shut up from complaining, and that he has not even the liberty of groaning out the wrong which is done him. An occasion is offered you, and that a great one, most illustrious Cromwell, of succouring the calamities of your country. I do not inquire into the reasons of your changing the government; I only praise your affection for liberty, and your noble atchievements in the establishment and confirmation of it. For though a discerning person may be more moved with the causes of events, than with the events themselves; it is better for a stranger to abstain from searching and examining into secret causes, which ought not to be rashly traced or censured: it is enough for him, who could not be present in the councils, to ponder the events, which are perspicuous. Yet this need not be imputed to ignorance or sloth, but to prudence and modesty.

Moreover, tho' it would be ridiculous to estimate the judgments of advisers by events, and to measure either these by their successes, or those by their opinions; since it is not in our power to know what will happen: it is nevertheless not at all unreasonable to acknowledge and revere certain judgments of a superior providence in events, which often suffers counsels rightly projected to miscarry, and sometimes conducts actions precipitately undertaken to a prosperous exit. I do not say this to disparage the causes of changing the government, but that I may recommend my sense of the alteration; and so commemorate those events alone, which your valour hath rendered the most happy. In so doing it will appear, that he to whom matters have so prosperously succeeded, employed all his studies and actions, not without the divine occurrence, for the common utility *.

When

---

* There seems to be an affected obscurity in this and the preceding paragraph, which is owing to the uncertainty people were in with regard to Cromwell's intentions upon the dissolution of the long parliament.

APPENDIX.

When England had roufed herfelf at the name of liberty, and her citizens began to fly together at the public fignal, you, moft illuftrious Cromwell, perfuaded yourfelf not to ftand neuter; but to give up all your faculties and ftudies to one party. You had not forgot the judgment of Solon, "that if any one ftood neuter in a fedition, he fhould be put to death." Even Cicero was moved by this fentence, when, quitting the moderation of Pomponius Atticus, he devoted himfelf to Pompey's party. You thought that he, who follows no party, muft be proud, or covetous, or ambitious; that he endeavours to keep his own, and to turn every event to his private advantage: yet, when his country is rent into parties, fuch a man has no medium wherein to be fecure. As you forefaw this, you engaged on the fide of liberty, and brought with you a great weight of prejudice and fortune to the patrons of that glorious name. They efteemed you a Cato for the fanction of their caufe, a Cæfar for their companion in war. Their caufe was liked by many, becaufe you approved it.

But when they faw you engaged in battle, every one prognofticated to you the victory. You fought mixed with princes, and was among them the prince. All admired to fee fo many military virtues blaze forth of a fudden, which had hitherto been hid in the bofom of your foul. So to draw up, to fet the battle in array, to begin the onfet, to encompafs, to 'urge, to drive, to overthrow, to difperfe the enemy, was what we had read of in books, but faw performed only by you. The endowments you difcovered, were thought hardly poffible to be contained in one man. As they could not be more in number, you enlarged and made them more confpicuous.

You paffed gradually thro' the other military offices to that of general, left any fhould affign your honours rather to fortune than defert. You arrived at them more flowly than the common wifhes defired, and was dragged to dignities by a fort of violence. Yet furrounded and coveted thus on every fide, your employments came on fast and thick, as the necessities of the commonwealth grew up and multiplied. In a few months you atchieved so many great exploits, that other the most famous captains could hardly parallel them in whole ages. Wars sprung out of wars, and you was absent in none: the state of affairs took different aspects, and you looked to them all. You steered the helm at every break, when the commonwealth, agitated by various motions, rose high in waves and surges, and when any other would have been swallowed up in the tempest.

Prudence, as well as fortitude, is requisite in the art of war. The antients therefore feigned, that Pallas issued armed out of the brain of Jupiter; to intimate, that arms prosper by counsel, and judgment is to be strengthened by arms: and Homer, in singing that war which was of all others the most famous, gives Nestor to Agamemnon, and Polydamas to Priam (though one had an Achilles, and the other a Hector) that he might shew of what service prudent counsels are, in the conducting of military affairs.

In both these, most noble Cromwell, we find you to have excelled, throughout all the wars you have undertaken. Discerning, ready, judicious, valiant, deliberate, expeditious, sagacious, crafty, careful, attentive; you foresaw every accident, prevented the meditated blow, dared the greatest danger, eluded the most artful stratagem, embraced and improved every opportunity. Other mens councils lay open to you, but yours to none: you perceived the designs of all men, while no man perceived yours till he saw them accomplished. Like lightning, you struck before the thunder was heard, and even before any one could discern the cloud big with the fiery embryo. Superior in this to the Roman Fabius, because Hannibal observed his thunderbolts in the clouds before their irruption: none was aware of yours, but by the stroke, and the ashes they left when they fell.

Great in fortitude, as in counsel, you weighed the hazards of war as if you feared them; you went thro'
them

them as if you defpifed them. Before danger, wary; in it, undaunted. Every imputation of rafhnefs, every fufpicion of incapacity or negligence, you prevented by your action, your prefence of mind, and your attention to every circumftance.

With thefe arts, whilft yet a private captain, you firft approved yourfelf among the generals. They could perceive you to be fet at the head of the war, and that victory attended where-ever you charged. To obey was your firft bufinefs, that you might bring difcipline to the office of general, which you was fpeedily to enter on. Nor did it feem a favour conferred by the commonwealth, but a reward rendered to your merit.

With what fkill, with what intrepidity, did you fight againft the enemy at Edgehill! by the confeffion both of your own army and of the foe, you obtained there the pre-eminence among your brethren. At Marfton-Moor how did you flay, how did you difperfe, a body of the moft defperate adverfaries; and, bringing back your troops from the purfuit, rout another party of them, which had broken the other wing of your own army! You, a fingle captain only, was equal to all the troops befide. But in that moft famous battle fought by you at Nafeby, what an example did you give of an excellent commander, and a gallant warrior! Nor did the generals of the enemy dread you more, than your own loved and admired you. Thofe called you Ironfides and the favage, thefe the waxen and the gentle Cromwell.

Your valour was not the lefs wonderful, in that it was dreaded by the enemy, than in that it was not envied by your friends. From an enemy, a man is preferved by arms; from a rival, not even by innocence. But fuch was the felicity of your virtue, moft illuftrious general, that it fhone forth envied by none, countenanced by all. No man is ufed to envy any one, but him whom he imagines he is able to emulate: but who would dare to emulate, who would think to imitate, one that has exceeded all example? No man that

that is beloved suffers envy. You, by your modesty and management, have rendered yourself amiable to all. You arrogated nothing to yourself; you detracted nothing from others. The actions you demanded for your own part, but left the fame of them to your fellows; the danger was yours, the glory theirs.

Valour and favour are the two things which usually prepare the way to the highest honours; but, tho' the first be sufficient to deserve, it does not always secure them: for when honours are to be conferred by a commonwealth, he who has not the citizens benevolence, will never be able to acquire them. Cromwell was raised to the highest honours of the commonwealth with this single prerogative, that he was recommended by Fairfax, the greatest general of the age, and appointed by the commonwealth to succeed him. Fairfax did not dread, that his own lights should be eclipsed by the splendor of his successor, nor did Cromwell doubt but he should come up to the expectation which so great a general had raised. England found within herself an Atlas and a Hercules, with equal shoulders, and with equal constancy; both friendly and steady, the one in giving, the other in receiving, the burden of the commonwealth.

Having taken upon you the military command, you over-run three kingdoms with a continued course of victories. And what kingdoms were they? Islands shut up by the sea, stored with men and arms, and fortified against foreign invasions? Ireland, all over horrid and warlike, vomiting up arms and armed men: Scotland, the mansion of an unconquered nation, a martial school, and even terrible in its very name: England, a generous country, the mother of heroes, the region of palms, the seat of laurels, the mount of trophies, whose hills and promontories are crowned with spoils gathered from her numerous enemies. These nations, unpassable to so many generals, pervious to you alone the invincible Cromwell, have owned themselves tamed and subdued. You over-ran, you vanquished them, while another could hardly travel

travel them thro'. That which happened once to Cæsar, by reason of his celerity, "to come, to see, to overcome," happened often to you with redoubled glory. Cæsar lighted on the most dastardly foes; you on the most rough and stubborn enemies. In battles, you acted like thunder; esteemed it your business to strike where there was force to resist; thought it mean to hurt yielding and gentle things. You fought for rugged and untamed natures. You, who hated delicacies at home, how could you be delighted with an effeminate victory abroad?

And as if fortune were obedient to your wish, she chose for you the fiercest battles, the sharpest enemies. Witness, to omit others, that memorable fight at Dunbar, in which you attacked, and broke, and scattered, a most well-appointed army, abounding with hardy commanders and soldiers, gathered from all parts of Scotland. So great was the slaughter of that battle, that the heaps of dead not only filled the field, but stagnated it with blood. Nor fell there only the bodies of the soldiers, but likewise the spirits of the whole nation. For that is to be reckoned a true victory, which is extended beyond the fight, which disarms and dispirits the living, runs on from the battle over the country, and, by the fame of it, compels cities, districts, and provinces to surrender. Innumerable towns, forts, castles, struck by the report, as by a piece of ordnance, fell into the hands of the English. Yet the once most strong, well-fortified, and populous city of Edinburgh, with her almost impregnable castle, offered to put a stop to the current of the victory. But, when she saw Cromwell, she was struck on a heap, and submitted. The castle only, trusting to her situation and garrison, would not yield; and prepared new matter of military praise for our general. You besieged it so judiciously, and so vigorously, that, tho' the enemy made a gallant defence, you soon brought them to submit. In the same moment the standards were beat down from the top of their walls, and the rest of the neighbouring towns were subdued. Not more revolted, ed, after the bloody battle of Cannæ, to Hannibal, than, after the storming of Edinburgh castle, yielded to Cromwell. Other fortresses followed, as if they had been appendages to it. Where-ever your conquering forces approached, palms were growing for you. Above others shews itself the victory in Fife, won under your auspices, and to which you opened a way by a famous adventure, ferrying over the Forth with a happy audacity.

I come to your last and greatest victory, that of Worcester, which may be compared to all the sharpest battles of past ages. The Scots had brought together from all sides their wealth, forces, and strength, adding a new hope to their old despair. Ready to throw the last dye, they prepared to engage the more vigorously; to fight, first, for their country; then, for their honour; and, lastly, for their lives. You, Cromwell, baffled all their attempts, broke their force, wearied out their strength, dispersed their troops, and, in one battle, finished all the war. By this victory you subdued Scotland, tamed Ireland, freed England; refreshed, established, confirmed the commonwealth. In that day there plainly appeared to be in you as much skill of military affairs as you can possess, as much valour as you should, as much felicity as you ought to have, when you would overcome an enemy. All, which industry can do, was then in your power. Fortune, who is her own mistress, had devoted herself to you only; seen elsewhere to command, in your camp to serve, she who suspends wars with her own brow, obeyed the least nod from you.

I remember but six generals in past times, and one of late years, who, when they had waged many and great wars, always came off conquerors. You only, added to the seven, can make the eighth, and be alone the compendium of them all. The magnanimity of Alexander, the valour of Camillus, the constancy of Scipio, the force of Cæsar, the skill of Belisarius, the fortitude of Scanderbeg, the violence of Gustavus Adolphus, all unite in you: you excel all of them, in

that

that wherein they most excelled; and there is now seen in Cromwell, not only the name of a great general, but even of valour and felicity themselves.

Martial praises however, though they may be more splendid and specious, are not therefore more solid and excellent, than those contained in works of virtue. The difficulty is greater in the exercise of these than in military affairs, since with other accomplishments we may overcome others, but with these only ourselves; which is so much the more honourable conquest, that some of the best orators have said, "they who conquer others may still be compared to men, but they who overcome themselves are very like to God." A general who wants the virtues, tho' he may excel in military glory, will often hurt the commonwealth, or cast a blemish on his own reputation. But they who have been famous both for military glory abroad, and the praise of virtue at home, have not only preserved and extended the commonwealth, but also acquired immortal fame to themselves. Such is the power of virtue, that men of this character must be not only dear to their fellow-citizens, but also amiable to their very enemies. Of this character, most noble Cromwell, do I esteem you to be: for so many virtues have flowed together in you, and those so great and splendid, that they seemed to have contended about adorning you, and, when they had adorned you, to have vied among themselves for the primacy.

And first, let us consider those virtues which serve to restrain the depraved assaults and tumults of the mind. There is nothing less in our power than the affections of this sort, which live in us. You could not help being obnoxious to these: but for the most part you so contained yourself, that, without taking away any thing from nature, you throw off much from vice, by continually watching and opposing these affections, when no tokens of the conflict outwardly appeared. Who ever saw you elated with pride? Who ever, burning with anger? Who, inflamed with lust? Yet occasions of this sort frequently offer themselves to one who
is

is a warrior, a general, and a conqueror: but in all these cases you so carried yourself, as if you were only your own master. You commanded yourself, before you injoined any thing to a soldier. You suppressed your own anger, before you set right a person that was mistaken, or punished one that was wicked. Your mind being prepared and purged from desires, you put away from you lust and avarice.

For a leader of those virtues which are exercised towards others, you made use of prudence: nor did you only consider what was due to every one, but what was becoming yourself, and agreeable to others; nor barely perform that which was just, but administer that which was equitable and generous. To remove an injury, to repel a force, you thought a trifling virtue; but, to lift up the miserable, to comfort the afflicted, to enrich the necessitous, you reckoned was a true and solid kind of goodness; nor did you desire to be applauded for your hatred to vices, but commended for your love to virtues.

In the highest licence of war nothing was lawful to you, but what was so in the nature of things; nothing pleased, except what was honest. You held your soldiers to their duty, not by force or authority, but by example. The laws of war were wrote in your countenance, they were silently carried about in your aspect. Words were idle, where the lessons were given in works. The soldiers never wanted of their pay, because you abated of your own to make it up. They who needed nothing for themselves, desired something for you; you who made them not only moderate, but abstinent. You first brought religion into the army, and taught your soldiers to war most against vices and irregular desires.

That general will at last know how to destroy the enemy, who can find how to preserve his own soldiers. No general was ever more tender of his soldiers than you. You loved them, abroad in the battle, and at home in their quarters, as your own children. You watched carefully against all their inconveniences, inquired

quired into their neceffities, prevented their intreaties, foreftalled their fighs. A man under you might be difpleafed, but certainly he could not complain. Did a foldier lie before you wounded with a random fhot? You leaped from your horfe, ran up to him, and took a part of his grief to yourfelf. If he wanted a bed, you fpread under him your own cloke, which, for the affection it was done with, felt fofter than down. To another you offered your arms, and laid him, folded in them, to your breaft, and, out of your inborn love, more nobly animated him with the throbbings of your heart. You pufhed not your horfe with greater force to the deftruction of an enemy, than you checked and pulled him back to preferve your own foldier. In the battle you inured your hand to flaughter; in the camp, to preferve life. You judged no man to be your enemy, longer than he exercifed both hatred and arms againft you. Fighting, and unwilling to be conquered, you drove, you bore him down: fallen, and overcome, you raifed, you cherifhed him.

There was nothing fo hateful to you as rapines and burnings. You thought it an impiety to rage beyond death, againft a private perfon; beyond furrendry, againft a public place. You wifhed to take towns by capitulation, not by ftorm. You made no man guilty through private hate, or wicked through rafh fufpicion, that fo you might take vengeance of him; but rather feighned an innocence for many, that they might efcape the punifhments appointed for them. This one kind of diffembling, which borders on piety, highly pleafed you.

With thefe virtues you have extinguifhed all envy in the foe; procured love from your friends; obtained the favour of all. What Pompey the great found, in a fevere illnefs at Naples, when the whole city feemed to be fick and to recover with him; that have you experienced from your friends, when, after fo many victories, a dangerous diftemper affailed you, which was no fooner reported over the Englifh dominions, but fuddenly a deep fadnefs feized the minds of all, and
the

the whole nation seemed to be in danger with you. In the wishes of all, life was unanimously decreed for you, on whom the welfare of the commonwealth was founded. You began to amend; and, being out of danger, removed the gloom from every countenance. As the world looks gay with rays every-where diffused over it by the sun, so all England was exhilarated by the news of your recovery. Cities, forts, towns, castles, villages, grew warm with gratulations; both the highest and the lowest leap'd for joy; and the citizen and the soldier alike danced and triumphed, as if the strength that you had regained, had been his own property.

This, tho' great in itself, seemed to portend something greater. The gods assenting, the citizens calling you, all the people uniting in your favour, you have ascended to the highest point of military empire; not blindly and rashly, but slowly and gently, through the degrees of offices and virtues; that so, born and formed the father of your country, you should preserve and not destroy it; advance, and not depress it; amplify, and not diminish it. You freed the citizens not only from fear, but also from suspicion, when you dissolved a parliament, composed of the most grave and wealthy persons, because it did not so much consult the interest of the people, as to reduce the commonwealth to be subject to its own will. You discovered certain tokens of a perpetual domination; that they were minded to keep their own acquired power, and to carry on the administration of public affairs more for their own private ends, than with the consent of the people; that they had not performed their faith plighted to their country, by electing senators out of all the provinces, nor were likely for the future to perform it. You found more among them like Cæsar; who retained the dictatorship, than like Sylla, who laid it down. Fired with a love of virtue, and of your country, you flew to help it; and, because the thing was full of hazard, you added might to right, and, entering the court with the authority of a general,
broke

APPENDIX. 329

broke up a great, a rich, a full, a solemn parliament, in a moment.

I do not consider here either your magnanimity, or prudence, or celerity, or felicity; but your regard to right and faith, and your study of liberty. There is nothing to be feared from that citizen, who hath shewn himself a vindicator of right, an overthrower of ambition, an expeller of impotence. He is to be cleared of all suspicion, who, when he drove out others, resolved to extirpate those vices which grew up to the hurt of the commonwealth. There will be no room to fear his government for the future, whose arms are hurtless, and whose force is moderated. He will act more innocently in peace, who hath gone thro' the war blameless. He who clad in a general's robe abstained from injury, vested in a prince's gown will promote all manner of justice. He who deserved well of his enemies, cannot deserve ill of his country.

On you alone, most noble Cromwell (than whom no man dares wish or think of any thing more great), the riches, the fortunes, the hopes of England are all built. The looks, the eyes of all its citizens, big with the highest expectation, are cast upon you. Nor is it England only, but all Europe, and the universal world, that turns up its thoughts to you; you, the sole object of their minds. Posterity, which depends on you, will not only admire your actions, but require the reason of them. It behoves you not only to satisfy your own conscience, but also the expectation and desire of the whole world. Represent the heroic virtues of that idea, whereof I have shewn you to be the example. In the greatness of your mind, act the Alexander; in your military skill, the Pyrrhus; in your valour, the Scipio; in your authority, the Papyrius; in your ardor the Marcellus; in your prudence, the Fabius; in your subtilty, the Hannibal; in your constancy, the Æmilianus; in your felicity, the Cæsar. Towards your citizens, shew yourself a Camillus, a Pompey, an Agesilaus, an Agis, an Epaminondas. Towards your

enemies,

APPENDIX.

enemies, exhibit a Brasidas, a Lysander, a Rutilianus, a Metellus, a Gylippus, a Luctatius. In your faith, stand forth a Regulus; in your abstinence, a Fabricius; in your moderation a Curtius; in your integrity, a Cato; in your patience, a Themistocles; in your gravity, a Cimon. To sum up all, INSPECT YOURSELF. You alone are sufficient to express the virtues of them all. Comport yourself as you have hitherto done; for you are HE, who, unless you deviate from yourself, cannot be a bad man; if you imitate yourself, cannot but be THE BEST.

FINIS.

INDEX.

A.

AGitators, grow troublesome to Cromwell, 90, 91. declare against the king, 91. reason of their being set up, 119.
Algerines, admiral Blake makes a peace with them, 187.
Army, draw up a charge of high treason against eleven members of the house of commons, 81. grow jealous of Cromwell, 84. protect the parliament, 87. offended with Cromwell, 88. draw up a declaration, and a vindication of their proceedings, 119, &c.
Ashburnham, Mr. negotiates for the king, 92.
Alston, sir Arthur, commands in Drogheda, 38.
Authority, in a magistrate, when it ceases, 15.

B.

BArkstead, Mr. his relation of Cromwell's interment in Naseby field, 212.
Bate, his character of Cromwell's regiment, 20.

Berkeley

INDEX.

Berkeley, sir John, receives a message from Cromwell, concerning the king, 83. Cromwell discourses with him in favour of his majesty, 84. An account of what passed between Cromwell and him upon the former's leaving the king's interest, 92, & seq.

Bishops, king Charles's, their character by lord Falkland, 222. note. and by a late author, 223, n.

Blake, admiral, sent to the Mediterranean, 187. concludes a peace with Algiers, 189. destroys the ships and forts at Tunis, ib. exacts 60,000 l. of the grand duke of Tuscany, ib. sends home sixteen ships richly laden with effects, 190. with Montague blocks up the forts of Cadiz, ib. where they destroy the plate-fleet, ib. destroys another plate-fleet in the Canaries, 191. dies off Plymouth, 192. his character, ib. regard for the honour of his nation, 193.

Bourdeaux, Mr. embassador to Cromwell, his harangue, 210, &c.

Broghill, lord, a conversation between Cromwell and him, 97. one of the committee to persuade Cromwell to accept the title of king, 256, & seq. talks to Cromwell of restoring the king, 161. stopt by Cromwell when going over to the king, 206. goes to see Ormond with the protector's leave, 207.

Burnet, his remark on the state of Scotland after Cromwell's conquest of it, 76. what he says concerning the charge against the king, 104. concerning the king's death, 105. and Cromwell's part in it, 107.

C.

CÆSAR, his dictatorship better than the preceding times, 142. dignifies the titles of dictator and imperator, 177.

Calamy, Mr. opposes Cromwell's single government, 135, n.

Cambridge,

INDEX.

Cambridge, Latin verses writ there on Cromwell's death, 310.

Capel, lord, Cromwell's speech against him, 131.

Cardenas, de, embassador from Spain to Cromwell, 180.

Carthagena, Cromwell had his eye particularly thereon in his West-India expedition, 187, n.

Cavaliers, how Cromwell managed them, 166.

Chancellor of Scotland, his speech against Cromwell, 113, &c.

Characters, different ones of men who act from the same principles, 2.

Charles I. king, his concessions to the parliament, 10. Goes to Scotland, ib. pompously received at his return to London, 11. A rash step of his that began the rupture between him and the parliament, 14. sets up his standard at Nottingham, 15. motives of seizing him by the army, 78. a design to restore him by means of the independents, 81, 82. better pleased than in the hands of the presbyterians, 82. receives a dutiful address from the army, ib. his indiscretion and haughtiness ruin him, 85. his high consideration of himself, 86. Wellwood's character of him, ib. escapes, by Cromwell's advice, to the Isle of Wight, 91. reasons of Cromwell's abandoning his interest, 92, & seq. his hypocrisy to Cromwell, 96, & seq. every thing contributes to his fall, 99. votes of the parliament in his favour, 101. put a stop to by Cromwell, 102. brought to Windsor, and votes passed for his trial, 103. charge against him, 104. his death, and the errors of his reign, 106. his insincerity towards the parliament, 108. bills which he refuses to pass, 125, n. compared to Cromwell in his person and acquirements, 213. in his natural abilities, penetration, and manner, 215. why so extremely popular among the clergy, 216, n. his piety, virtue, and affability, ib. his humanity, good-nature, and personal courage, 218. his sincerity and enthusiasm, 219. a martyr to the pride of the ecclesiastics, 222. his justice in the civil administration, and zeal to his country, 223, repeatedly

violated

INDEX.

violated his coronation-oath, 228. acts of usurpation he committed, ib. laid aside parliaments, 229. what his judges were, ib. insincere in his declarations to parliament, ib. distrusted by his friends, 230. his heroic death no proof of his sincerity, 231.

Charles II. king, crowned in Scotland, 64. his proceedings there ib. marches into England, whither Cromwell follows him, 67. stops at Worcester, where Cromwell comes up with him, 68. loses the battle of Worcester, 71. escapes into France, 72. a report of his restoration, which Cromwell converses upon, 160. makes proposals to Cromwell, which are rejected, 162, n. a gentleman converses with him in the dark, which Cromwell knows of, 207.

Charles Gustavus, king of Sweden, Cromwell's favourite ally, 202.

Clarendon, lord, his character of Cromwell's troops, 27.

Chelsea-college, the use Cromwell designed it for, 206.

Cooper, a story of his related by Mr. Locke, 123.

Commons, house of, remonstrate on the state of the nation, 12. See parliament.

Commonwealth, instituted after the king's death, 129.

Cosins, bishop, several remarkable particulars concerning him, 224, n.

Council of officers, their declaration, 144. n. a list of them, 146. n.

Council of state, a list of the members of it, 130. dissolved by Cromwell, 138.

Council, protestant, in opposition to that de propaganda fide at Rome; project of such an one by Cromwell, 206.

Cowley, Mr. Abraham, prejudiced against Cromwell, 234. examination of his discourse concerning Cromwell's government, 234, & seq.

Cromwell, colonel John, attempts to work on his cousin in the king's favour, 105.

CROM-

INDEX.

CROMWELL, OLIVER, inconsistent manner of treating his character, 4. his name no dishonour to the English nation, 5. his descent, 6. education, 8. first rise to popularity, ib. his zeal for the grand remonstrance, 13. discourse thereon with lord Falkland, ib. had designed to go to the American plantations, ib. raises, and artfully proves a troop of horse, with which he recommends himself farther, 18. made lieutenent-general, does wonders, and is in great danger, 19. character of his regiment by Bate, 20, n. his own account of the reformation he brought into the army, ib. is instrumental in winning the battle of Marston-moor, 22. gains the name of Ironsides, 23. misrepresented by Sir William Dugdale and lord Hollis, ib. is envied and opposed, but keeps his ground, and does farther service, 23. commands both horse and foot with equal ease, 25. his success in the battle of Naseby, ib. difference between his troops and the king's, 27. all that Fairfax atchieved ought to be ascribed to him, ib. in great peril at Naseby, 29. his success after that action, ib. suppresses the clubmen, advises the storming of Bristol, and takes several places, 30, 31. how employed between the first and second civil war, 32. his part in the second war, 33. he wins the battle of Preston, 34. marches into Scotland, and settles affairs there, ib. at his return receives the thanks of the parliament, 35. offered the command in Ireland, which he accepts with reluctance, ib. provides expeditiously for the discharge of his commission, 36. sends succours to Dublin, who raise the siege before his arrival, 37. arrives at Dublin, ib. reviews his army, 38. takes Drogheda by storm, ib. puts the garrison to the sword by way of terror, ib. does the same at Wexford, 39, 40. good effect of these severities, 40. refuses to go into winter quarters, ib. takes Ross, and receives the submission of other places, ib. defies Ormond, 41. attempts Duncannon, ib. and Waterford, ib. retires into winterquarters, ib. is sent for to England, 42. but yet

takes

INDEX.

takes the field, 42. reduces several places, ib. Storms Gowram and Kilkenny, which both surrender, 43. excuses himself to the parliament, 44. sets down before Clonmell, 45. takes it by storm, ib. rises to prodigious interest, 46. called home by a new order, 47. goes to London in triumph, 48. persuades the council to a war with Scotland, ib. his speech to general Fairfax thereupon, 49. is made captain-general in the room of Fairfax, 51. sets out for Scotland, ib. his reception on the way, 52, 53. enters Scotland, and forbids all injuries to the natives, 53. after attempting unsuccessfully to draw the Scots to a battle, is attacked by them in his quarters at Musleborough, 54. routs them, ib. defies general Lesley, ib. marches backwards and forwards, 55. is in danger, ib. is in great distress at Dunbar, 56. how he heartens his officers, 58. totally routs the Scottish army, 59, 60. draws up a narrative of that victory, 60. takes possession of Edinburgh town, 61. summons the castle, ib. besieges it in form, 62. takes it, 63. his proceedings in Scotland, 64. falls sick, but recovers, and takes the field again, 65. sends forces into Fife, who win a battle, 66. takes St. John's town, 67. follows the king into England, 68. comes up with him at Worcester, 68, 69. wins the battle of Worcester, 71. his letter to the parliament thereupon, ib. marches in a triumphant manner up to London, 74. receives the thanks of the parliament, and has large grants made him, 75. conclusion of his military character, 77. defended from the charge of cruelty, ib. reason of his having the king seized, 78, & seq. designed to play him off against the presbyterians, 81. and to restore him by means of the independents, 82. behaves openly to his majesty, ib. his message and discourses to Sir John Berkeley. 83. suspected thereupon by the army, 84. marches to Westminster to protect the parliament, 87. his zeal for the king offends both the parliament and the army, 89. to secure himself, he sends away the king, and abandons his interest, 90,

INDEX.

90, 91. quiets the levellers, 92. what passed between Sir John Berkely and him upon his quitting the king's interest, 93, & seq. more ambitious views ascribed to him than he really had, 95. story of his being deceived by the king, 96. a discourse on that subject between him and lord Broghill, 97. every thing contributes to his rise, 99. grows violent against the king, ib. speaks against him in parliament, 100. writes against addressing him, ibid. prevents the parliament's acting in the king's favour, 103. what he said concerning proceeding against the king, ibid. and a breach of trust in monarchs, 104. no commonwealth's man, but in earnest when he treated with the king, 106. how far the king's death to be imputed to him, 107; a proficient in the art of governing parties, 112. too hard for the earl of Manchester, 115. whom he succeeds in his command, 116. his views in promoting the self-denying ordinance. ib. speech in favour of it, ib. n. recommended by Fairfax to the parliament, 117. being suspected by the parliament, he sets the army against them, 118. sets up the agitators, and why, 119. which secures him, and terrifies the parliament, 121. inveighs in the house against the army; but, being suspected, flies to it, ib. eludes a charge in the house by dissimulation, 122. steals out of the house upon another charge, 123. suppresses the levellers by his personal bravery, 124. 125, 126. attempts to reconcile parties, and deals craftily with them all, 127. & seq. speaks in the character both of a general and a member of parliament, ib. his pretensions to devotion one of his great engines, 129 made one of the council of state, 130. his speech against lord Capel, 131. holds a conference about settling the government, ib. relation of that conference, 245. has another with Whitelock on the same subject, 133. relation of it, 247. exasperates the army against the parliament, 136. which he dissolves by force, 137. has a conference with the city divines, 135. writes to cardinal de Retz,

INDEX.

136, n. diffolves the council of ftate, 138. advantages of thefe bold proceedings, 139. what his panegyrift fays of them, 140. n. his protectorfhip better than the commonwealth, 143. calls his firft parliament, ib. form of his fummons, 144, n. which paffes the inftrument of government, 147. unites the three kingdoms, ib. his oath and inauguration, as protector, 150. calls his fecond parliament, 151. fpeech to it, ib. calls his third parliament, 155. which debates upon the government, ib. and afterwards offer him the crown, 157. after much deliberation he refufes it, ib. his conferences with the commons committee thereupon, 255, & feq. how terrified from accepting the title of king, 157. n. what he fays to lord Broghill of king Charles II. 161. applied to privately and ineffectually in behalf of that prince, 161, n. confirmed protector by the humble petition and advice, ib. fubftance of that inftrument, 162. eftablifhes the other or upper houfe, which weakens his intereft in the lower, 163. makes a fpeech to both houfes in the regal ftile, 165. diffolves them upon their debating his authority, ibid. defence of thefe arbitrary fteps in him, ibid. his management of the feveral parties, 166. & feq. plots againft him, and his lenity to the confpirators, 169, & feq. his adminiftration very little ftained with blood, 173. inftitutes major-generals, 174. but foon fuppreffes them, ibid. a general view of his government at home, 175. inftitutes a college at Durham, 176. account of that inftitution, ib. n. his tendernefs of the clergy, ib. dignifies the title of protector, 177. his war with the Dutch, 178. grants them a peace upon hard conditions, 179. takes part with the French againft Spain, 180. whether in this he acted confiftently with the intereft of his country, 181. extract of his manifefto relating to the Spanifh depredations, ib. & feq. fends a fleet againft Hifpaniola and Cuba, 185. which only takes Jamaica, ib. fends Blake to the Mediterranean, 187. extract from the

INDEX.

Craftfman relating to his West-India expedition, ib. & feq. concludes his alliance with France, and his ships destroy the plate-fleets at Cadiz, and the Canaries, 190, 191. extract from a speech of Mr. Pulteney's concerning his manner of returning infults, 194, & feq. fuccefs of his arms by land, 197. Dunkirk delivered up to his troops, 198. further reflections on his alliance with France, 199. his defign to quit the French, and efpoufe the Spanish intereft, upon feeing the balance of power changed, 201. his great power and intereft with foreign ftates, ib. his rigid juftice towards the Portuguefe embaffador's brother, 202. will not fuffer the French king to call himfelf king of France, 203. obliges the duke of Savoy to favour his proteftant fubjects, 204. faves certain Huguenots in France, ib. his defign of a college in oppofition to that de propaganda fide at Rome, 206. his letter to the prince of Tarente, 205. &c. his univerfal correfpondence, and impenetrable fecrecy, 206. has fpies every where, 207. trufts none but his fecretary Thurloe, and him not always, ib. his meffage to France about the bufinefs of Dunkirk, 208. which not only fecures the place, but produces a folemn embaffy to him, 209. cardinal Mazarine's and Mr. de Bourdeaux's compliments to him, 210. he dies poffeffed of fovereign power, 211. conjectures about the place of his interment, 212. third of September fortunate and fatal to him, 213. compared to king Charles, in his perfon and acquirements, ib. in his natural abilities, eloquence, penetration, and manners, 214. Sir Philip Warwick's picture of him, 215. n. in his piety, virtue, and affability, 217. in his humanity, good nature, and perfonal courage, 218. in his fincerity and enthufiafm, 219. in his adminiftration of affairs, 223. and zeal for his country, 226. his character fummed up, 232. remarks on Mr. Cowley's difcourfe, by way of vifion, concerning the government of Oliver Cromwell, 234, 240.

D.

DANES, upon what terms admitted into alliance with the English, 201.

Depredations, Spanish, as set forth in Cromwell's manifesto, 182.

Derby, countess of, defends and surrenders the Isle of Man, 75.

Drogheda, taken by storm, with a terrible slaughter. 38.

Dryden, Mr. his heroic stanzas on the lord protector, 295, & seq.

Dublin, siege of, raised by colonel Jones, 37.

Duffus, lord, obliged to surrender St. John's town to Cromwell, 67.

Dugdale, Sir William, accuses Cromwell of cowardice, 23.

Dunbar, Cromwell and his army in distress there, 56, 57, battle of, won by Cromwell, 58, 59.

Dundass, Sir William, defends Edinburgh castle against Cromwell, 61. delivers it up, 63.

Dunkirk, siege and battle of, 198, 199. reflections on the sale of it, 199. a design to trick Cromwell of it, 208.

Durham, a college instituted there by Cromwell for the convenience of the northern students, 176.

Dutch, a war between them and the English, 178. which produces several bloody fights at sea, ib. 179. sue to Cromwell for a peace, ib. who grants them one upon very severe conditions, ib.

E.

ECHARD, his story of a private application from king Charles II. to Cromwell, 161, n. his panegyric on Cromwell's government, 175.

Edinburgh castle, siege and surrendry of, 61, 62, 63.

F.

Fairfax, general, his character, 27. all his succeſs to be aſcribed to Cromwell, ib. is againſt a war with the Scots, 49. Cromwell attempts to ſatisfy him, 50. lays down his commiſſion, 51. and is ſucceeded by Cromwell, ib.

Falconbridge, lord, Cromwell's ſon-in-law, ſent with a ſolemn embaſſy to France, 201.

Falkland, lord, extract of a ſpeech of his concerning the biſhops of his time, 222, n.

Fife, a battle there, won by Cromwell's lieutenants, 66.

Fifth-monarchy-men, how managed by Cromwell, 168.

Fleets, Spaniſh, deſtroy'd by Cromwell's, 190, 192.

France, ſues for Cromwell's friendſhip, 179. who takes his part againſt Spain, 180. whether this was doing right, 199.

G.

Gage, a prieſt, informs Cromwell how weak and wealthy the Spaniards were in America, 181.

Gerard, Mr. beheaded for a plot againſt Cromwell, 169.

Gillebrand, an almanack-maker, proſecuted by Laud for leaving the popiſh ſaints out of his kalendar, 224, n.

Government, conferences on the ſettling of it, 131, 133, 245, 247.

Gowram, taken by Cromwell, 43.

Grievances, public, inquired into, and by whom, 10. new ones, 11.

Grimſton, Sir Harbottle, charges Cromwell ineffectually in the houſe of commons, 123.

H.

Hewet, doctor, executed for a conspiracy against Cromwell, 173.
Hispaniola, the English fail in their attempt thereon, 185.
Hollis, lord, accuses Cromwell of cowardice, 23.
Huguenots, French, saved by Cromwell from punishment, 204.

I.

Jamaica, taken by Penn and Venables, 185.
Jews, admitted by Cromwell into England, and why, 206.
Inaugurations, Cromwell's two, 150, 163.
Instrument of government, substance of it, 147, & seq.
Jones, colonel, raises the siege of Dublin, 37.
Joyce, cornet, the story of his seizing the king at Holmby-house, 78, n.
Ireland, state of that kingdom when Cromwell was sent there, 35.
Ireton, left by Cromwell his deputy in Ireland, 46. his success there, ib. a zealous commonwealth's man, 106. drives on the king's death, 107.
Ironsides, Cromwell so called, 23.
Isles, British, completely reduced to the parliament's obedience, 75.
Judges, king Charles's, their character, 223.

K.

Kilkenny, taken by Cromwell, 44.
Killing no Murder, dedication of the pamphlet so called, 171, n.

King,

INDEX.

King, no more juftifiable when he exceeds his authority than a conftable, 16.

L.

Lambert, general, wins a battle in Fife, 66. contefts the paffage at Warrington-bridge. 68.
Laud, archbifhop, licenfes popifh and forbids proteftant books, 223, n. profecutes an almanack-maker, 224, n.
Lawyers, Cromwell advances the moft able, 175.
Lenthal, Mr. William, reproved in the houfe of commons for cenfuring the long parliament, 17.
Lefly, general, fends an equivocal meffage to Cromwell, 55. avoids an engagement, which Cromwell feeks, ib. againft fighting at Dunbar, 58. routed there, 59.
Levellers, quelled by Cromwell, 91. fuppreffed by his perfonal bravery, 124. & feq. their declaration to the general and parliament, 124. how managed afterwards by Cromwell, 168.
Locke, Mr. his thoughts concerning refiftance to a prince, 15, 16, 17. a ftory of his concerning Cromwell, 123. his verfes on Cromwell, 295.
Lockhart, Mr. Cromwell's embaffador to the French court, his remonftrances there, 197, 204, 208.
Londoners procure votes in their favour, 87.
Loretto, church of, the Romans in pain for it, 185.
Ludlow, a faying of Cromwell's related by him, 118, n. fufpects Cromwell, and what he fays to him thereupon, 128. what he fays of Cromwell's being terrified from accepting the kingfhip, 157, n.

M.

Major-generals, inftituted and fuppreffed, 174.
Manifefto, Cromwell's againft Spain, 181.

Mardyke,

INDEX.

Mardyke, taken by the English and French, and delivered up to the former, 197.

Marston moor, the battle there, 22.

Mazarine, cardinal, engages Cromwell to the French interest, 180. writes to Turenne about the importance of his friendship, 197. complains of Cromwell, but at the same time complies, 207. his compliments to Cromwell, 209. of whom he stands greatly in awe, 210.

Members, the five, demanded by the king in a hostile way, 14. eleven, impeached by the army, 81.

Mexico, viceroy of, with his lady, perish in an engagement off of Cadiz 190.

Milton, his remark on the inconsistency of what was said by king Charles's friends, 91, n. Latin secretary of Cromwell, 176.

Mob, London, insult the parliament, 87.

Montague, admiral, with Blake, blocks up the port of Cadiz, where the Spanish plate-fleet is destroyed, 190.

Montrose, marquis of, his unfortunate letter from Scotland causes the king to break off the conferences at Uxbridge, 109, & seq. copy of that letter, Append. No. I. 265.

Morland, Mr. detects Willis to the king, 207. like to be killed by Cromwell, 207.

Morgan, major-general, commands the 6000 English in Flanders, 197. sets down before Dunkirk, 198. prevents the French from raising that siege, ibid. wins the battle of Dunkirk, 199. upon which the town surrenders, ib.

N.

NAseby fight, account of it, 25. the king's lost in it, 28. consequences of it, 29. Cromwell said to be buried in the field where it was fought, 211.

Nismes,

INDEX.

Nifmes, a tumult there, which Cromwell prevents the ill effects of, 204

O.

ORleans, father, what he fays of the characters of Fairfax and Cromwell, 27. what of Cromwell's conduct in Scotland, 55.
Ormond, marquis of, routed, 37. defied by Cromwell, 41.
Other houfe, in imitation of the houfe of peers, eftablifhed by Cromwell, 63. lift of its members, 164, n.

P.

PAnegyric on Cromwell by the Portuguefe embaffador, quoted, 25, 28, 35, n. 140, &c. tranflation of the fubftance of it, 311, & feq.
Pantaleon Sa, don, the juftice done on him by Cromwell, 202.
Parliament, Britifh, fenfe of one concerning refiftance, 17.
Parliament, the long, character of it, 9. &c. breaks with the king, 14. infulted, and protected by the army, 87. offended at Cromwell, 89. pafs feveral votes in the king's favour, 100. which Cromwell renders ineffectual, 103. terrified by the army, and fend to treat with it, 120. Cromwell diffolves it by force, 137.
————Cromwell's firft, 143. which paffes the inftrument of government, 147. his fecond, 151. Cromwell's fpeech to it, ib. his third, 155. which debate upon the inftrument of government, ib. offer him the crown, 157. which after deliberation he refufes, 160. his conferences with their committee upon that fubject, Append. No. II. 255, & feq. diffolved, 165.

Penn

INDEX.

Penn, vice-admiral, commands in a West-India expedition, 185. takes Jamaica, ib. put in the Tower, 186.

Penruddock, colonel, executed for an insurrection, 170.

Petition and advice, the humble, confirming Cromwell in the protectorate, 162.

Plots against Cromwell, 132, & seq.

Portugal, forced by Cromwell to send an embassador to beg for peace, 201.

Prejudices, party, reflections on them, 1. effects of them in the instance of our own troubles, 3.

Presbyterians, how managed by Cromwell, 167.

Preston, battle of, won by Cromwell, 33.

Protector, lord, Cromwell made so by the instrument of government, 147. his inauguration, 150. dignifies that title, 177. which signifies more in him than either king or emperor, ibid.

Puffendorf, a remarkable instance related by him concerning Cromwell, 203.

Pulteney, Mr. extract from a speech of his relating to Cromwell's manner of negociating, and returning insults, 194, 197.

Q

Quaker, English, complains to Cromwell of having his ship taken by the French, 195. Cromwell procures him satisfaction, and how, 195, 196.

R.

Rainsborough, colonel, a leader of the levellers, 124.

Remonstrance of the state of the nation, account of it, 12.

Representative, list of that summoned by Cromwell, 253.

INDEX.

Republicans, how managed by Cromwell, 167.
Refiftance to a king, when lawful, 15, & feq.
Retz, cardinal de, receives a letter from Cromwell, 136, n.
Rofs, taken by Cromwell, 40. bifhop of, hanged, 45.

S.

SAlmon, Mr. what he fays of Cromwell, 219. n.
Savoy, duke of, obliged by Cromwell to fpare his proteftant fubjects, 204.
Scotland, remarks on the ftate of it after Cromwell had reduced it, 76.
Scots, rife of the war between them and the Englifh, 47. write to the Englifh parliament upon the march of Cromwell's army, 32. terribly terrified upon his entering Scotland, 53. beat at Dunbar, 59, 60. and at Worcefter, 71. their lofs there, 72.
Self-denying ordinance, an account of it, 23. Cromwell's views in promoting it, 116.
Slingfby, Sir Henry, executed for a confpiracy againft Cromwell, 173.
Sovereignty, by birth-right, a vain idea, 5. why continued in particular families, 6.
Spain endeavours to buy Cromwell's friendfhip, 180. but without fuccefs, ib. manifefto againft that kingdom, 181.
Sprat, Mr. his poem on Cromwell's death, Appendix, 297—309.
Stayner, captain, deftroys the Spanifh fleet off of Cadiz, 190. burns their fhips in harbour at the Canaries, 191.
Syndercomb, Miles, his plot againft Cromwell, 173.
Synnot, colonel, commands in Wexford, 39.

T.

T.

TAAFE, lord, governor of Rofs, 40.
Tarente, prince of, Cromwell's letter to him, 205, n.
Temple, Sir William, his account of Cromwell's defign to abandon the French and efpoufe the Spanifh intereft, 200.
Thames, river, Cromwell's body faid to be funk in it, 212.
Thurloe, Mr. John, the only man Cromwell trufted, and him not always, 207.
Titus, colonel, writes a pamphlet called "Killing no Murder," 171. dedication of it to Cromwell, ib. n.
Tunis, the forts and fhips there deftroy'd by Blake, 189.
Tufcany, grand duke of, pays admiral Blake 60,000l. ibid.

V.

VAudois, perfecuted, and their caufe efpoufed by Cromwell, 204.
Venables, commands the forces in an American expedition, 185. put in the Tower, ib. Cromwell's inftructions to him, 186, n.
Voltaire, Mr. de, what he fays of king Charles, and the ftate of England under him and Cromwell, 226, n.
Vowell, Mr. hanged for a plot againft Cromwell, 169.

U.

UXbridge, treaty of, an account of breaking it off by means of a letter from the marquis of Montrofe, 108, & feq.

W.

W.

Waller, Mr. his story of Cromwell's manner of treating the enthusiasts, 221. his obligations to Cromwell, 234. panegyric on him, 287—292. poem on Montague's fight at sea, 292—294. on the protector's death, 309, 310.

Wariftoun, occasions the battle of Dunbar, 58.

Wellwood, doctor, his character of the long parliament, 9. &c. affirms Cromwell to have been in treaty with the king, 99. his account of breaking off the treaty of Uxbridge, 108, & seq.

Wexford, taken by storm, and the garrison put to the sword, 39.

Whitelock, Mr. his opinion of Cromwell delivered to the chancellor of Scotland, 114. his conferences with Cromwell about settling the government, 132, 246, 247, & seq. his remark on the dissolution of the long parliament, 138, 139.

Wildman, major John, his declaration against Cromwell, 173.

Williams, bishop, articles against him, 224, &c.

Willis, Sir Richard, brought over by Cromwell to betray the correspondence of the royal party, 207.

Worcester, Cromwell comes up with the king there, 68. battle of, won by Cromwell, 69, 70.

Wren, bishop, forbids talking on religious subjects, 223, n.

The END.

BOOKS *printed for* L. DAVIS *and* C. REYMERS.

I. THE HISTORY of ENGLAND, as it relates to Religion and the Church, from the earliest Accounts to the present Century. Comprehending a clearer and more connected View of the Progress of our ecclesiastical Constitution; the Preservation of our Rights and Liberties, and the Rise and Declension of the Power of the Popes in *England*, than any other History extant. By F. WARNER, L. L. D. Rector of Queenhithe, London, and of Barnes in Surrey; and Chaplain to the Right Hon. the Lord Keeper. In Two Volumes Folio, Price 1l. 16s. half bound.

II. A COLLECTION of STATE-PAPERS, during the Reigns of HENRY VIII. EDWARD VI. Queen MARY, and Queen ELIZABETH. From 1540 to 1570. Published from the Originals left by CECIL Lord BURGHLEY, now at Hatfield House, in the Library of the Right Hon. the Earl of SALISBURY. 2 vols. Price Two Guineas bound.

III. TRAVELS in EGYPT and NUBIA, by FREDERICK LEWIS NORDEN, F. R. S. Captain of the Danish Navy. Translated from the original Edition, published by Order of his Majesty the King of Denmark; and enlarged with Observations from ancient and modern Authors that have written on the Antiquities of Egypt; by Dr. PETER TEMPLEMAN. Elegantly printed on a fine Writing Royal Paper, and a new Type, in Two Volumes Folio.

IV. The same Work printed in one Volume OCTAVO, with Plates, Price bound Six Shillings.

V. A VOYAGE to SOUTH-AMERICA, describing at large the Spanish Cities, Towns, Provinces, &c. on that extensive Continent. Interspersed throughout with Reflections on the Genius, Manners, Customs, and

BOOKS *printed for* L. DAVIS *and* C. REYMERS.

and Trade of the Inhabitants; together with the Natural History of the Country. And an Account of their Gold and Silver Mines. Undertaken by Command of his Majesty the King of Spain, by DON GEORGE JUAN, and DON ANTONIO de ULLOA, both Captains of the Royal Navy, Members of the Royal Societies of London and Berlin; and corresponding Members of the Royal Academy at Paris. Translated from the Original Spanish. Illustrated with Copper-Plates. In Two Vols. Octavo. Price 12s.

VI. MONTESQUIEU's Rise and Fall of the Roman Empire; a new Edition, in Octavo, Price 5s.

VII. The BEAUTIES of ENGLAND, comprehended in a Pocked Volume; or a succinct View of the chief Villages, Market-towns, and Cities; the Seats of the Nobility and Gentry; Antiquities, Remains of Palaces, Monastries, Camps and Castles; the Two Universities; and the Cities of London and Westminster. The whole divided into the respective Counties, and intended as a Travelling Companion, pointing out whatever is curious both in Art and Nature. Third Edit. Price 3s.

VIII. VOYAGES and TRAVELS in the LEVANT, in the years 1749, 50, 51, 52: Containing Observations in Natural History, Physick, Agriculture, and Commerce. Particularly on the Holy Land, and the Natural History of the Scriptures. Written originally in the Swedish Language by the late FREDERIC HASSELQUIST, M. D. Published by order of her present Majesty the Queen of Sweden, with an Account of the Author. By Sir CHARLES LINNÆUS, Physician to the King of Sweden, and Member of all the learned Societies in Europe. Octavo, with a Map. Price bound 5s.

IX. OBSERVATIONS on ITALY, by Two Swedish Gentlemen. Translated from the French by Dr. NUGENT. In Two Vols. Octavo. Price 12s.

Books *printed for* L. Davi *and* C. Reymers.

X. The HISTORY of PARAGUAY, tranflated from the French of Father Charlevoix. In Two Vols. Octavo. Price 12s.

XI. The POLY-OLBION, with the other Poetical Works of MICHAEL DRAYTON, Efqr. a celebrated Writer, cotemporary with Shakefpeare, collected and publifhed in 1748, in one volume, Folio, and in four Volumes, Octavo, at the Price of 2l. 2s. in Sheets, are now propofed to be fold, either Edition, at 1l. 1s. bound and lettered,

Drayton's Poly-Olbion ftands celebrated as the moft accurate and entertaining Defcription we have of England and Wales: It gives an authentic chorographical Account of all the Tracts, Rivers, Mountains, Forefts, &c. together with the moft remarkable Stories, Antiquities, Wonders and Rarities of this Kingdom, taken from our old manufcript Hiftories, and illuftrated with the judicious Notes of the great Selden, which contain an infinite Variety of curious and recondite Learning, and have given fuch Weight and Authority to this Piece, as to have fupported it in the Efteem of all good Judges for above a Century.

www.ingramcontent.com/pod-product-compliance
Lightning Source LLC
Chambersburg PA
CBHW020238240426
43672CB00006B/570